PC-DOS/MS-DOS

User's Guide to the Most Popular Operating System for Personal Computers

PC-DOS/MS-DOS

User's Guide to the Most Popular Operating System for Personal Computers

Alan M. Boyd
of
Microsoft Corporation

BANTAM BOOKS
TORONTO • NEW YORK • LONDON • SYDNEY • AUCKLAND

PC-DOS/MS-DOS: USER'S GUIDE TO THE MOST POPULAR OPERATING SYSTEM FOR PERSONAL COMPUTERS
A Bantam Book / August 1985

Cover design by J. Caroff Associates, Inc.

Throughout the book, the trade names and trademarks of many companies and products have been used, and no such uses are intended to convey endorsements of or other affiliations with the book.

Book design by Nicola Mazzella.

ISBN 0-553-34231-2

Published simultaneously in the United States and Canada

Bantam Books are published by Bantam Books, Inc. Its trademark, consisting of the words "Bantam Books" and the portrayal of a rooster, is Registered in U.S. Patent and Trademark Office and in other countries. Marca Registrada. Bantam Books, Inc., 666 Fifth Avenue, New York, New York 10103.

PRINTED IN THE UNITED STATES OF AMERICA

HL 0 9 8 7 6 5 4 3 2 1

To Heather

Contents

Introduction

This book is an edited compilation of the articles that I wrote for the *Softalk for the IBM* magazine under the name of "System Notebook." It is a reaction to a demand for back issues that cannot be met in any other way. When the magazine first went to print, the IBM Personal Computer had only just appeared. Luckily, I had been familiar with its operation for several months before it was released, and was privy to many of the secrets of its operation.

Even back in early 1982, I began to notice that the type of person involved with the IBM Personal Computer was different from those who bought earlier personal computers, such as an Apple II or a Radio Shack TRS-80. The new user was more professional, definitely less of a hobbyist, and considerably more "up-market."

At the same time, the new user was intelligent in his own right—not particularly as a computer hobbyist, but as an innovator in his own field. I therefore set about to provide the type of information that would be appreciated by such a character. I determined to cut away much of the technical jargon from the articles to reveal the functional side of DOS, rather than the technical side.

I felt that the average user would first want to learn how to use his computer to perform the tasks that it was purchased for. Then, with that mastered, he would be daring enough to dig a little deeper. There would be a desire to know "why" as well as "how."

Most people who purchase a personal computer do so to solve a problem. The problem might be an overworked staff, a tight expansion budget, a desire for greater personal productivity, or simply a need to keep up with the times. However, when most people walk out of the computer store and unwrap their computers, they realize after only a few minutes that what they have just bought is not a solution to their problems—rather it is a whole set of new problems. They are faced with the realization that in order to solve the problem for which the computer was purchased, they must first overcome the mysteries of computerese.

Generally, the literature that is available for these users is either very simplistic or overly technical. On the simplistic side, there are many books available for those in the process of purchasing a personal computer. These books explain the basic terminology used to describe the various components and are designed for the enterprising consumer so that he will know what to look for when shopping for a personal computer.

At the other end of the scale, there are also many books that teach programming or other more appealing applications such as spreadsheets or word processors. These books tend to be well written, although they generally cater to a more technical audience—either to professional programmers who moonlight on their PCs, or to very smart fourteen-year-olds.

Stuck in the middle between these two groups are the vast majority of PC owners. *Softalk for the IBM* catered to those users who took the plunge and actually bought a PC. Most of the other magazines cater to the other two groups, primarily the former. Since the magazine was targeted to owners, it was reasonable to expect that every reader actually owned a PC. The articles, and hence this text, are designed to be read while sitting in front of your PC.

Between when the articles were first started in January 1982 and the release of this book, the PC has gone through several major incarnations—from the original PC to the PC-XT, to the PC*jr,* and finally to the PC-AT. So, too, the operating system that is the subject of this text has gone through several generations. To date, there have been three major releases of DOS: version 1, version 2, and version 3. Since versions 2 and 3 are essentially supersets of version 1, it is recommended that you read the entire section on version 1; everything in that section is appropriate, even if you only use version 2.

The second section, which deals with version 2, is only necessary if that is the version that you use. Version 3.0 is the only release of version 3 that is covered. Version 3.0, however, is functionally identical to version 2.0. If you are still using version 1 (either 1.0, 1.05 or 1.1), it is highly recommended that you upgrade to version 2.1. It is not recommended that you upgrade beyond version 2.1, unless you have a particular need for a specific function of a higher version.

DOS is a continually evolving product. Features will be added at a somewhat furious pace. In order to take the best advantage of your PC, you should always keep the operating system current at the highest version number that covers your needs.

Acknowledgments

It is not an easy job to meet the pace of the personal computer industry head on, and undertake a book at the same time. I would therefore like to thank the many people who helped me prepare the series of articles and put them together into this book. First and foremost, my thanks go to Craig Stinson, Kevin Goldstein, Kathey Talley-Jones, and the rest of the editorial staff at *Softalk*. At Microsoft, the MS-DOS crew who let me pick their brains, and the management staff, Bill Gates in particular, who encouraged me. Among the many others to whom I owe thanks are Nahum Stiskin for the insight (and the shoes), Tim Paterson for the initial design, and Ginger for letting me stay up late. Last, but by no means least, I owe a debt of gratitude to the capable staff at Bantam who put this book together in record time, particularly Deborah Aiges, Susan Crouch, Jono Hardjowirogo, Nicola Mazzella, and Jim Walsh.

PART I

DOS Version 1

CHAPTER 1

The IBM Personal Computer

The PC, as the IBM Personal Computer is generally known, is the first of a new generation of personal and small business computers. It blends some of the more desirable features that surfaced during the earlier "traditional" microcomputer industry with innovative features and attractive, functional packaging. Certainly there may be more sophisticated, more powerful personal computers available or on the way, and no computer can be all things to all people, but no other can lay claim to the title "the IBM of personal computers."

International Business Machines, which according to *Fortune* magazine, was the eighth largest corporation in the United States in 1982 and the sixth largest in 1983, and the largest computer company in the world, has introduced what many industry experts consider to be more than just another personal computer. The PC, when it was initially introduced, was an endorsement, a recognition of the very existence of the microcomputer industry.

This acknowledgment that the adolescent, hobbyist-oriented, personal computer is important enough to attract the attention of the world's largest computer company indicates that the personal computer industry is here to stay. It also indicates that more people will be interested in coming to terms with and learning how to master personal computers in general, and the PC in particular.

Newcomers to personal computing will be confronted with the weird and wonderful terms and concepts that "veterans" take for granted. This book is dedicated to those newcomers, although it won't ignore the needs of those pioneers who already experienced the joy that was personal computers before the PC—back when some of the most successful computers were designed and built in the garage and laughed at by the so-called experts.

Many of the original features and concepts that were introduced on the Radio Shack TRS-80, the Apples II and ///, and even the original Altair, the first personal computer, have found their way onto the PC. The overall performance of personal computers has, of course, increased by leaps and bounds since the early days, but it is interesting to note that IBM traded pure speed, which most people associate with computer performance, for something more important: standardization. Since its introduction, the PC has become not the standard to beat, but the standard to match.

The PC is certainly more powerful than its predecessors. Perhaps the most important of its features is simply the fact that nothing was omitted from the design. Earlier competitors were designed with such glaring flaws as a keyboard that didn't have lowercase, or a minimal 40-column screen that couldn't be used for business letter writing, or software that didn't tolerate typing errors.

Whereas many of the earlier personal computer manufacturers simply ignored the needs of the user, IBM has managed to maintain a balance between what the technical market wants and what the commerical market really needs—the computer that no one loves, but many use.

The aim of this book is to bring the user who is not a professional computer scientist closer to the IBM PC by explaining how it can be used to its fullest capabilities—in plain English with as little "computerese" as possible. Most of the information and examples cover the software part of the PC, focusing on the operating system.

Some technical areas will be covered, from beginner level through to programmer. Admittedly, not everyone purchased a PC to jump in and program it. In fact, most purchasers, or "end users" as the industry insists on calling us, will not be interested in programming at all. For those people this book should help explain a great deal of the background behind some critical parts of the system: what their fundamental use is, where they came from, why they are there in the first place, and how they can best be used. A minimum of technical expertise will be assumed.

The Hardware

Most of this book will focus on the software part of the PC, since that is the part that by its very definition, has been left open to user participation. Very few people will be interested in designing hardware interfaces or peripheral cards for the PC, but many will be interested in either running off-the-shelf commercially available software packages, programming their own applications, or customizing existing applications to better suit their own needs. The hardware part of the PC does require a short introduction, however, since a cursory knowledge of the hardware is helpful for a full understanding of the software.

The PC consists of a microprocessor, several peripheral processors, main user memory, expansion slots, peripheral cards and devices, and the electrical systems to make them all work. The microprocessors selected by IBM for the PC family are from the Intel 8086 series. The PC-AT uses an Intel 80286 while all the others in the family use the Intel 8088. Apart from a few minor differences they both operate the same way. They are 16-bit microprocessors, which means that they generally work with 16 bits, or pieces of information at a time.

To a computer, a piece of information is represented digitally; that is, it is either a zero or a one. How the computer converts this simple *binary* system into the information that it processes is quite a simple task, but it is not necessary to understand this process to use the computer. As an analogy, it isn't necessary to understand the intricacies of fuel injection to be able to drive a car.

The "main user memory," as it is called, consists of several chips located on the main circuit board (often called the "motherboard"), and also any add-on memory cards that are plugged into the PC. This memory is the area in which the microprocessor stores information that it is processing. The particular technology utilized for these memory circuits (called RAM—for random-access memory, also known as read/write memory) requires that a constant electrical voltage be supplied in order for the chips to "remember" the information stored in them. Whenever the computer is turned off, any information in this memory is lost.

When the power is turned back on, this memory is blank. This means that the main user memory is really only used to store transient information, such as programs, temporary data, and valuable data that will later be transferred to a disk file for long-term storage. It is the ability of this type of memory to be erased and used for another purpose that gives the computer its inherent general-purpose nature.

There is another way of storing information in silicon chips. This technology is called ROM, for read-only memory. This type of memory is fixed and doesn't require an electrical voltage to retain stored information. Once it has been programmed it cannot be changed, and when the power is turned off, ROM doesn't lose its contents.

In the PC the ROMs have been programmed at the factory by IBM. They contain a version of the BASIC language, the diagnostic test programs that are run every time the PC is turned on, and several other programs, including a part of the operating system, that are used for more complex tasks.

For long-term storage, or storage of information and programs, information is transferred from the main user memory to floppy diskettes inserted in the PC's disk drives, or to a fixed disk that cannot be removed. Information stored on either of these devices is nonvolatile. That is, when the power is disconnected from the PC, information or programs stored there are kept intact. For all intents and purposes, the disk can be thought of as a specially shaped magnetic tape, since it performs substantially the same operation.

The PC also consists of several circuit-card holders along the back panel. These slots are generally used for expanding the PC by adding peripheral equipment such as printers or telephone modems. One of the most complained about items on the PC is the number of slots available. Of the five slots available on the standard PC, one is normally used for the disk-drive interface card, one for the video interface card, and one for a printer interface card. That really only leaves two additional slots for future expansion.

All of the components that are programmable are integrated into a single unit under the control of a very important piece of software called the operating system. To make the PC work for its living doesn't require learning about bus structures or interpreting hardware timing diagrams. Instead, the best approach for anyone wanting to control the hardware components of the PC is to learn to use the software that comes with it. By mastering the operating system, the user can master each of the individual components and have them perform technically amazing tasks on demand.

The Software

Since IBM has the dominant position in the computer industry, it is safe to assume that no matter in which direction they take any of their computers, they will set a standard for the rest of the industry. There is no reason to doubt that this will also be true for the PC. The fact that IBM has adopted several existing (non-IBM-developed) standards in the software for the PC sets a precedent for the company. It is an indication of their seriousness, as well as their willingness to endorse the work that others have done in the field, and enforces the individual components' claims of being "standard."

The most obvious of these is the ROM-based version of Microsoft's BASIC, the most popular computer language in the world, and the most common piece of software in the personal computing industry. This language is distributed with every PC and will probably be used at some time by all programmers, professional or casual, since the language is designed to be suitable for either.

BASIC is an interpreted language. That means that a program can be entered into the computer and operated right away, without having to go through any of the fuss of compiling which other languages require. This means that it conforms very well to the "train-of-thought" school of programming, which can be very powerful in the hands of a beginner. Although no particular knowledge of computer programming is being assumed, we will encounter BASIC several times during this discourse.

The other important program is the disk operating system, PC-DOS, or simply DOS. Although there are alternatives to this particular operating system, DOS offers performance characteristics unmatched by the other systems. Even though they sell other operating systems as well, IBM has made it abundantly clear that this is the operating system that they will support by offering applications software packages that run under DOS for accounting, word processing, financial planning, and the like.

Executives of IBM have also made it clear that "upward compatibility" —the ability to take software with you when you upgrade to a larger, better system—is of great importance to them. It can be assumed that DOS will be around for a long time. It is also evident that most software houses who are writing software for the PC will want their packages to be compatible with IBM's, and they are also using DOS.

CHAPTER 2

The PC Operating Systems

On very large computers, where many people can use the system at the same time, there is a need for some kind of order, so that one user doesn't interfere with any other user. This order is brought about by a very low-level and highly technical program whose purpose it is to manage the many users and make the most efficient use of the available memory and peripheral equipment. This program is known as the "operating system" (OS).

The operating system is perhaps the most important piece of software running on any computer. It is the program that ties all the hardware components together and makes them appear to the user as an integrated system, as opposed to a set of components. It manages the keyboard, video display, disk drives, printer, and any other component that is attached to the computer. In large computer installations it also manages the allocation of resources among the many users of the system.

The OS tackles the mundane tasks associated with data and file manipulation, so that you need only issue very general, easily understandable commands, and need never be technically specific. These commands tend to be words that have real-life English meanings, such as "load," "save," "copy," etc.

For example, to read a file from a floppy disk into memory, you issue a simple operating system command such as **load.** You do not need to know how the computer stores information on the floppy disk, how it is coded or decoded during the transfer, or even where on the disk it is stored. The operating system takes care of all these details—often called housekeeping—automatically.

In smaller computers such as the PC, the operating system is known as a "disk operating system," or DOS for short. This name came about due to the fact that smaller computers rely heavily on the external storage afforded by floppy disks. Much of the software development that goes into creating a DOS concerns itself with the manipulation of these disks. Therefore, most of a DOS's function is associated with the input and output of data to and from disk drives.

Smaller computers are essentially unusable without some sort of mass-storage device. Since disk drives are currently in vogue, operating systems tend to be designed around them. Earlier generations of personal computers made heavy use of other forms of removable storage such as cassette tape and punched paper rolls.

When the PC was first announced by IBM, the people there somehow managed to confuse the issue of operating systems in the eyes of the general public, particularly those already familiar with the subject. They offered not one but three operating systems for the PC. Two of these are standard operating systems that have existed for years and are available from IBM on an optional basis, and the third, PC-DOS, is a new operating system, designed specifically for the PC and similar computers.

Since the introduction, IBM has announced several other operating systems for the PC family. Before we delve into the world of PC-DOS, let's find out more about the alternatives.

The Operating System Alternatives

The problems associated with different operating systems are somewhat analogous to the problems created in the videotape industry by the Beta and VHS tape formats available for videocassette recorders. Software written for one operating system will generally not work with any other.

IBM demonstrated an inordinate amount of common sense in offering three operating systems for the PC at its introduction. On the surface they appear to have done this to give commercial software development houses the ability to transport their applications packages from the old world of 8-bit microcomputers to the new 16-bit systems such as the PC.

The process is not quite as simple as it may first seem and much misunderstanding still abounds about this. Nevertheless, at least some links do exist to the familiar territories of the past, allowing software developers to move their existing products over to the PC. As a result software became available in a relatively short time and all of the meaningful software that existed in earlier 8-bit systems—particularly the Apple II and CP/M—was quickly available for the PC.

The three operating systems available from IBM when the PC was announced are the CP/M-86 system from Digital Research, the p-System, developed at the University of California at San Diego (UCSD) and marketed by SofTech Microsystems, and PC-DOS, a variant of MS-DOS, developed for IBM by Microsoft Corporation.

These operating systems offer a spectrum of choices for the software developer, with an emphasis on an upward migration path for existing 8-bit software applications. Since there had been so much software developed for the older 8-bit systems, IBM made it as easy as possible for developers to bring their software to the new larger market.

To the average owner of a PC, the selection of an operating system should be determined by the commercial availability of applications software packages, such as word processors, spreadsheets, database managers, etc., that address his or her specific needs. The operating system should not get in the way, should be as transparent as possible to the user, and should not play any part in the selection of applications.

However, one of the operating systems is required, since all software applications require one or another of them. Needless to say, there is no limit to the number of different operating systems that can be made to work with the PC, although it is not very convenient for a user to have to learn several different conventions to do the same thing with several different operating systems.

To better understand the position of each of the operating systems available from IBM, it is important to understand the reasons why IBM offers these operating systems in particular, what the role of each was to be, and what purpose they have served in the past. As is typical for IBM, and not so typical for the microcomputer industry in general, the criteria for selection of these operating systems was not based purely on their technical abilities, but on quite subtle marketing reasons that are not particularly important for the user.

The UCSD P-System

The origins of the p-System can be traced back to the arrival of the Pascal language from Europe and its ready adoption into academia in the United States, particularly at the University of California at San Diego (UCSD) campus. Here, a group at the university's Institute for Information Science, under the direction of Kenneth Bowles, saw an opportunity to create a comprehensive programming environment in and around the language.

Bowles and his students recognized that the effort required to write a Pascal compiler with an integrated operating system for every one of the many computers on the market would be considerable. So they developed a method for engineering these systems that would allow them to transport the bulk of the software from one machine to another without having to rewrite it each time. This was the genesis of the p-System.

The p-System utilizes a somewhat unique scheme that makes it very easy to write software on one type of computer and transport it to another. It does this by implementing a translator program on each different computer. This translator works by emulating some hypothetical, nonexistent computer. Of course, this hypothetical computer operates the same way on all real computers. It is known as a p-machine, and the translator as a p-machine emulator.

Software written on any of the language compilers on the p-System is internally different from other types of software. The software cannot be run directly on any normal computer. However, it can be run on a p-machine, or any computer that can emulate a p-machine. Inside the computer, the p-System languages produce programs that consist of what is called p-code, or pseudo-code. The p-System available for the IBM PC consists of such a p-machine emulator and several language compilers that produce p-code.

The obvious advantage of such a system is that it produces software that is free from the constraints and limitations of any particular family of microprocessor. Software developed under the p-System on an IBM PC can most probably be transported to, say, an Apple II running the p-System with little or no modifications. There are disadvantages, though. Since the computer spends as much time emulating the p-machine as it does running the applications program, its performance is seriously compromised. Also, this level of software portability is a benefit not to the end user but to the software developer. A user of an IBM PC usually cares very little whether or not his or her software will run on an Apple II.

The other distinct advantage of the p-System has been its ready adoption by the academic community. The p-System offers the academic world a standard programming environment, such that students can learn to program in Pascal on a large minicomputer and then switch to a microcomputer, and have the environment change as little as possible. This means, for example, that they do not have to undertake the learning of an entirely new editing program, with a new set of commands and instructions, every time that they move to a new computer. The same case can be made for the assemblers, compilers, and utilities available under the system. Currently, the p-System is available for several families of microprocessors and also some larger computers.

The p-System is, at the same time, more and less than simply an operating system. It is not conducive to the types of high-performance work usually undertaken by the other operating systems—CP/M or PC-DOS—in that it is not a simple matter for a programmer to work with the operating system directly. This type of work is usually undertaken through one of the high-level languages such as Pascal or FORTRAN. On the other hand, the p-System incorporates its own set of compilers each of which produces the same type of pseudo-code. Initially the system was implemented around UCSD Pascal, but now there are p-code versions of FORTRAN and BASIC available.

Overall, the p-System does offer some advantages over the other alternatives. It gives software developers an opportunity for writing transportable software, but it takes its toll in performance—being abysmally slow. The other major advantage is its ease of use. As a teaching system it has been adopted by many colleges and universities, and consequently there is a large body of literature available, most notably for the Pascal language. However, once a programmer has mastered the p-System languages, he will most probably move on to the more powerful "native" languages available on the PC. Less than 1 percent of all PC users have purchased the p-System, and useful software that runs under it is difficult to find. In fact, the p-System seems to have eliminated itself as a real choice for an operating system.

CP/M-86

CP/M-86 has its roots in its 8-bit predecessor CP/M, which stands for control program/monitor. CP/M was originally developed by Gary Kildall (founder of Digital Research, the supplier of CP/M) in 1974 when he was working as a consultant to Intel, the developer of the 8080 microprocessor. Initially it was designed to interface Kildall's own home-brewed system with his PL/M compiler. When Intel rejected CP/M as a commercial product, Kildall went out on his own and formed Digital Research to bring the product to market.

By 1975 several companies, including Altair, Polymorphic, and Processor Technology (then the big three), were marketing microcomputers. Few companies, however, offered compatible disk drives to go with their computers. Add-on disk drives were being sold by third parties, though, and many of the earliest disk-based systems were hybrids of several manufacturers' components. In this hobbyist-oriented mix-and-match world of early computers, CP/M emerged as the standard—the lowest common denominator that would allow many of these systems to share the same software. Ironically, CP/M's most salient feature was the fact that it used IBM standard disk formats.

Several manufacturers quickly adopted CP/M for their systems and shipped it as their "standard" operating system. As the years went by, a large software base compatible with CP/M was developed, and the position of the operating system moved from being a hobbyist-oriented system to being the standard medium for most business software applications packages. Internally, however, CP/M changed only marginally over the years, and did not attempt to push the state of the art much further than the very earliest version. In fact, to this day the code necessary to talk to punched paper tape readers is still a part of CP/M, although such tape readers have long since been abandoned for use on microcomputers, having been replaced by disk drives.

CP/M-86 is a translation of the original 8-bit product onto the 16-bit Intel 8086 microprocessor. The PC uses the 8088 microprocessor (compatible with the full Intel 8086 family of microprocessors); CP/M-86 will run on any processor in that family. The objective of CP/M-86 on the PC is obviously to offer a migration path from the 8-bit systems to the PC to make it easy for all of the independent software vendors to move their applications packages up from CP/M.

Internally, CP/M-86 functions more or less identically to CP/M. The operating system is logically divided into four distinct parts. The part that the user sees is called the CCP, or console command processor. This is the part of the operating system that interprets commands typed on the keyboard and passes the information to the remainder of the system. There are a number of commands built into the system but most commands reside on disk and are read into memory when they are invoked.

The BIOS, or basic input/output system, is the part of the system that is hardware-dependent, and therefore varies with each implementation. It is the BIOS that interfaces with the various hardware components attached to the system. The BDOS, or basic disk operating system, is the section that manages the disk filing system and allocation of disk space. The last section is called the TPA, for transient program area. It is this section that is used to hold whatever applications program or high-level language is being used under CP/M.

For a user of CP/M there are two ways to "talk" to the system. The first method is to issue commands by typing them on the keyboard. As mentioned earlier, there are two types of commands: built-in commands and what are known as transient commands (usually stored on a floppy disk). To the user the only difference is that the operating system must first read a transient command from the disk before it can run it. The advantage of this system is that commands, in the form of transient, disk-resident programs, can be added to the operating system to customize it to a particular application.

Commands are used to perform tasks like formatting blank disks, copying files from one disk to another, duplicating disks, examining the contents of a disk file by displaying it on the screen, erasing files from a disk, renaming files, configuring the system for a particular set of hardware, passing information between the various components of the system, and invoking an applications program.

The second way to use CP/M is to make what are known as operating system calls. This is the method that programmers use to interface applications programs directly to CP/M. Operating system calls are performed by passing certain codes to CP/M and then "jumping" to the operating system. This method of communicating with CP/M is to be avoided by anyone not familiar with assembly language programming. High-level languages that run under CP/M usually take care of these calls for the user. Operating system calls are used to perform tasks such as reading the keyboard, dispatching messages to the screen or printer, reading and writing blocks of data to and from disk, moving data from one device to another, and maintaining the disk directories.

CP/M-86 functions in a manner that is just about identical to the earlier CP/M, which is both a blessing and a curse. It is a blessing because software developers don't need to learn a whole new set of commands, or indeed a whole new operating system, when they move from 8 bits to 16 bits, making the transition easy. It is a curse because CP/M still suffers from the infuriating lack of "user-friendliness" and outdated capabilities for which it has always been criticized.

Although CP/M-86 seemed to hold much promise as the operating system of choice when it was first introduced, the software development community has largely ignored it. This seems to be a reaction to the late introduction of the product and the price IBM chose for it. It would appear that, in all, less than 3 percent of all PC owners use the CP/M-86 system.

PC-DOS

PC-DOS is the new "nonstandard" operating system that IBM has made available for the PC. IBM has chosen to make it their standard for the PC. This is evident by the fact that all the applications software and "native" languages that IBM ships require and support PC-DOS. In light of the relative merits of introducing a proprietary operating system as opposed to a standard operating system, how can this make good business sense for IBM? Why has IBM chosen a newcomer over a host of standards? Perhaps a brief look at the history and capabilities of PC-DOS will shed some light on this apparent mystery.

DOS, as IBM calls the operating system, began its life as the brainchild of Tim Paterson of Seattle Computer Products. Known originally as 86-DOS, it was a complementary product for the SCP 8086 microprocessor card for S-100-type systems. It allowed owners of the card to interface their computers to the host of disks and other peripherals available, a situation much analogous to the beginnings of CP/M in the early 1970s. Paterson, who is primarily a hardware engineer, actually developed 86-DOS out of frustration. He simply could not wait any longer for the CP/M-86 operating system that Digital Research was at that time developing. So he went off and did his own.

To make it easier for the independent software vendors to move their applications programs from the 8-bit world to the PC, Paterson designed the interfaces to the operating system in a manner that made it look very similar to CP/M. To do this, all he had to do was use a similar structure for the system and use the same calling conventions, the rules governing the interface procedures that programmers use.

He wrote the system in 8086 assembly language, so that it would be faster than CP/M-86, and using CP/M as a conceptual model, he designed an operating system that had all the benefits that can be derived from a more powerful 16-bit microprocessor, used much of the same style as CP/M, but overcame many of the serious technical limitations of CP/M. The result was a new generation of single-user operating systems, upward compatible with much existing software, and just as easy to convert CP/M software to as CP/M-86 itself.

As the contracted vendor of IBM's PC-DOS, Microsoft recognized the value of Paterson's work and licensed the product for distribution. In a later development, Microsoft bought the system outright. Turning 86-DOS over to their own operating systems group, then headed by none other than Tim Paterson himself, Microsoft produced PC-DOS, and designed all of their languages to run under it. The results are evident on the PC—an integrated family of languages and operating systems that chart the direction ahead for IBM.

In a related occurrence, Microsoft made the operating system available to the general public and other computer manufacturers under the name MS-DOS. Other computer manufacturers quickly adopted MS-DOS as their operating system, including such giants as Wang Labs, NEC, Fujitsu, Zenith, and Texas Instruments. It was also quickly adopted by relative newcomers, such as Columbia Data Systems, Compaq, Hyperion, and Victor, who were looking to make their machines as compatible with the PC as possible.

So now there is an operating system available on many of the new 8086- and 8088-based computers that is known by several names—86-DOS, PC-DOS, SB-86, Z-DOS, MS-DOS (and even as SCP-DOS and DOS-86 in some areas), and simply as DOS by IBM. All are the same, simply a rose by various names. However, the fact that it is known by several names has tended to confuse the issue.

MS-DOS has, since its initial selection by IBM, become the dominant operating system for the 16-bit single-user type of microcomputer, with the list of manufacturers who offer it sounding like a who's who of the computer industry. With the exception of a few minor CP/M-86 diehards, it is now safe to say that MS-DOS is available on every single Intel 8086- and 8088-based computer system. Recent polls have shown that more than 96 percent of all the software available for these systems requires MS-DOS. It can be assumed that 100 percent of PC owners use PC-DOS. Since it is so universal, it is the one program that all PC owners should learn to use.

Already it is clear that all PC users who want to use *Multiplan, VisiCalc, 1-2-3* by Lotus, Peachtree's or BPI's accounting packages, *EasyWriter,* or any of the IBM-supplied software must familiarize themselves with DOS, if only for the purposes of making backups or formatting new data diskettes.

Most people already familiar with CP/M or CP/M-86 will find that DOS behaves in a very similar manner. On the other hand, it does work considerably faster and has managed to remove many of the limitations that were imposed by CP/M, which, after all, was designed almost a decade ago. The enhancements include better error-recovery procedures, more powerful, flexible file characteristics, and a faster, more efficient file structure.

To the casual user, however, the most noticeable enhancement of DOS is that there is no need ever to "log-on" disks. This removes the necessity of resetting the operating system after disks are changed, so that the user will never have to experience the dreaded "BDOS ERR READ ONLY" situation common to CP/M users which often leads to the loss of valuable data or many hours of work. The advanced error-recovery features are another interesting enhancement. With CP/M it is possible, and in fact very easy, to lose valuable data simply by pressing the wrong key at the wrong time; with DOS this intolerable situation no longer exists. Those users who never experience life under CP/M are blessed in that they will not have to "unlearn" the habits of that system.

In general, DOS is much friendlier than CP/M, substituting a set of more intuitive command syntax for the "backward," counterintuitive approach employed by CP/M. With its additional power and features, DOS is the obvious choice for any PC user. IBM is attempting to make sure it is the universal operating system on the machine, as is evident in the price of DOS compared to the price of either of the other two operating systems. Perhaps part of IBM's strategy for operating systems can be recognized by the fact that they demand the lowest price for the operating system that is the most powerful of the three.

The choice of operating systems is up to the end user, but it is assured that DOS will be used on the vast majority of PCs. Any user who wishes to use IBM-supplied applications software will have to learn DOS, its structure and commands, and it is this subject that we will look at in depth in the next chapter, and in the rest of this book. Once DOS is understood, even the most casual user will be able to make use of the many powerful applications programs that are on the market.

CHAPTER 3

The Basics of PC-DOS

Secretaries with responsibilities for accounting data entry, managers and professionals who want to use a spreadsheet such as *Multiplan* or *1-2-3,* and both casual and professional programmers will need to know how to use DOS. The secretary will need to know how to format blank diskettes and make backup copies, the manager may want his *Multiplan* reports integrated into a report that was done on the *Multimate* word processor, and the programmer will want to have his or her programs work with the operating system so that the all-important data files they produce can be accessed and used by other IBM DOS-based programs. All users, in fact, will need to learn at least the basics of DOS. That will be our subject for this chapter—the basics of DOS.

What Is DOS?

The IBM disk operating system manual offers a simple explanation of what the disk operating system is and does. As a prerequisite to working with DOS, it is strongly recommended that the user read at least the introduction to that manual. What the manual does not do is go into details of what is happening inside the computer when you issue a DOS command, nor does it give a clear picture of what DOS "looks like" internally. Sadly, it is also lacking in detail about how to use the operating system and how processes can be speeded up.

The DOS manual is primarily a reference manual. Even though the IBM documentation is hailed industrywide as the best documentation yet to surface for a small business computer, there is still a noticeable shortage of tutorial material. This chapter will attempt to fill in many of the holes in IBM's documentation. These holes are usually the result of IBM taking for granted that all PC users will know more than they do about computers in general. We will go through the simple basics of DOS, from starting the system to understanding the underlying principles.

Since many people may (justifiably) feel that they already know how to do these basics, the subjects will be made more interesting by the inclusion of some of the lesser-known facts about DOS, particularly the differences between DOS and older, more well known operating systems. Since DOS is superficially similar to some of these older systems, many users may simply assume that DOS is no more capable than these. As will be seen, DOS may look familiar on the outside, but inside, DOS has many surprises.

Starting DOS

When the IBM PC is equipped with one or more disk drives, the startup procedure becomes quite complex. When the power switch is set to the *on* position, the PC will run through a self-check, and if all is functioning, it will then turn on one of the disk drives and go looking for the operating system. The disk drive that it turns on is known as the A drive.

The process of starting the operating system by placing the DOS disk in drive A and turning the computer on is generally called *booting* the system. This term comes from the theoretical ability of being able to pick oneself up by the bootstraps! To the computer this translates into the ability of the operating system to start itself from a minimal amount of information. After all, if the operating system is stored on the disk, how can the computer read the operating system from the disk?

The information required to boot DOS is stored on one of the read-only memory (ROM) chips inside the computer; it is called a "bootstrap loader." This is a very short program that starts the disk drive running by turning the motor on and then sending the disk reading head (similar in function to a combination of a record stylus and a cassette tape head) to a predetermined position on the disk where it knows that it will find a slightly longer program. This longer program is then read into user memory. Its function is, predictably, to read yet a longer program off the disk. The net result is that the bulk of the operating system is read in off the disk whenever the computer is started. This entire procedure takes only a few seconds. The long delay that preceded this is caused by the diagnostic program checking the hardware for malfunctions.

DOS consists of several definable parts, some of which can be customized by the user for a particular application. The first of these parts is called the "boot record." This is the short program that the bootstrap loader loads into memory, and it is this program that is responsible for further loading the rest of the DOS into memory. On some disks, called nonsystem disks, the boot record is replaced with an error message. This is the error message that you see when you try to start (boot) the system with a non-DOS disk. A more detailed discussion of the boot record will follow in the next chapter.

The rest of DOS is then loaded from the disk, where it is stored in two parts. The first part is the program that interfaces the operating system with the programs stored in the system ROM, and it is called the BIOS interface. The second part is the main body of the operating system itself. Finally, another program called the "command processor" is loaded and the system is started.

Once DOS is placed in memory by the boot operation, it is available for use either by an operator typing commands at the keyboard or by a program making "calls" to it. Most people who use DOS will really only be aware of it when they type in commands to perform system-related functions, such as formatting blank disks or invoking other programs. In this mode of operation the user is talking to the command processor, and all other parts of the system appear to be transparent. When a command is issued to invoke another program, such as advanced BASIC, for all intents and purposes it seems that the operating system has gone away, but, in fact, the bulk of the system is still resident. It has simply slipped into the background, and is called by BASIC when its functions are required.

Files

One of the primary functions of DOS, or any operating system for that matter, is to handle all the mundane tasks associated with file manipulation. In order to fully grasp the power of DOS, a complete understanding of these files is necessary.

DOS stores all the information that it is given in files on the disk. They relate physically to the disk in much the same way that individual tracks are laid out on a long-playing record album. Files can contain either data or programs. DOS itself is stored in files on the disk, as is BASIC and the demonstration programs that come on the DOS master disk. When a file is created, the user gives the file a name, and DOS then manipulates the file by that name. There are specific rules for naming DOS files, and a set of conventions that should be obeyed.

The full name for a disk file, called a file *specification,* consists of three parts. These parts are called the drive designation, the file name, and the extension. These are used in the format:

d:filename.ext

where *d* is the drive designation, *filename* is the name that the file was given, and *ext* is the extension. The colon and the period must be used as shown.

The drive designation is a single character that is used to tell DOS on which disk drive the file that is being accessed is located. If your system has a single disk drive, it is not necessary to enter the drive designation or the colon. Disk drives are referred to in alphabetic order; for example, the first disk drive is referred to as A:, the next B:, then C:, etc. Note that the drive letter can be either upper- or lower-case, and that the colon is always used as part of the drive designation. When you first enter DOS, you will be "logged on" to drive A: Typing another letter and a colon will then log you on to that designated drive.

If you wish to access a file on the drive that you are already logged on to, it is not necessary to supply the drive designation, since DOS always automatically defaults to the drive that you are currently logged on to, called the logged or active drive. If you want to access a file on a disk drive other than the currently logged drive and you don't want to log on to that drive, you must specify the drive designation as part of the file specification.

The file name is any name that you want to specify consisting of up to eight characters. The characters that can be used to make up the file name are all of the alphabetic characters a–z, the numeric characters 0–9, and many of the punctuation symbols that are available on the keyboard. The following punctuation symbols may be used in a legal DOS file name:

& # @ ! % [} _ ' ( ) -

Since the period (.) is used to separate the file name from the extension, it obviously cannot otherwise be used in a file name. For the same reason, since it is used in the drive designation, neither can the colon be used. For similar reasons, as we shall see later, neither the ? nor the * may be used in a file name and the \ < > and | symbols cannot be used. For reasons that are too complex to go into now, it is not recommended that the percent (%) character be used in a file name. In general, you should avoid any use of punctuation symbols in a file name—if possible.

The actual name given to the file is entirely up to you, but the name should be used to give some idea of the nature of the contents of the file. When creating a file name, you should try to take advantage of all eight character positions that DOS makes available for file names—otherwise DOS will fill them in with blanks. Once you are more familiar with DOS, you should establish and use a specific set of guidelines for naming DOS files to take advantage of some of the more subtle features of DOS, which will be discussed later.

The extension is a three-character block that is generally used to indicate what type of file it is and what form the contents of the file take. DOS adds its own extensions to certain types of files if they are not defined by the user. For example, a file containing a BASIC program will be given the extension .bas.

The following extensions have specific meanings to DOS:

.bak	DOS created backup file
.bas	BASIC program file
.bat	batch processing file
.com	external command file or program
.exe	executable command file or program
.hex	special file for use with **debug**
.map	special listing file used with **link**
.obj	object code file from compiler
.rel	object code file from assembler
.tmp	temporary file created by DOS

Other file extensions can be created and used by the user arbitrarily. For example, many word-processing programs use the extension .txt to indicate that the file is a text file. Similarly, the extension .ndx could be used to indicate that the file contains an index, .dbf might indicate a database file, and .rep might be a report. In a situation where more than one user is accessing a single disk, the file extensions could be the initials of each user or any other code name.

The Joker's Wild

One interesting feature of DOS is its ability to use *wildcards* in conjunction with commands that access files by name. These wildcards are the two characters mentioned earlier that cannot be used in a file name or extension—? and *.

The ? is a single-character wildcard and when included in a file specification (filespec) it will cause the command to refer to a file with any character in that position. For example, if two files named file1.txt and file2.txt were to be deleted using the **erase** command, you could type

```
erase file1.txt
```

and then

```
erase file2.txt
```

However, the single command

```
erase file?.txt
```

could be issued. The ? can be used anywhere in the file name or extension, and can be used repeatedly. However, instead of using it to describe whole words, the * is used. The * means *all*. For example, if all the files with the extension .bad are to be deleted from the disk, the command

```
erase *.bad
```

can be entered. Similarly, if a program is being used that generates many files with the same file name but with different extensions, and all of these files are to be erased, the * can be used in the extension. Suppose that a program is being used that generates the files named data.one, data.two, and data.thr. To erase all of these files at once, the command

```
erase data.*
```

could be used. Of course, if the files data.for and data.fiv are also on the disk but they are not to be erased, the wildcard cannot be used.

If, for whatever reason, all the files are to be erased from a particular disk, the command

```
erase *.*
```

is used. Some thought should go into the naming scheme that you use for files so as to best take advantage of wildcards.

*The **Dir** Command*

DOS keeps track of all the files on each disk by maintaining a directory on a special part of the disk. The directory can be displayed by typing the **dir** command. Along with the file names, the **dir** command instructs DOS to display the size of the file in bytes (characters) and the date on which the file was created. File names and wildcards can be used with the **dir** command to give selective listings of the directory.

As often happens on a full disk, the directory will be too long to fit on a single screen, causing much consternation as it scrolls off the top of the screen. If, in such a situation, a listing of all the BASIC programs on a disk (.bas files) is needed, DOS can be given the command:

```
dir *.bas
```

This will cause a listing of all the .bas files to be displayed on the screen. The command

```
dir *.com
```

will cause a list of all the files on the disk with the extension .com to be displayed.

DOS Commands

The preceding examples show the uses of two DOS commands **erase** and **dir**. These two were selected as an introduction to the concept of DOS commands because they are the most simple of all the commands available and each responds with an immediate and definite action. Either of these commands can be typed at the keyboard and DOS will respond with the appropriate action. These are both examples of the use of DOS in the "immediate mode." Immediate commands can be typed into the PC whenever the DOS prompt > is visible. The prompt is always preceded by the active disk drive letter, e.g., A> indicating that drive A: is the currently active drive.

The two examples quoted happen to be examples of *internal* commands—that is, these commands are built into DOS and are loaded into memory whenever DOS is loaded. There are, in fact, two different types of DOS commands—*internal* and *external*. The only difference is that internal commands are loaded into memory when DOS is loaded, and external commands are loaded into memory each time, and only when, the user wants to use them.

External commands are stored on the DOS master disk in files given the extension .com. To invoke an external command, the process is identical to that of internal commands—i.e., the name of the command is typed on the keyboard after the DOS prompt. For example, the DOS command to change the internal time of the PC is **time** and is entered after the prompt:

```
A>time
```

Note that even though the command itself is stored on the disk in the file called **time.com,** there is no need to type the extension **.com.** It is actually immaterial if the .com extension is entered, whether the command is an internal command or an external command. Either way, if the .com extension is entered it is simply ignored. Since it is totally redundant, it is a habit that is not usefully employed.

When you enter the name of an external command such as **time,** DOS will read the information from the file, which in this case would be **time.com,** and perform the task, in this case prompting for the time to be entered on the keyboard. When this is done, the internal time will be updated and DOS will then return to the prompt, awaiting another command. Of the seventeen commands supplied with DOS version 1.0, nine are external commands and eight are internal.

The internal DOS 1.0 commands are:

(batch)
copy
dir
erase
pause
rem
rename
type

The external DOS commands are:

chkdsk
comp
date
diskcomp
diskcopy
format
mode
sys
time

Other than the fact that DOS must first read external commands from the disk, to the user there are no differences between the two.

The obvious advantage of having the external command system is that any competent programmer can add his or her own DOS external commands simply by writing them using the macro assembler or any of the native language compilers of the PC and storing them in .com files on a DOS disk. In fact, that is exactly how the languages and many of the applications programs are stored. For example, to invoke advanced BASIC, the user types **basica** at the keyboard. DOS then looks for an external command called **basica.com** on the disk, and if it finds it, will load and execute the command. The result is that the user is then placed in advanced BASIC. This process will be examined in greater detail in a later chapter. For now, a basic understanding of the mechanism behind the internal and external DOS commands will suffice.

CHAPTER 4

Creating and Duplicating Diskettes

When most disks are purchased, they are blank, virgin disks and have no magnetic marks written on them. Going back to our record-album analogy, this would be like having the blank plastic without any tracks or even grooves on it. Before they can be used with DOS, they must be specially prepared. This preparation is known as *formatting* or, as some people call it, *initialization*.

Some disks may be purchased already formatted, usually at a premium, but it is always best to format them on your own system, or the system they are to be used on. This assures that the magnetic marks are in synchronization with your particular disk drives. Minute variations in speed between two disk drives may mean that DOS will have to try several times before it can read information off a disk. Large variations in speed are cause for alarm and indicate that your disk drives are due for servicing by a professional.

The process of formatting a disk is relatively trivial, but is, of course, highly necessary. Without the magnetic marks on the disk, DOS would not be able to find its way around on the surface. It would not be able to write information to a disk or read any information off it. Fortunately, DOS can take care of the formatting process all by itself when so instructed.

Not quite so trivial, and just as important, is the process of duplicating a disk, commonly called "making a backup." This process is essential for anyone who is writing valuable data onto a disk. Whether it be business information or a fun program that you are writing, always back up important disks. Again DOS makes it easy to perform this, since it has a utility command that takes care of it for you.

*The **Format** Command*

The **format** command is the first command that should be learned, since it is both the most creative and potentially the most destructive of all the DOS commands. **Format** is an external command stored on the master disk in the file **format.com.** It is used to format blank diskettes for use with DOS version 1.

When DOS version 1 formats a disk, it breaks the surface into 40 concentric tracks. Each track is subdivided into 8 sectors, each the same size. These sectors are capable of holding up to 512 bytes each. Consequently, the total storage capacity of a single-sided disk is 40 × 8 × 512 bytes, or 163,840 bytes—about the equivalent of thirty typed pages of information.

Some of the disk space is required by DOS to store the directory and certain other information about the files on the disk. More space is required by DOS if a copy of the operating system itself is to be placed on the disk. By placing the operating system on the disk, the disk becomes a *master* DOS disk. That is, the PC can be booted with that disk. Some users prefer to have all of their disks be masters, but this is not really necessary. In fact, master disks have considerably less space available for data storage than data disks due to the space taken up by the operating system itself. It is better to have DOS reside on only those disks that will be used when the system is first turned on.

Disks that do not have a copy of the operating system placed on them are sometimes referred to as *slave* disks, or data disks. One point frequently misunderstood by PC users is that once a disk has been formatted as a slave disk, it *cannot* simply be turned into a master. This is due to the way in which DOS allocates space on the disk.

When DOS version 1 formats disks, it assigns each track a number from 0 to 39, and each sector is given a number from 1 to 8. The reason that the track numbering system starts at 0 instead of 1 is that DOS uses the first track largely to maintain the disk directory tables. So normally this track is not available for the storage of user information. Track 0, sector 1, is used to store the boot record mentioned earlier. This boot record is different for a master and slave disk. In a master disk the boot record contains the code necessary to read the rest of DOS into memory during the boot process. On a slave disk the boot record contains the error message that appears when you attempt to boot the system with a nonmaster (slave) disk.

Track 0, sector 2, contains a table known as the file allocation table (FAT). The FAT is used by DOS to keep track of which sectors on the disk are currently being used for file storage. In a later chapter we will take a closer look at the FAT. Track 0, sector 3, contains an exact duplicate of the FAT. If, for any reason, DOS has a hard time reading the first copy of the FAT, it will attempt to read the second copy.

This is a particularly interesting feature of DOS which contrasts sharply with similar operating systems that keep only one single copy of the allocation table on disk; in such a system, if one single bit is incorrectly set by whatever means, from magnetic interference to dirt or dust damage, the entire disk may be rendered unusable and may have to be reformatted. In a situation like that, if the disk contains valuable information, it may be lost entirely. Unfortunately, Murphy seems to set the rules for this kind of problem—the more valuable the data, the easier it is to lose it! It is heartening to see that DOS is sensitive to this need by supplying a second copy of the FAT on every disk.

Track 0, sectors 4–7, contain the actual disk directory. The directory has space allocated for 64 entries. Each entry manages the storage information for one file and is 32 bytes long. Consequently, the entire directory is 64 × 32 bytes, or 2,048 bytes (2K) long. Every directory entry contains information about a particular file, including its file name and extension, the date that the file was created, and a pointer to the sector that contains the start of the file. It is from this directory that DOS derives the information that is presented on the screen when the **dir** command is entered.

On a slave disk the remaining sectors—track 0, sector 8, through track 39, sector 8—are available for user file storage. A quick count will indicate that in this optimum situation there are a total of 313 free sectors on a newly formatted single-sided diskette. Since each sector can store 512 bytes, this means that such a disk has a total of 160,256 bytes available for data storage. The other 3,584 bytes are consequently not available and can be considered as overhead.

On a master disk there must be other space allocated for storage of the operating system itself. As mentioned earlier this data is stored in two system files. These system files are always stored in the exact same disk locations so that the boot code always knows exactly where to find them. This explains why master disks cannot be made out of data disks as an afterthought. If this was attempted, any data residing in these sectors would most probably be erased or overwritten.

Track 0, sector 8, through track 1, sector 3, contains the system file ibmbio.com and track 1, sector 4, through track 2, sector 8, contains the file ibmdos.com. Therefore, for master disks there is another disk space overhead of 8,704 bytes. A further amount of disk space is then allocated to the file command.com. Since this file can be replaced by a user-developed program, it is not actually considered as pure overhead, although the command.com supplied with IBM DOS version 1.0 does take up a further 3,231 bytes. In all, a master disk will have approximately 157,025 bytes free for user data storage.

The process by which master disks are created is slightly different from the normal formatting procedure. To format a disk for use as a data (slave) disk, all that is required is that the **format** command be used. DOS will then prompt for the disk drive containing the blank disk to be formatted. Enter the drive specification and the ever-required colon and the **format** program will begin to format the blank diskette.

Once you are better acquainted with the process, you can speed things up a bit by specifying the target drive along with the **format** command. For example, if the DOS master disk is in drive A: and you are logged on to it, and the blank disk is in drive B:, then you can shorten the process by entering the command and the argument—which in this case would be the target drive specification—on one line by typing:

```
format b:
```

DOS will then load the **format** program from the master disk and prompt the user to enter a blank disk in drive B:. Pressing Return then starts the formatting. When it is done, DOS will prompt to ask if there are other disks to be formatted, and if so to enter another blank disk. It is usually a good time saver to format several disks at one time. Once all the disks are formatted, press the *n* key when prompted and DOS will return to the command processor, awaiting another command.

To create a master disk, DOS has the facility to set a "switch" in the command. This switch takes the form of a **/s,** which stands for *system*. This tells DOS to transfer the system files that differentiate a master disk from a slave disk after the format process is complete. The command to create a master or system disk in drive B: would therefore be:

```
format b:/s
```

The difference between the two processes is that DOS now transfers the operating system files to the diskette in drive B: after it has written the formatting marks and directory information onto the diskette. A disk created in this manner would be usable to boot the system when it is first switched on.

When you have finished formatting a disk, it is good practice to issue the **dir** command to make sure that it has formatted correctly. If the message "no files" comes back, you know that the disk has been formatted correctly. Sometimes, though, DOS will not be able to format a portion of the disk correctly. In cases like this, DOS will mark the offending tracks as unusable in the FAT. This means that these tracks will not be used to store data, assuring better data integrity. In version 1 of DOS, the unusable tracks will be allocated to a hypothetical file named badtrack in the directory, so that they cannot be accidentally allocated to a user's file.

As a last word about the **format** command, it was mentioned that it could be the most destructive of all the DOS commands. For obvious reasons, it should be clear that disks containing valuable information can quite easily be accidentally wiped clean by the formatting process. To guard against this, make sure that all your diskettes are clearly labeled; if the information on the disk is very important, use a write-protect tab over the cutout on the left side of the disk. This prevents DOS from accidentally writing to the disk or formatting it if the wrong command is typed.

*The **Diskcopy** Command*

The next DOS command that we will examine is the **diskcopy** command, whose function is obviously to make copies of a particular disk. **Diskcopy** acts as a bulk copier for making duplicate backup copies of entire disks. The copies, or target disks, are exact images of the original, or source disk. With version 1.0 of DOS target disks must first be formatted prior to using **diskcopy.** DOS also has a **copy** command that is used for transferring specific files from one diskette to another. **Copy** can also be used to create backups of important disks, but since it works with one file at a time it is considerably slower than **diskcopy. Copy** will be examined closely later.

The syntax that must be used for **diskcopy** introduces us to a syntactical approach that DOS takes that differs from the method many people learned to use with older operating systems, such as the CP/M operating system. To illustrate, the syntax used by DOS to copy the source diskette in one drive to the target diskette in another is

```
diskcopy d: D:
```

where *d:* is the source disk drive specification and *D:* is the target disk drive specification.

This is actually quite an intuitive, logical method of specifying the source and target. For example, if the contents of the diskette in drive A: are to be copied to the diskette in drive B:, the command

```
diskcopy a: b:
```

is given. This can easily be remembered mnemonically as "copy a: to b:." CP/M, on the other hand, worked logically backward from this, and is consequently somewhat counterintuitive and difficult to learn for both unsophisticated and sophisticated users alike.

Operators who have become familiar with CP/M will no doubt remember the frustration this accorded them during the initial phase of learning the operating system and its commands. Rather than having to learn a new system, CP/M users will have the harder task of having to "unlearn" an awkward system. In all, the result is that DOS brings more intuition to play than its early predecessors.

Conveniently for those who have a single-drive system, **diskcopy** will function as either a single-disk or dual-disk copy program. When only one disk drive is attached to the system, **diskcopy** will read as much information into memory as it can hold and then prompt the user to exchange diskettes so that it can write to the target disk. It will cycle through this process until all of the data have been copied from one disk to the other. This may mean that you have to swap disks several times. Take care during this process to make sure that you keep track of which disk is which, otherwise you may wipe out your original.

Since **diskcopy** copies whole tracks at a time, it will also copy DOS itself. Therefore, if a backup copy of a DOS master disk is to be made, there is no need to first format the target disk as a master disk. In other words, when formatting a disk for use with the **diskcopy** command, there is never any need to use the /s switch in the **format** command.

Using the **format** command and the **diskcopy** command, most users should be able to make backup copies of any important disks. In its documentation IBM advises that, wherever possible, backup copies of disks should be used, and originals should be kept on file. This approach should ensure that valuable disks will never be lost.

Anyone who has been using or operating a personal computer in the past is well aware of the pitfalls that await the inexperienced user. The accidental erasure of valuable software or data is perhaps the most frustrating of these. In any office environment where people are using a PC on a daily basis, the latter part of the day should be employed to back up the day's work. As time-consuming as it may appear, it is not nearly as time-consuming, or costly for that matter, as having to reconstruct accidentally lost data.

CHAPTER 5

The Internal Commands

We've seen how to use several of the most basic commands that are part of DOS version 1.0. Let us now restrict ourselves to the type of command that all users will need to be familiar with. These are the utility commands used to make backup copies of files, erase files from a disk, and change the name that a file was given. In the language of DOS they are the internal commands—**copy, erase, rename,** and **type.**

As was explained earlier, these commands are built into the DOS module that is loaded into memory whenever the system is booted. Therefore, they are always resident in memory and can be invoked by simply typing the command name at the keyboard—along with whatever arguments, if any, are required by the particular command. Other DOS commands, known as external commands, are resident on the master disk and are read into memory from disk each time they are invoked. One consequence of this is that the internal commands are available when the system is booted with any user-created master disk, regardless of whether the other DOS command files have been transferred to the disk or not.

In the last chapter it was explained how to format a blank disk with the **format** and **format /s** commands, and how to copy the contents of one disk to another using the **diskcopy** command. **Diskcopy** is, of course, an external command, and will probably be used less frequently than the internal **copy** command. As we will see, there are distinct differences between the two.

*The **Copy** Command*

The **copy** command is an internal DOS command used to transfer individual files from one disk to another—or even to the same disk. During the copy process the name of the copied file may be changed. The primary use of the **copy** command is to make backup copies of individual files. Backing up important data files is highly recommended and is the single most important deterrent against accidental erasure of valuable data.

There are several syntactical forms for the **copy** command, depending on the particular function being performed and the disk-drive configuration used. In all of these variations one important determinant is the default or logged drive specification. As was seen earlier, a disk drive is logged on by typing the letter corresponding to that disk drive and the ever-required colon. For example, to log on to the B: disk drive, the command

```
b: [Return]
```

is typed. In each of the examples presented, we will assume that we are logged on to drive A: unless otherwise stated.

The first form of the **copy** command is:

```
copy filespec
```

The **filespec** referred to takes the form of

```
d:filename.ext
```

as was seen earlier. To illustrate this, let us assume that we are logged on to drive A: and that we want to copy a file named sample.txt from drive B: onto the disk in drive A:. To accomplish this we would type:

```
copy b:sample.txt
```

This has the effect of reading the file sample.txt from the disk in drive B: into memory and then writing it onto the disk in drive A:. If the file is too big to be read into the available user memory, as much of the file as will fit into memory at one time will be read in and then written to the target disk. This cycle will then continue until all of the file has been transferred.

The second form of the command can be illustrated by an example that does the reverse of this; it copies a file from the logged drive A: to the disk in drive B:. The syntax of the **copy** command to accomplish this would be:

```
copy filename[.ext] d:
```

The *d:* in this case is the drive designation of the target drive—the drive containing the disk onto which the file is to be copied. This is best illustrated.

Using an example comparable to the one preceding, let us assume that we are logged on to drive A: and that we are to copy a file named sample.txt from drive A: to drive B:. The syntax of the command required would be:

```
copy sample.txt b:
```

This is easily remembered mnemonically as "copy sample.txt to b:."

Combining these two examples, we can see that any file can be copied from one drive to any other drive. In a situation where there are more than two disk drives, the syntax remains the same. For example, if we are logged on to drive A: and have to copy a file named sample.txt from drive B: to drive C:, the command format would be:

```
copy b:sample.txt c:
```

Another way of accomplishing the same result would be to log on to drive B: first, issue the command

```
copy sample.txt c:
```

and then log back on to drive A:. This method does add a few more steps to the process and is not quite as efficient as the preferred method. However, the result is the same, and the method of accomplishing this result is left up to you—use whatever method is most comfortable.

The next form of the **copy** command results from a situation whereby a file must be transferred from one drive to another and the name of the file must be changed. The full syntactical format for this type of command can be described as:

```
copy filespec filespec
```

In this case, the first *filespec* is the name and drive designation of the file that is being copied from, the source file, and the second *filespec* is the name and drive designation of the file that is to be created, the target file. To illustrate this, let us assume that we are logged on to drive A: and that we are to copy the file sample.txt from drive A: to drive B:, and at the same time change the name of the new file to backup.txt. The command format would be:

```
copy sample.txt b:backup.txt
```

To further illustrate, let us assume that we are to copy the file sample.txt from drive B: to drive C: and again rename it. In this case, the command would be:

```
copy b:sample.txt c:backup.txt
```

In the first example the drive designation (A:) for the source drive was omitted because it was the currently logged drive. If there is ever any confusion, there is no harm done in entering the drive designation, even if it is redundant. It does mean entering more characters than are actually required, but if it helps to clarify the task, then it really does perform a function.

The second example illustrates an interesting feature of DOS: the ability to create a backup copy of a file on the same disk as the source file. This is accomplished either by leaving off the drive designations, or by making them both the same, depending on whether you are currently logged on to that drive or not. For example, to make a backup copy of the file sample.txt on drive A: and call it backup.txt, the command would be:

```
copy sample.txt backup.txt
```

If the file was on drive B:, the command

```
copy b:sample.txt b:backup.txt
```

would be used. It is easy to see that if a backup copy of a file is to be created on the same disk as the source file, then the newly created file must be given a file name or extension that is different from the original source file. Otherwise, DOS would not accept the command, since it would lead to the unacceptable situation of having two files on the same disk with the same name—a situation that DOS would not be able to work with. If this is attempted, DOS will return the error message:

```
File cannot be copied onto itself
0 files(s) copied
```

Another interesting feature of the **copy** command is its ability to accept commands that incorporate the wildcard characters discussed earlier, ? and *. As you may remember, these characters can be used as wildcards in file names. By including wildcards in the file names, the **copy** command can copy multiple files at a time. The simplest example of the use of these wildcards would be the situation in which all the files on the source disk were to be copied to the target disk. The command format for this type of **copy** would be:

```
copy *.* b:
```

This would achieve substantially the same effect as using the **diskcopy** command, in that all the files from the logged drive would be copied to drive B:. During the process all the file names would remain the same.

Similarly, if all the files with the same extension were to be copied from the logged drive to drive B:, the command would be:

```
copy *.ext b:
```

It can quickly be seen that the use of wildcards in the **copy** command can be used to your advantage. For example, if the file example.txt is to be transferred from the logged drive to drive B:, and at the same time the name is to be changed to example.bak, then you could type:

```
copy example.txt b:example.bak
```

Or the shorter

```
copy example.txt b:*.bak
```

can be used. Similarly, if all the text files with the extension .txt are to be backed up onto the same disk and given the new extension .bak, the command

```
copy *.txt *.bak
```

can be used.

Before leaving the **copy** command, a short discussion on the differences between the internal **copy** *.* command and the external **diskcopy** command is in order.

Although both of these commands appear to perform the same task, there are real differences in both the method and the result. As we saw, the **diskcopy** command makes an exact duplicate of the source disk. Therefore, if the source disk is a master, or bootable, disk, the target disk will also be a master.

Not so in the case of the **copy** *.* command. This command will only copy the nonsystem files, and will not create a master disk. In fact, there is only one situation in which use of the **copy** *.* command to copy an entire disk makes more sense than use of the faster **diskcopy** command. That is the case where file access is being hampered by the nonlinear distribution of file space on a disk. This can happen when a disk is used often, or when files are erased from a disk and then the disk is used to store other data.

To understand this situation, it is necessary to understand a little of how DOS actually allocates disk space for files. When DOS gets a request to allocate disk space to store a file, it allocates sectors on a first come first served basis. That is, whenever a file requests more space from DOS, DOS will allocate the next available sector from the file allocation table (FAT). This means that disk files will probably not be distributed sequentially on a disk, but may be scattered around a disk in a seemingly random manner. This situation is aggravated when files are erased from a disk, freeing up disk sectors. The next time a file is written to that disk, DOS will allocate the first available sector. The sector will most probably be one of the sectors freed during the erasure. The result is that the file will be scattered in a seemingly random fashion over many sectors and tracks. The most noticeable exception to this is when a file is written to a fresh disk. Then it will be given a sequential block of sectors.

This, of course, is precisely what the **copy** command does—it writes files, in total, to a disk. Therefore, another use of the **copy** command is to "straighten out" the file allocation for a particular set of files.

This would be used on a disk where DOS takes what may seem like a longer time than normal to access a particular disk file. It is especially helpful when disk files are used to store an index of some sort, where that index then points to data contained in another disk file. Indices that are stored in sequential sectors on a disk may perform considerably better than their randomly written counterparts.

We can summarize by stating that it is worthwhile creating new versions of disks using the **copy** *.* command when the disk is updated frequently with new data, or if many files have been erased from the disk. Occasional use of the **copy** *.* command may shorten the data access time for that disk.

One final note about the **copy** command for those DOS users who may have used the CP/M operating system in the past. **Copy** substantially replaces the CP/M PIP command, and for most purposes performs in an identical manner. The most obvious difference between the two is the order of the arguments, and, as stated earlier, CP/M users will have the more difficult task of unlearning the logically backward approach of CP/M in favor of the more intuitive syntax of DOS.

The other obvious difference between the DOS **copy** and the CP/M PIP is that **copy** is an internal command. One of the extremely annoying aspects of using the PIP command was that since it was an external command, there had to be a copy of PIP on the disk before it could be used. In many cases, this meant that before you could copy a file using PIP you had to copy PIP itself. Not so with the DOS **copy** command.

There are other, more advanced uses for the **copy** command, as we shall discover later, but since they involve some of the more complex features of DOS, we shall defer them until we have established a good base of understanding for the universally applicable DOS commands.

*The **Erase** Command*

The **erase** command is an internal DOS command whose purpose is to remove the named file or files from a disk. The specific format for the **erase** command is

```
erase filespec
```

where *filespec* is the file specification for the file or files to be erased. For example, to remove the file example.txt from the disk in drive B:, the command

```
erase b:example.txt
```

would be entered. As with the **copy** command, wildcard characters can be used in a filespec to specify a number of files to be erased. For example, to remove all the files with the extension .bak from a disk, the command

```
erase *.bak
```

would be entered. To erase all the files from a disk, a particularly drastic measure, the command

```
erase *.*
```

is entered. This is a command that should be treated with kid gloves. Before you erase all the files from a disk, be certain that this is really what you want to do by looking at the directory (with the **dir** command) and scanning the files to make sure there are none you want to keep. Use of such a command is tantamount to reformatting the disk.

The **erase** command cannot be used to remove the system files from a diskette. That is, it will not operate on the files ibmbio.com, ibmdos.com, or badtrack. It will, however, remove the file command.com if so directed. If you elect to remove this file from a disk, you must replace it with another file by the same name. Otherwise there will be no way to communicate with DOS via the keyboard, since command.com contains the command line interpreter, the link between the visual command line and the operating system. This is not something that can be done by the beginner; a user-supplied command.com must perform many important functions.

When the **erase** command is invoked, it does not actually remove the files from the disk. It marks the files as erased and frees up the sectors that they use in the file allocation table for use by other files. As other files require space, DOS will allocate the first available sector for use by those files. So, the erased data is never actually eradicated from a disk until it is overwritten by DOS.

It is quite possible to reconstruct an erased file by hand—providing that DOS has not written anything to the disk in the interim. However, this is a very difficult and time-consuming process, unless you use one of several utility programs available on the market that perform this function. Of course, such a utility program will only work on a disk if it has not been written to after the accidental erasure.

For those using their PCs in an environment where unsophisticated users are handling valuable data files, such a utility would certainly pay for itself if it ever needed to be used. However, it is best to assume that whenever files are erased from a disk, the data are no longer on the disk. Therefore, you should use the **erase** command with the utmost caution, particularly when using it in conjunction with wildcard characters, since it is potentially one of the most destructive commands in the operating system.

*The **Rename** Command*

The **rename** command is an internal DOS command used to change the name by which a file is stored on the disk. The general syntax for the **rename** command is

```
rename filespec filename
```

where *filespec* refers to the current name and drive designation of the source file, and *filename* refers to the new name that is to be given to it. For example, to change the name of the file oldfile.txt on drive B: to newfile.txt, the command is:

```
rename b:oldfile.txt newfile.txt
```

The wildcard characters ? and * can be used in conjunction with the **rename** command, simplifying the preceding example to:

```
rename b:oldfile.txt new????.*
```

Or even

```
rename b:old*.* new*.*
```

providing that oldfile.txt was the only file on the disk whose name started with the characters old.

If a drive designation is given to the new name it will be ignored. Of course, it is meaningless to rename a file on a drive other than the drive on which the file is located. **Rename** simply alters the contents of the directory, substituting the new name for the old, and does not do anything to the data in the file. Obviously, the new name must obey all the rules for DOS names.

There is one situation in which, theoretically, the use of the **rename** command could lead to disaster—when the new name you give the file is the name of a file that already exists in the directory. This will lead to the intolerable situation of having two files on the disk with the same name. The consequence of this will be that you will only be able to access the file that was created first, since that will be the first file with the given name that DOS will find when it searches through the directory.

This is a situation in which many owners of the popular Apple II computer may have found themselves, since the disk operating system on that computer does not guard against such a situation. Luckily, DOS protects the poor, unsuspecting user by not allowing such a terrible situation to arise. If you try to rename a file by giving it the name of a file that already exists, DOS will return the error message:

```
Duplicate file name or file not found
```

*The **Type** Command*

The last DOS command that we shall examine in this chapter is the **type** command. **Type** is an internal DOS command whose function is to examine the contents of a file by typing it out, either on the video screen or to a printer. This gives the user a method of examining the contents of a file without modifying them. This method can only be used for files that contain ASCII characters, and cannot be used for program files or other binary-type files. ASCII files are those files that contain data. Characters are stored as binary numbers—each number representing a specific character. Each of the 256 binary combinations represents a character. Some of these characters are *control characters* and do not print on a printer or a video screen. However, they can tell certain devices to perform particular tasks. For example, a Control-g tells a printer to ring its bell, or when sent to the video screen tells the computer to beep. Other control characters perform functions such as clearing the screen, or on a printer issuing a page eject or changing the character sets to be displayed, or worse, something totally unpredictable with another device.

Data files will generally contain no such control characters; they will consist mainly of the letters of the alphabet, the digits 0–9, punctuation marks, and some simple control characters used for formatting, such as a carriage return, a line feed, or a tab character. The **type** command is designed to work with files such as these.

On the other hand, program files—those files that contain the programs, DOS commands, or other code—store binary representations of codes that do not represent the letters of the alphabet. Attempting to **type** such a file will have totally unpredictable results, since a code that represents a simple program statement may also be the same code that tells a printer to switch from text mode to graphics—or something equally bizarre! For safety's sake, do not attempt to **type** files that do not contain data; do not attempt to **type** files with the extensions .com, .exe, .hex, .map, .rel, or .obj. Doing so will result in unpredictable action on the part of the computer.

Don't misunderstand: it is quite impossible to do any physical damage to your system by doing so, but it could have unpredictable results, particularly if peripheral equipment is attached.

Conversely, it is perfectly safe to type files with the extensions .bat, .asc, and .dat, or any file that is generated by an applications program known to contain data—particularly those files that are generated by word processors or other text editors.

The general format for the **type** command is:

```
type filespec
```

This is relatively straightforward—there is only one file involved. Wildcard characters, therefore, cannot be used with the **type** command, since their presence makes a file name ambiguous, indicating that more than one file may be named. **Type** requires that the filespec be unambiguous. If a wildcard character is used with **type,** DOS will perform the action on the first file that fits the filespec. When it has typed that file, it will terminate and return to the command line.

Again, this command is best illustrated with an example. To examine the contents of a file named example.txt, located on the disk in drive B:, the command

```
type b:example.txt
```

would be entered. This would cause the contents of the file example.txt to be displayed on the video screen. In order to stop the scrolling, press the Ctrl key and the Num Lock key simultaneously. This causes the action to halt, and it will remain so until you press any other key. This key combination (Ctrl-Num Lock) will suspend the operation of the computer in almost any program—any program in which the programmer has not deliberately programmed around it and thereby eliminated its function.

Another special key combination is Ctrl-PrtSc. This function is invoked by pressing the Ctrl key and the PrtSc (printscreen) key simultaneously and causes all output to the video screen to be output to the printer at the same time.

By pressing this combination, and then invoking the **type** command, the contents of a file can be dumped to the printer as well as to the video screen. All of this can actually be accomplished by entering one line. For example, to dump the contents of the file example.txt on drive B: to the printer, the command

```
[Ctrl-PrtSc]type b:example.txt
```

could be entered. When the operation is done, the printer can be disconnected by again typing the Ctrl-PrtSc combination. This combination has the effect of toggling the printer on and off.

The **type** command will not do anything to attempt to format the contents of a file that is to be dumped either to the screen or to a printer, with one exception—tabs. It will, of course, recognize carriage returns and line feeds, and when it encounters a tab character it will advance to the next eight-column start. That is, all tabs are expanded to spaces consistent with tab stops every eight columns. This may not be consistent with the tab stop arrangement under which the document was prepared, but there is no way for the **type** command to determine what that arrangement was, so it compromises with its own tab stop arrangement of one tab stop every eight columns. Other than this, the document will appear exactly as it is stored on the disk.

CHAPTER 6

The External Commands

At this juncture we have reached a crucial milestone on our way to understanding the software side of the PC. Up to now we have seen how to perform all of the basic functions associated with DOS. These include formatting blank disks, making backup copies of entire disks, copying files from one disk to another, changing the names by which files are stored, deleting files from a disk, displaying the contents of a file, and reading the directory of a disk. These are all of the functions that everyone who uses the PC wil have to learn at some point.

They are the functions that are required learning for anyone who wishes to use applications software packages—the primary reason that most people purchased a PC in the first place. In the jargon of computerese, they are what is known as "housekeeping" tasks. The rest of this book will focus on areas that are not required understanding for PC users, but nevertheless are of use to anyone who cares to take the time to learn them.

Most of the DOS commands that are used on a less frequent basis are stored on the DOS master disk as external files. These commands are stored in .com files. As was seen in chapter 2, that is the only difference between them and the more commonly used internal commands. One consequence of this structure is that these commands are not always available on demand. Either the DOS master disk must be inserted in the disk drive or the files containing the commands must be copied from the DOS master disk onto a user-created disk.

The first area we are going to examine concerns the PC's ability to handle date- and time-related functions. Timing is a very important part of any type of computer equipment, and the PC is no exception. Today's microcomputer chips and their related circuitry operate at speeds that are quite literally running up against the physical boundaries of space and time. The numbers that are quoted for the timings of these chips are often quite staggering, but will probably mean little to the average user.

In many computers and operating systems, timing functions are carried out without the user knowing about them. In the PC, however, some of the characteristics of the internal timing have been left open to user manipulation. This means that users can access timing information via software and can use this information in their programs, or can have programs take control of the PC at specific times.

DOS, which, after all, is simply a program running on the PC, makes use of the timing information in some very interesting ways. In the command interface, for example, this facility is demonstrated in the two external DOS commands—**date** and **time.** Before we look at the commands in depth, though, let's examine a little of the background behind how the PC relates to time in general.

The heartbeat of the PC is produced by an internal clock—a crystal timer to be exact. This clock produces a pulse with a frequency of 14.31818 MHz. That is, it pulses over 14 million times per second. This is the heartbeat from which all internal timing information is derived. Internal circuitry divides this pulse so that it can be used for various operations by driving various devices at different, although related, speeds. One such operation is the pulse that actually drives the Intel 8088 microprocessor chip that is the brain of the PC. This pulse is derived by dividing the clock signal by 3 to produce a 4.77 MHz signal. This is the speed at which the 8088 runs. Another use for the clock is to derive the 3.58 MHz pulse (14.31818 MHz divided by 4) that is used to produce the color burst signal required to drive a color television, RGB monitor, or composite color monitor.

The main clock is supported by a chip known as a three-channel timer/counter (an 8253-5 to be precise). Channel 1 of this counter is used to maintain an accurate time of day. In effect, this circuitry behaves as though it were a very accurate real-time clock built into the PC. The minimum accuracy of this clock is 1.05 µsc. This may seem like overkill! Using a super-high-speed counter simply to keep track of the time of day? However, it does give the PC the ability to perform tasks based on time, and can also keep track of when files are written to disk.

DOS accesses this timer and converts the number that is stored there into a format that we mere humans can read directly as time and date. Whenever you boot the PC, the first thing that you must do is seed this timer with some point at which it can start. This is done by entering the date. This date is then used as the base date for the counter.

The current time of day is not asked for in version 1.0 of DOS, although the option to set the time when the system is booted is included in the later version 1.1. If it is not directly entered, it is set to zero. The internal clock would then take on the function of an elapsed-time indicator, since its starting time was set to zero. In this mode it can show how long you have been glued to the keyboard during any one stretch. DOS also uses the time and date to "time and date stamp" any files that are created. In version 1.0 of DOS the time of creation is not stored. This is, in fact, a feature of version 1.1. Let's take a look at time and date in a little more detail.

*The **Time** Command*

Time is an external DOS command that is used to display and set the internal system time information. The ways in which DOS makes use of the time information have changed dramatically between DOS version 1.0 and version 1.1. In version 1.0 the internal time is set to zero when the system is booted. The internal timer therefore becomes an elapsed-time indicator, indicating the difference in time between whenever the system was booted and the current time.

DOS version 1.0 itself never actually uses the internal time, although any applications program that is running under DOS can make use of it. DOS version 1.1, however, makes extensive use of this information. The rest of this discussion, then, really only applies to DOS version 1.1 and, of course, any later versions.

This internal information is used by programs other than DOS to transfer control for timing-dependent jobs. DOS uses the timing information to time-stamp files. Whenever a user creates a file and then writes the file to disk, DOS (versions 1.1 and later) enters the system time of creation in the directory along with the file name and other information about the file. When that file is then changed by modifying the information that it contains, the time information is modified. This is a particularly helpful characteristic for those who have very large storage devices such as a Winchester-type hard disk drive attached to their PCs.

One of the problems of working with any large mass-storage device is that the medium is not usually removable. Therefore it is extremely difficult to make backup copies of the information. Several alternative solutions exist for this dilemma, ranging from the use of a second hard disk (very expensive and not very cost effective) to backing up onto floppy disk (very cost effective but very time-consuming).

Using the time-stamping facility, it is quite easy for a programmer to create an incremental backup system, a program that can be used to back up only those files that have been modified since the last backup. Such a program would compare the date and time stamps of the file that is to be backed up with the date and time stamps of the last backup of the file. If they are the same, there is no need to perform the **copy** process. If they are different, the **copy** program would proceed.

The disk-resident **time** command is used to both display and alter the internal system clock. It is invoked simply by typing the command at the keyboard with the DOS master disk in the disk drive. DOS will read the command from the time.com file and execute it. The result is that the system time is displayed on the screen and you are prompted to enter the new time. For example:

```
time
Current time is 07:10:55.51
Enter new time:
```

The time displayed is in the format hours (on a twenty-four-hour scale), minutes, seconds, and fractions of a second. As is obvious, with a resolution of microseconds it is quite easy for the PC to maintain the time down to the hundredth of a second. If you simply press Return, the time will not be changed. If you wish to set the time to something else, enter it as:

```
hh:mm:ss.xx
```

The internal time will be updated to whatever you enter as soon as you press the Return key. Note that there is actually no need to enter the full time all the way down to fractions of a second. If the time is three-fifteen in the afternoon, all that need be entered is 15:15. If it is exactly four o'clock, simply enter 16. DOS accepts any part of the time and leaves the accuracy of the entry up to the user.

*The **Date** Command*

Date is an external DOS command that is used to both display and change the internal system date information. Date information is used to stamp files created under both DOS version 1.0 and version 1.1.

When DOS is first booted, the user is prompted to enter the date. Since all files created are date-stamped, it is always advisable to enter the proper date. Failure to do so may lead to unpredictable consequences with some applications software packages. Inside, DOS only understands dates that are later than January 1, 1980. Of course, there were no DOS systems running previous to that date. If, for whatever reason, you wish to display or change the internal date of the system, enter the **date** command and DOS will first display the current date and then repeat the same prompt that it displays when booted. If you wish to modify the date, enter it again in the format:

```
mm-dd-yy
```

The upper limit for dates turns out to be 12–31–99, which tends to limit the useful life of DOS to less than fifteen years. Fortunately, there will most certainly be a better version of DOS available before then (?). Unlike the **time** command, the entire date must be entered. DOS will not accept a partial date.

*The **Sys** Command*

The DOS manual describes **sys** as a command to transfer the operating system files from one drive to another. This could lead to confusion since it has already been established that the DOS **format d:/s** command both formats the target disk and then writes the system files onto it. Why then is there a need for the **sys** command? Most people have assumed that it is to modify a disk that was created with the simple **format** command—a nonsystem disk—into a DOS master disk. However, whenever this is attempted DOS returns the error message:

```
No room for system on destination disk
```

What function, then, does the **sys** command perform? To understand the raison d'être for **sys**, a little foray into copyright law is required. DOS is a copyrighted piece of software. It is copyrighted first by Microsoft Corporation, the owners, and then by IBM, the licensor. No other person or company is allowed to distribute PC-DOS without first arranging a distribution license from IBM (currently not offering such a license). As a consequence of this, it is not legal for a software manufacturer to distribute copies of the operating system on a program disk.

Many software distributors want to make it as easy and painless as possible for a user to install a newly purchased software package on his or her machine. The best method to accomplish this is to distribute a disk that has been formatted with the **format d:/s** command, but from which the system files have been erased. In this way software vendors do not have to distribute the DOS system files on their disks and are therefore in compliance with federal copyright laws and are not giving away a piece of software that is the legal property of IBM.

This would mean that the purchaser, who should have already paid for DOS, and is therefore a legitimate owner of the operating system, has to perform the operation of writing the system files onto the disk. DOS has already prepared the disk, so there is room for these system files in the proper place that they should be stored. If you remember from a past chapter, it was described how and why DOS does this.

It is expressly for this purpose that the **sys** command was created. When a new piece of software is purchased to run under DOS, the procedure for making it into a DOS compatible, bootable disk is generally as follows:

1. Format a blank disk with the simple **format** command.
2. Copy the contents of the purchased disk onto the newly created disk using the **diskcopy** command.
3. Transfer the system files from the DOS master disk to the new disk using the **sys** command.
4. Place the purchased disk in a safe place and use only the backup disk. Never write anything onto the purchased disk.

There are other ways in which this same result can be accomplished, but sometimes other methods may not work correctly. Before doing this, always consult the documentation that should come with any software package.

There are some software packages that do not need DOS, including some of the packages that utilize sophisticated software protection schemes. This type of disk does not allow the purchaser to make backup copies. Use of the **sys** command on a copy-protected disk may cause irreparable damage. Always read the documentation before writing the system files onto a disk.

Another creative use of the **sys** command is to update the operating system on a disk from an old version to a new version. If you had previously created several DOS master disks using version 1.0 of DOS and you wish to upgrade them to the version 1.1 that you just purchased, use the **sys** command. In this way you could alter all of your old master disks, so that you use only the most recent version of the operating system. However, this is not recommended practice.

Whenever you go through a process as radical as updating your operating system, you should always prepare a completely new set of disks. These new disks should be prepared under the new version of the operating system to ensure complete compatibility. This way, if you ever have to revert to the older version because some software does not work correctly under the new version, you still have your old disks intact.

CHAPTER 7

Verifying Data

The process of verifying data is as important to guaranteeing safe data as making backup disks or keeping duplicate copies of files on a disk. In fact, making backups and verifying the results should really be thought of as one single activity. DOS supplies two powerful tools to check on the integrity of backup files and disks. These tools should be used to verify the copy procedure every time it is used on important data and files. If an error is encountered, the copy should be run again.

Most nonprofessional users quickly learn that this is the only way to handle data. The problem is that it usually isn't quick enough or easy enough. Unfortunately, many suffer from bitter experiences, such as losing several hours, or even days, of work. Simply accept the fact that it must be done.

The verification process has been perceived, in the past, as being the first hurdle to using computers. The making of backup disks is perceived as being totally acceptable and something that must be done, but verifying the process is usually treated as being a lot of work to accomplish little. This is the wrong attitude. If the verification process ever turns up one single error, then, as we shall see, it was worth the effort.

To make matters a lot more simple, we'll see in the next chapter that DOS has ways of making repetitive processes like formatting, copying, and verification much more fun by making it much less work.

*The **Diskcomp** Command*

The **diskcomp** command is an external command stored on the DOS master disk. Its purpose is to compare the contents of two disks to see if they are the same. Usually **diskcomp** is invoked after you have made a backup copy of a disk using the **diskcopy** command, as explained earlier. It would then be used to check that the copy was completely successful. **Diskcomp** is a track-by-track comparison, rather than file by file. It reads whole tracks of data into memory from each disk and then compares them, byte by byte. If discrepancies are found on any track, the bell will ring and the offending track number will be displayed on the screen.

Diskcomp can be used with either a single-drive or a dual-drive system. The syntax is as follows:

```
diskcomp d: [d:]
```

The second *d:* is optional. If only one drive designation (or indeed no drive designation since it will default to the logged drive) is entered, the command will perform a single-drive comparison, prompting the user when to swap disks. If two drive designations are entered, it will perform a dual-drive comparison and the user will not have to switch disks.

Diskcomp is actually an excellent command to illustrate some of the concepts that have already been learned. If possible, try the following example on your own PC.

The disk that we are going to use in this particular example is the DOS version 1.0 master disk, although a similar scenario can be created with any master disk. Place a DOS master disk in drive A: and boot the system. Enter the proper date, and where appropriate time, and DOS will display the A> prompt.

Next, take a blank disk and format it in drive B: by use of the **format b:** command. When this is done, copy the entire contents of the master disk, which should be in drive A:, onto the new disk in drive B:, using the command:

```
diskcopy a: b:
```

This essentially creates a copy of the DOS master disk in drive B:. When this is complete, type the following:

```
diskcomp a: b:
```

The computer will respond with:

```
Insert first disk in drive A
Insert second disk in drive B
Strike any key when ready
```

Press a key and the compare procedure will start. If the **diskcopy** process has performed correctly, you should get back the result:

```
Diskettes compare ok
```

If you didn't get this result, repeat the process until you do. If you consistently fail, there is probably something wrong with your disk drives and you should consult your dealer. Most of us should have gotten this far.

Now, let's deliberately change the contents of the duplicate disk. There should be a file on the disk by the name of comm.bas. Look at the file contents with the **dir** command to make sure. Then delete this file from the duplicate disk by typing:

```
erase b:comm.bas
```

When this is done, again invoke the **diskcomp a: b:** command. This time, when it is run, it will return the message:

```
Compare error(s) on track 00
```

This indicates that there was a discrepancy on track 0. However, since the comm.bas file was the very last entry in the directory, it is highly unlikely that it is stored entirely on track 0, particularly in light of the earlier discussion on the use of track 0 to store the directory and the operating system files. Let's go a little further and find out more about this strange condition.

Delete all the files from the duplicate disk by typing **erase b:*.*.** Then perform the comparison again by typing **diskcomp a: b:.** Again, only one error will result.

Here, we have just seen proof of the fact that the DOS **erase** command never actually erases data from a disk; it simply marks it as erased in the directory and frees up the sectors that the erased file was occupying by marking them as available for further use in the file allocation table. Since the directory and file allocation table are maintained on track 0 of a disk, this is the only area where the **diskcomp** operation will find differences—hence the result we saw.

This demonstrates both the usage and the interpretation of the **diskcomp** command. It is an excellent command for use in verifying the integrity of a backup procedure and should be used directly after every backup operation. If files are deleted from the disk, however, it will only show that the directory has been changed. So don't assume that because a **diskcomp** procedure only returns one compare error that the difference between the two disks is negligible.

DOS provides **diskcomp** as a verification procedure for backups created with the disk-oriented **diskcopy** command. It should be obvious, then, that the **comp** command is the complement of the file-oriented **copy** command.

*The **Comp** Command*

Comp is an external DOS command that is used to compare individual files. In general, **comp** is used immediately after a backup copy of a file is generated as a verification of the data integrity. Where the **diskcomp** command compares an entire disk, sector by sector, the **comp** command compares individual files. The files may be on different disks or on the same disk. The syntactical format for the **comp** command is:

```
comp d:filename d:filename
```

The first drive designation (d:) is mandatory if the file does not exist on the currently logged drive—as with all other DOS commands. The second drive designation is necessary if the second file is not resident on the currently logged drive. If the second file name is not entered, DOS will assume that you want to compare two files with the same name. Of course, in this case, the two files must be located on different disks, since two files with the same name cannot exist on a single DOS version 1 disk.

For those who are intimidated by having to enter long command lines, the **comp** command has an easy mode. By simply entering the **comp** command, a user will be stepped through the process of entering the necessary information. The PC will respond with:

```
Enter primary file name
```

Type in the name of the original file and press Return. The computer will then prompt:

```
Enter 2nd file name or drive id
```

Type in the name of the backup copy of the file, along with the drive-designation letter and colon if it is not located on the logged drive. If the file has the same name as the original file, there is no need to retype it. Simply enter the drive designation and colon and press Return.

Comp will then read the first file into memory, or part of the file if it is too big to fit, and then a similar part of the second file. It will then perform a byte-by-byte comparison of the two files. If the files are obviously different in nature, the **comp** process will be halted.

The first indication of extreme differences between two files is, of course, different file lengths. **Comp** first checks to make sure that the two files are the same length. If they are not the same size, DOS will return the error message:

```
Files are different sizes
```

It will then prompt the user to enter other file names. To exit the **comp** command, press Return.

If **comp** finds differences in two files, it will display them on the screen. The display format for a difference is:

```
Compare error at offset 9E
File 1 = 44
File 2 = 2E
```

The offset is the number of bytes after the beginning of the file in which the discrepancy was discovered, and the two numbers after the File 1 and File 2 designations are the contents of the two different bytes. All of the numbers are in hexadecimal—that is, base sixteen—notation.

When **comp** discovers ten discrepancies between the two files, it will conclude that the files are radically different and will abort the compare process. In this case, the process will be halted and the message

```
10 mismatches - aborting compare
```

will be displayed. Luckily, there is a very easy way to demonstrate this facility, since there are two files with different contents but with the same length on the IBM-supplied DOS master disk. The two files both contain music information for the sample programs contained on the disk and are called pop.bas and forty.bas. To compare them, enter:

```
comp pop.bas forty.bas
```

Note the results.

The wildcard characters * and ? can be used with **comp,** but a multiple-file compare will not be done. Instead, only the first set of files that match the ambiguous file names will be compared.

Anytime an important file or an entire disk is backed up, such as at the end of the day in an accounting department, or after a master *Multiplan* template has been prepared, it is worth the few seconds that it takes to verify the integrity of the backup using either the **diskcomp** or **comp** command.

If, for any reason, the compare turns up errors, immediately recopy the disk or file and retry the comparison. A few seconds spent doing this is well worth the effort, particularly if the file contains information that is important.

For those who have graduated to later versions of DOS, there are better ways of setting up data verification. However, they are not available to DOS version 1 users. Whatever version you are using, it is still better to learn how the **comp** and **diskcomp** commands work. You'll never know when they might come in handy.

CHAPTER 8

Batching

Computers are marvelous tools for the application of solutions. These solutions are usually associated with business, engineering, or scientific problems. In order to reach these solutions, computers are often used to automate processes that we mere human beings would consider as being immensely time-consuming—calculating, adjusting, recalculating, testing. . . . Such rote tasks are generally becoming more and more the domain of the computer, freeing mankind for the performance of other, more meaningful tasks.

Many first-time users of personal computers are quite astounded at the speed at which these machines can perform ordinarily lengthy and time-consuming tasks, such as sorting long lists of names. Few ever ask if they can go any faster. They are always pleasantly surprised to find that one of the best areas in which to apply computer technology and power is the operation of computers themselves. The art of making a computer take care of all the work is not practiced frequently enough in the software industry. DOS, however, brings with it tools that are powerful when applied in this area.

Let's examine a simple operation that many of us encounter on a daily basis—the operation of backing up a disk. What discrete steps does this operation consist of? Well, first we must format a blank disk, using the **format** command. Then we invoke the **copy** or **diskcopy** command, depending on our requirements. Finally we should run a verification of the data disk by using the **comp** or **diskcomp** command.

In other words, we use a total of three different DOS commands. Every day a conscientious user must enter the same string of commands, taking care to make sure that each command has been entered correctly and with the proper syntactical structure. This seems to be a very simple case of a rote function—one of those tasks at which computers excel.

DOS has the built-in facility to remember a series of commands and invoke them when the operator enters a single command. This capability is known as *batching*. Quite simply, a new command is created that is really a "batch" of individual commands. This batch capability is defined in the IBM DOS manual as an internal DOS command. Batch, however, is very different from any of the other DOS commands, in that there is no keyword associated with it, although it is true that all the capabilities of the batch system are available in a manner similar to the other internal commands.

The batch command operates, not by entering **batch** such as you would to invoke any other internal DOS command, but by entering the name of a specially prepared batch file that is stored on the disk. So, even though the facility to perform batch functions is internal to DOS—in that the code that performs the batch function is always stored in memory when DOS is booted—it does require that a file be present on the disk. These special files contain a series of DOS commands, exactly as they would be typed at the keyboard, and are stored in the disk directory as batch files. That is, they are given the extension .bat.

Creating Batch Files

Those users who have already purchased a word processor such as MicroPro's popular *WordStar* program may already be familiar with the creation of files. Some users may even have used **edlin,** the line-oriented mini editor that is supplied with DOS. Whatever method you are using to create files under DOS is perfectly acceptable for the purpose of this exercise. However, for those who have yet to discover this trick, let me give you a quick preview of a feature that we will discuss in more detail later.

Due to a feature of DOS that we shall learn much more about later, called "redirection of standard I/O," a user can treat the keyboard as though it were a file. This may seem a little odd at first until the consequences become clear. Since the keyboard actually generates a stream of characters when a user is typing at it, there are actually many similarities between the keyboard and the structure of a file, which after all is also a stream of characters.

A little creative thinking tells us that if we can treat the keyboard (or "console" as it is known in computer jargon when used in conjunction with the video screen) as a file, we can use the **copy** command to create a backup of the character stream that the file consists of. In fact, this is perfectly feasible.

In DOS the keyboard and video screen are given the special reserved name con:, for console. By copying this "file" to a named disk file, we can actually trap all the characters typed at the keyboard in the disk file. The command to perform this task is

```
copy con: filespec
```

where *filespec* is the complete specification of the file in which we wish to store the character stream.

For example, if we want to create a file that consists of a very short letter to a friend, and we want to store the file on the disk in drive B: under the name letter.fil, we enter the command:

```
copy con: b:letter.fil
```

Anything that we type on the keyboard will then be written out to disk and stored under that name.

When we finish typing the letter, we need to enter a special character so that DOS understands that the file is complete and that we want to return to the normal DOS mode where commands can be typed in and executed. To do this we enter the standard character that DOS uses to mark the end of a disk file. This character is normally a Ctrl-z, entered by holding down the Ctrl key and simultaneously pressing the *z* key.

Conveniently, in this particular mode, DOS turns the F6 special function key into the equivalent of the Ctrl-z. Pressing the F6 key and then the Return key will terminate the **copy** command and return control of DOS to the user. DOS actually marks the end of a file on the disk by storing the special Ctrl-z character as a terminator.

This is about the simplest method of creating DOS files. It is very quick and convenient and does not require any software other than the internal commands inherent in DOS itself. The only problem with this method is that once the Return key has been pressed, the previous line cannot be edited.

The editing features of DOS can only be used on the current line. Therefore if you miss a mistake and press Return, the file is essentially useless and will have to be reentered. However, for very short files, such as the batch files we are discussing, this method is perfectly acceptable.

A Simple Batch File

Perhaps the best way to consolidate this information is to perform a simple example of batch file processing. For the purpose of this example we will assume that you have a dual-drive system. Disk drive A: will contain the DOS master disk or a copy thereof, and disk drive B: will contain a freshly formatted disk with no files yet written on it.

Enter the following commands exactly as shown:

```
copy con: b:testfile.bat
dir a:
dir b:
copy a:*.* b:
dir b:
```

Then press the F6 key. This will cause DOS to enter a Ctrl-z file-terminator character into the file, marking the end of it. It will display this on the screen by showing the ^z sequence, which is DOS's standard method of describing control characters.

Press Return, and DOS will write out the characters that you have typed to the file testfile.bat on drive B:. As is usual, when the **copy** command finishes work, DOS will display the message:

```
1 File(s) copied
```

In order to verify that there was a file created, issue a **dir b:** command. Then enter the **type b:testfile.bat** command and DOS will obligingly display the contents of the file. We now have a batch file containing a series of simple DOS commands stored on the disk in drive B: under the name testfile.bat. In order to invoke any batch file, we simply type the drive, if needed, and the file name without the .bat extension. In this case, to invoke the batch processing of these commands, we would enter the single command:

```
b:testfile
```

When controlled by a batch file, DOS behaves as if the commands were being individually typed at the keyboard instead of coming from a disk file. The net result will be that the newly created **testfile** command will display the directory of drive A:, followed by the directory of drive B:. It will then copy all the files from drive A: to drive B:. Finally, it will display the newly created contents of drive B:.

Essentially we have created a new DOS command called **testfile** whose function is to perform the previously mentioned steps. We have, however, shortened the process. If we were to perform the process by typing each and every character every time, we would need to enter a total of thirty-five keystrokes. Using the batch capability, we have reduced this burden to ten keystrokes!

The newly created "meta-command" could have been given any name that was appropriate, with a length from one to eight characters. This may not seem like such a terrific savings, but when long processes that are done on a continual basis are automated using the batch-processing ability, considerable time and effort can be saved.

As another interesting aside, you may have noticed that it took the PC close to four minutes to perform this simple batch operation. This is time that the computer may free the operator to perform more important and productive tasks, such as getting a cup of coffee. Obviously, well-planned batch files may alleviate many operators from long stretches of rote computer operation.

It is possible to create a new DOS command that will perform any series of functions just by stringing together DOS commands.

Going back to the example that was discussed earlier—the formatting of new blank disks and the procedure for creating backup disks—it is easy to see that we can create a simple batch file to perform the series of functions as though they were a single function. A batch file containing the commands

```
format b:
copy *.* b:
```

will perform exactly that function. Unfortunately, the **format** command is an interactive command. Since it is potentially destructive, it will not proceed without operator approval. The command first prompts the user to insert a blank disk and press Return. When the formatting process is over, it will ask if another disk is to be formatted.

The responses to these commands cannot be stored in a batch file, but must be entered on the keyboard. This prevents runaway batch files from simply destroying everything in sight. The operator, however, is not asked to enter any pertinent information. You simply verify that the next sequence of events is actually supposed to happen.

This leads us to a very interesting situation. What happens if an operator enters the name of the wrong batch file, and there are no interactive stages in the command? Can the batch process be stopped? Of course it can. There is a very simple mechanism whereby any batch process can be terminated. This is done by pressing the Ctrl key and simultaneously pressing the Scroll Lock/ Break key. DOS will display the prompt

```
Terminate batch job (y/n)?
```

and wait for a response. If you press the *y* key, the batch process will end and the normal DOS system prompt will appear, returning control to the user.

The Autoexec.bat File

The file name autoexec.bat is actually a very important reserved name in the DOS world. Its function is different from any other batch file. When DOS is first booted, it performs several checks. One of these checks is to determine if there is a file on the disk by the name of autoexec.bat. If there is such a file, DOS immediately transfers control to that file without stopping at the command line as it usually does.

The commands that are contained in an autoexec.bat file can be made to take over the operation of the computer as soon as it is booted. Such a process is generally called creating a *turnkey* system (note the *n*). This is an example of the type of process that a computer expert would set up for a less sophisticated user, or an office manager might set up for his or her staff.

Many of the applications software packages that are on the market will utilize the autoexec.bat facility simply because it removes the need for a user to know the startup procedure for a particular piece of software. The startup is reduced to a simple set of instructions: insert the disk, turn on the computer. The autoexec.bat file takes over and automates the various steps that would normally have to be entered by the user.

One interesting by-product of the use of the autoexec.bat feature is that it bypasses the normal

```
Enter today's date (m-d-y):
```

prompt that is encountered when the system is booted. Of course any programmer designing an autoexec.bat file can simply insert the **date** command into the file, forcing the operator to enter the current date (or press the Return key to decline entering the date). This example brings up one issue that needs to be mentioned. Obviously, if external DOS commands are used in a batch file, they must be available on the disk! Otherwise the batch process will return an error message stating that the command was not found. DOS will then forge ahead and read the next command from the batch file. The consequences of not having the correct file on the disk, or having it misnamed, may be totally unpredictable, depending on the circumstances.

As a learning exercise, let me describe what is really an exercise in pure futility. Even though it doesn't actually do anything, it presents a unique opportunity to understand the operation of the batch file process. Imagine, if you will, a batch file stored on a disk by the name of autoexec.bat that contains nothing but the single command:

```
autoexec
```

When the system is booted with this disk, DOS will find that there is indeed a file by the name autoexec.bat. It will therefore pass control to the contents of that file. However, when the file is invoked, it simply sends out the command **autoexec.** This command will simply reinvoke the autoexec.bat batch file, returning control to itself. The result is a loop.

In a situation like this DOS will run itself round in circles ad infinitum. Although this exercise performs no useful function, it does demonstrate quite emphatically that batch files can be linked. That is, when a batch file is being processed, it may contain a command that actually invokes other batch files. Such a command would obviously be placed as the last entry in a batch file, since control would be passed from the batch file to the newly invoked file, and any command after the batch command would be ignored.

The consequences of this kind of power are usually not immediately recognized. It means that once a process has been established, usually as a sequence of DOS commands, it may be submitted to a batch file, or even to a "linked list" of batch files. Since batch files can be linked, DOS can actually be programmed in a very unusually structured manner. This kind of capability will be better understood with time as it is used.

Since the batch file capability is so radically different from all the other internal DOS commands, the wizards of DOS have actually added a few commands and features that only make sense when they are used with batch files. Let's take a look at some of them.

*The **Rem** Command*

So that a user can return to a previously created batch file and fully comprehend the contents, DOS provides the **rem** command. This command is totally useless for any function other than as part of a batch file. It is used to pepper batch files with remarks so that they can be better understood when read at a later date. DOS will simply ignore any command that begins with such a **rem** statement. Try typing a simple **rem** statement into the command line interpreter (at the A> prompt) to see what happens.

DOS ignored the entry, as though it were not there. The **rem** statement is a very convenient method of internally documenting the function of a batch file.

```
rem this is an example of a rem statement
```

*The **Pause** Command*

The **pause** command is an internal command specifically for use within batch files. When a batch file is being processed and a **pause** command is encountered, DOS will halt the batch process and display the message:

```
Strike a key when ready...
```

It will then suspend all operation until a key on the keyboard is pressed. This offers a very convenient method of determining whether some operator action is required before going on to the next step in a batch process.

For example, if for whatever reason, a process controlled by a batch file becomes too large to fit on a single disk, a **pause** command may be inserted into the batch process, enabling the operator to remove one disk and replace it with another. To make things a little clearer, DOS allows the **pause** command to be followed by an optional comment. If such a comment is detected, DOS will print it on the screen along with the **pause** identifier. This is best demonstrated with an example.

Assuming that you are working with a dual-drive system for the moment, create the simple batch file that follows. Its function is to print the directories of two separate disks on the screen. First, log on to drive A: and use the

```
copy con: myfile.bat
```

command to instruct DOS to save what is typed on the console in a file, on drive A:, by the name of myfile.bat. Then enter the following commands:

```
rem this is the file myfile.bat
dir b:
pause insert another disk in drive B:
dir b:
```

Follow this up by pressing the F6 special function key to mark the end of the file. DOS will then close the file myfile.bat, capturing the commands that you have just typed.

Make sure that you have a disk in drive B:. Invoke the newly created batch file by typing **myfile,** and watch the results. DOS will first display the directory of the disk in drive B:, as it is so instructed by the batch file. It will then pause, printing the message:

```
Pause insert another disk in drive B:
Strike a key when ready...
```

Do as it asks, and press any key on the keyboard. The batch process will then continue by displaying the directory of the second disk.

One interesting use of this feature of DOS is that it can work in conjunction with the batch file abort sequence as a step-by-step verification procedure. That is, by placing the statement

```
Pause press any key to proceed or ctrl-break
to terminate
```

after each (or any) statement in the batch file, the operator can be given the chance to terminate the process at each stage. When DOS comes across the **pause** statement, it will print the message and then wait for a key. If the operator wants to terminate the process for whatever reason, he or she can press the Ctrl-Break combination. DOS will then display the

```
Terminate batch job (y/n)?
```

prompt and wait for a key. If *y* key is pressed, the batch process will be terminated and control will be returned to the command line interpreter—the A> prompt.

One other interesting point can be made here. You may remember that in an earlier chapter it was shown that many DOS processes can be terminated by pressing the Ctrl-c combination. Ctrl-c, as it is called, is a key combination that is almost universally a termination signal in the world of computers. Just for consistency, it is no different with the batch file process. Consequently, the termination sequence could be Ctrl-c rather than Ctrl-Break. Either combination will halt the batch process and display the terminate prompt, although it is best to get into the habit of using the Ctrl-Break combination, since other software may not support the Ctrl-c combo.

Beware

No, *beware* is not a DOS command, but should be taken literally when using DOS batch files that contain commands with potentially destructive powers. The most obvious set of consequences arises when the user places an **erase** command inside a DOS batch file. If the wrong disk happens to be in the disk drive at the time, then damage may be done.

Another comical, but surprisingly effective, set of circumstances arises out of having a batch file erase itself! Just for fun try this one. Enter the following:

```
copy con: myfile.bat
rem this file erases itself
dir
erase myfile.bat
dir
^z (using the F6 special function key)
```

Then invoke the batch file by typing:

```
myfile
```

Not surprisingly, the batch file will issue the **dir** command, to which DOS will respond by displaying the directory of the disk. Next the batch file will erase itself. After it has finished this, it will go back out to the disk to find itself, so that it can retrieve the next command in the sequence. When it doesn't find itself, it will assume that the disks have been messed around with while it was away performing the first task. It will prompt the user to

```
Insert disk with batch file
and strike any key when ready
```

not understanding the consequences of having sent itself to the "bit bucket."

Using Batch Files with BASIC

To get a better idea of the doors that the batching capability opens, we ought to look at an example that demonstrates more fully the power and function of the system. This example makes use of BASIC, which, although not considered a DOS command, is a program residing on the DOS master disk. It is stored in a file with the .com extension, so that it can be invoked simply by having its name entered into the command line interpreter. DOS, however, treats it exactly as though it were simply another external DOS command.

When BASIC, or BASICA, is called from within a batch file, DOS will not give it any special treatment. That means that whenever the user is finished with BASIC, DOS will return control to the batch file, just as if it never left.

To illustrate this, let us build a simple batch file that performs a DOS function, calls the BASIC language, and then performs another DOS function. First make a backup copy of the DOS master disk. Then create a batch file by entering the following:

```
copy con: myfile.bat
dir
basica
dir
^z (using F6)
```

When this batch file is invoked, it will perform the **dir** command and will then load in the version of advanced BASIC, leaving the user in the BASIC command line interpreter. If you know any of the BASIC commands, you should try them out just to make sure that you are really in BASIC. If you don't know any BASIC commands, just type:

```
files
```

This is the BASIC version of **dir.** When you are convinced, type:

```
system
```

This is the BASIC command to return to the operating system. As soon as DOS takes control again, it will pass the process along to the batch file, exactly where it left off. The final **dir** command will be sent and performed.

Taking this yet a step further, let us actually create a batch file that strings together BASIC programs. Again, using a backup copy of the DOS master disk, enter the following:

```
copy con: myfile.bat
dir
basica ball
dir
basica samples
dir
^z (using F6)
```

Then invoke the new batch command by typing

```
myfile
```

and digest the results. DOS will first display a directory of the disk. Then it will load in BASICA and run the program named ball. Let this program run for a few minutes and then press the Escape key. This key tells this particular program that you are finished with it. It will therefore return control to the BASIC command line interpreter. Enter the command

```
system
```

to return to DOS. DOS will then obligingly display another directory, just to demonstrate that the batch file has taken over control again. It will then load and run the BASIC program called samples. This program will actually pass control to other BASIC programs as you can demonstrate for yourself. When you are satisfied, press Escape and return to the BASIC level. Enter the **system** command to return to DOS, and DOS will again perform a disk directory.

The batch file capabilities of DOS, as you can see, are quite powerful. In fact, many PC owners will probably have experienced the abilities of the batch command already. Many of the "canned" software packages available on the market make use of the batch file capability simply to start the program, so that the user need never actually have to learn the startup procedure. This, of course, is done by placing a file named autoexec.bat on the disk. In this file are placed the commands that would have to be typed to start the program.

In many cases it is a worthwhile endeavor to examine an autoexec.bat file when it is supplied with a commercial software product. It may help you understand how the software package that you have just purchased is structured.

One interesting example of the elegance of the batch file capability is the use that several commercial packages put it to. The disk is supplied with an autoexec.bat file containing the name of the program that will operate in 80-column mode. Also on the disk is another program file that is set up to operate in 40-column mode for those PC owners who do not have high-bandwidth monitors. Usually there will also be included a utility program. The function of this utility is simply to create the autoexec.bat file that will contain the proper startup procedure for your particular system.

If you tell this utility that yours is a 40-column system, it will create an autoexec.bat file containing the command to start in 40-column mode. If you tell it that you have an 80-column system, it will put the command into the autoexec.bat file that starts in 80-column mode. In this way, every time that you boot the system with your disk it will come up in the correct mode.

Filling In the Blanks

As we have seen, batch processing is quite a powerful tool for automating frequently performed tasks, such as backing up disks or formatting and copying a disk in a single operation. However, this kind of task is really general in nature. Once the batch file has been created, it is fixed in its purpose: it will perform the same task each and every time that it is invoked. Supposing, by way of an example, that we wanted to create a batch file that would format a disk in drive B: and then copy all the files with the .com extension from drive A: to the newly created disk. The commands in the batch file would be something like this:

```
format b:
copy a:*.com b:
^z
```

Then suppose at some later date we wanted to create a batch file that would do substantially the same thing, but instead of copying all the .com files, it would copy all the files with the .bas extension. This batch file would, of course, look something like this:

```
format b:
copy a:*.bas b:
^z
```

As you can see, they are really the same file, but with the extension .com in the former replaced by the extension .bas in the latter. In their current state they would take up the space of two files on a disk, which seems like quite a waste, considering how computers are usually good tools for combating such redundancy. It would certainly be nice to have just one batch file on the disk that was capable of performing both tasks. Predictably, DOS has such a feature.

DOS has the facility to remember up to ten parameters that the user can enter when invoking a batch file. These parameters are then used to replace the corresponding number of dummy parameters that are specified inside the batch file. The dummy parameters are represented inside a batch file by the percent character, followed by one of the digits 0–9. This facility is somewhat analogous to the wildcard facility that was discussed earlier, but it is more specific and usable only with the batch processing capability.

Lost? Well, don't worry, this happens to be one of those features that is easier to use than it is to describe. Let's look back at the pair of batch files that we set up earlier. Let's assume that we have both of these files on a disk stored under the names copycom.bat and copybas.bat:

```
rem this is                rem this is
 copycom.bat                copybas.bat
format b:                  format b:
copy a:*.com b:            copy a:*.bas b:
^z                         ^z
```

To invoke the .com copy program, we would type:

```
copycom
```

And to invoke the .bas copy program, we would type:

```
copybas
```

However, using the replaceable parameters just described, we can create one batch file that will perform either of these tasks on command. Such a file would contain the following:

```
rem this is the copyall.bat
format b:
copy a:*.%1 b:
^z
```

The %1 parameter is a dummy parameter. When such a batch file is invoked, the user must specify what the replacement for the dummy parameter will be. Assume that the batch file is named copyall.bat. If we wanted to copy all the files on the disk with the extension .com, we would have to define .com as the replacement parameter for the %1 dummy parameter.

This is done by following the batch-file name by a parameter list when invoking it. In this case, the command would be:

```
copyall com
```

Note that the period normally associated with the extension is not included in the replacement parameter, since it is already specified within the batch file. Including it in the command line as a parameter would mean that when the batch file sent the command, it would contain two periods, which would not make any sense to DOS. It doesn't matter whether it is specified within the batch file or within the replacement parameter, just as long as it is only specified once.

If we wanted to have the same batch file copy all the files on a disk with the .bas extension, we would enter:

```
copyall bas
```

DOS simply replaces the dummy parameter in the batch file with the parameter entered along with the batch command on the keyboard. Of course, a batch file such as the one described here is not limited to simply copying those two types of files. Any type of file can be copied by this batch file, simply by entering the particular extension. Try some variations and see for yourself.

One additional capability that really puts the icing on the cake is the ability to use the wildcard characters with a batch file containing dummy, or replaceable, parameters. To illustrate, try entering the following with the previous example batch file:

```
copyall *
```

The replacement facility will simply substitute the wildcard character * for the dummy parameter %1, causing the batch file to send the command:

```
copy a:*.* b:
```

This is the command to copy all the files on the disk in drive A: over to B:.

You may have noticed that the dummy parameter used in the last example was %1, although it was explained that the parameters %0 through %9 could be used. Why, then, was %1 chosen and not %0?

The answer is that %0 has a special meaning for batch file replaceable parameters; %0 is used to designate the name of the batch file itself. In the previous example, %0 would be equivalent to the batch command **copyall**.

Again, this is best illustrated by way of an example or two. Modify the .bat file copyall if you are using an editor, or if you are simply copying from the console, reenter it as:

```
type %0
copy a:*.%1 b:
^z
```

Then invoke it by typing:

```
copyall com
```

Note the results. DOS first replaces the %0 dummy parameter with the first command on the command line, which in this case is the **copyall** command. It then issues the command:

```
type copyall
```

Of course, the file is stored under the name copyall.bat, so no match could be found. Therefore, in one example, we have shown how the special %0 case works and at the same time demonstrated one of the more common pitfalls of using it. The solution would have been to initially enter the command

```
copyall.bat com
```

in which case the dummy parameter %0 would be replaced by copyall.bat. In this case the batch file would work correctly, since the .bat extension is simply redundant to everything except the replaceable parameter mechanism. First it would issue the command:

```
type copyall.bat
```

This displays the contents of the file. Then it would issue the command

```
copy a:*.com b:
```

thereby completing the function of the batch process.

Passing Multiple Parameters

Since DOS recognizes the dummy parameters %0 through %9, a total of ten parameters may be passed to a batch process, nine of which are specified by the user, with the %0 represented by the name of the batch command. The thought of building a batch file with ten dummy parameters seems immediately intimidating, but such a file can be built with a little thought. The function of such a file would be quite complex, perhaps overly so. However, the capability is there for all to take advantage of.

When DOS is told to process a batch file command and finds multiple parameters on the command line separated by spaces, it assigns each parameter in numerical order to a dummy parameter. That would mean that if you entered the following command

```
dothis *.bat readme.txt * foo.bar ??1 mac bak BASICA
samples
```

DOS would assign the parameters as follows:

%0—dothis	(the name of the batch file invoked would be dothis.bat)
%1—*.bat	
%2—readme.txt	(a popular name for important documentation files)
%3—*	(the wildcard character for all)
%4—foo.bar	
%5—??1	(a wildcard expression that could signify all files with an extension ending in a 1)
%6—mac	(a common extension used with the macro assembler distributed by IBM)
%7—bak	(a popular extension for backup files)
%8—BASICA	(the command normally used to invoke the advanced BASIC stored on the DOS master disk)
%9—samples	(the name of the sample BASIC program stored on the DOS master disk under the name samples.bas)

These parameters would be inserted in place of the dummy parameters in the batch file dothis.bat. Suppose that dothis.bat contained the following commands:

```
rem this is the batch file dothis.bat
```

```
dir a:%1
type %2
pause
copy %3.%6 b:%3.%7
erase %3.%5
type %4
%8 %9
^z
```

When the previous command is given, DOS will replace the dummy parameters with the replacements and essentially change the file into one that contains the following commands:

`rem this is the batch file dothis.bat`	(no change)
`dir a:*.bat`	(display all the directory entries with the extension .bat)
`type readme.txt`	(display the contents of the file readme.txt on the screen)
`pause`	(no change)
`copy *.mac b:*.bak`	(make a backup copy of all the .mac files onto drive B: and change the extensions to .bak in the process)
`erase *.??1`	(erase all the files on the disk with extensions that end in the number 1)
`type foo.bar`	(display the contents of the file foo.bar on the screen)
`BASICA samples`	(load advanced BASIC and run the BASIC program named samples)

This program is actually quite useless as a batch file in that it does not really perform any specific task that can be used over and over again for other tasks simply by changing the parameters. All it really does is demonstrate the concept of multiple replaceable parameters. This type of facility is not really much use to the novice or unsophisticated user. On the other hand, it is of particular use to programmers who work with either the macro assembler or any of the language compilers supplied by IBM.

For programmers it is not unusual to have to enter a list of parameters to instruct an assembler, compiler, or other software development tool. Frequently, the same parameter has to be entered several times. It is immediately obvious that the replaceable-parameter capability of the batch-processing system can offer a significant savings in keystrokes entered. This is particularly true of processes where a programmer may write part of a program, compile it, test it, discover bugs, and go back to editing it, starting the cycle over and over again.

During such a process the programmer naturally makes a routine backup copy of his or her file before compiling. Then, after compiling, the programmer reads any files created to specify errors found by the compiler. If any errors are found, the program has to be corrected and the process repeated. Let's look at a particular example of this more advanced use of replaceable parameters. It doesn't matter if you don't understand the commands, they are not really important. What is important is the amount of work that the batch file can handle when used in this manner.

For a programmer using IBM's macro assembler to invoke the assembly process, often three files (all of which may have the same file name but with different extensions) need to be described. This can result in entering commands like this:

```
masm b:myfile,b:myfile,b:myfile
```

Looks like a job for replaceable parameters. By first constructing a batch file something like this

```
rem this is asmfile.bat
rem first make a backup copy
copy %1.asm %2.asm
rem next assemble the source file
masm %2,%2,%2
rem finally read the assembler listing
type %2.1st
^z
```

and then invoking the file by issuing the command

```
asmfile a:myfile b:myfile
```

the programmer can save many, many keystrokes every time he or she wants to back up and reassemble the program. Typing this short command is the same as typing:

```
copy a:myfile.asm b:myfile.asm
masm b:myfile,b:myfile,b:myfile
type b:myfile.1st
```

Not only does it eliminate many keystrokes, but it makes sure that the necessary steps are performed each and every time, so that the chance of the accidental erasure of an important file is far less than when commands are manually entered every time.

One such batch file command that all users ought to have in their library is a command to copy and verify a named file. This batch file would batch together the **copy** and **comp** commands along with a replaceable parameter for the file name. It should be tailored to each person's particular use, but the basic functionality should be the same for all. The core should be a file that would look something like this:

```
rem this is the batch file copyver.bat
rem %1 is the file name to be copied
copy a:%1 b:
rem next verify the transfer
comp a:%1 b:
^z
```

This batch file is invoked by typing the new command **copyver** and the name of the file to be copied and verified. For example, if you wanted to transfer the file BASICA.com from drive A: to drive B:, you would enter:

```
copyver BASICA.com
```

Of course, the wildcard characters * and ? can be used in a replaceable parameter in exactly the same way as they are used in regular commands entered on the keyboard. Using the previous example, you could enter:

```
copyver *.*
```

This would transfer the entire contents of a disk from drive A: to drive B: and verify the results.

The Fly in the Ointment

As with most of the good things in life, there is a problem inherent in the replaceable-parameter scheme that needs airing. It is not exactly a problem, but more like a mild irritation. It stems from the fact that the percent character, %, is used to mark a replaceable parameter. This character is also a legal character for use in a normal file name (although it is recommended that you not use it, thereby avoiding this difficulty). You can imagine the confusion that would arise if you were passing parameters to a batch file and one of these parameters was a file specification that contained the character %!

Let's look at an example. Suppose, for whatever reason, we have a batch file with a replaceable parameter %1 that is to copy a file from drive A: to drive B: and verify the results. The batch file will always operate on files with the names scores%.txt and scores%.ndx, and will transfer them selectively, based on the parameter passed, which will represent the extension. The batch file, which we will call mytest.bat, will contain the following:

```
rem this is the file mytest.bat
rem %1 is a replaceable extension
rem first copy the file
copy scores%.%1 b:
rem then compare and verify them
comp scores%.%1 b:
^z
```

With this file on the disk, if we wanted to transfer and verify the file scores%.txt, we would enter the command:

```
mytest txt
```

This would instruct DOS to replace any %1 parameters encountered with the txt extension. However, whenever DOS encounters the **copy scores %.%1 b:** instruction, it gets confused. It cannot tell if the first % is a file name character, or if it is part of a replaceable parameter. In fact, when the batch file command is given, we see that the command

```
copy scorestxt b:
```

is issued. Since there is no such file, the message

```
0 File(s) copied
```

appears. And the batch instruction continues, again erroneously, with the **comp** operation.

To overcome this problem, a special condition is set up for just such batch files, and a simple rule has been created. The rule states that when a batch file is created and it contains a file name with a % character in it, the % character must be doubled, so that there is no conflict. When the batch file processor sees a file name with two consecutive % characters, it understands that this represents a single % in the file name.

So, using the same example, the batch file would now contain the following:

```
rem this is the file mytest.bat
rem %1 is a replaceable extension
rem first copy the file
copy scores%%.%1 b:
rem then compare and verify them
comp scores%%.%1b:
^z
```

This now resolves the conflict. When the batch file is invoked, the operation will execute in the way in which it was originally designed to be performed.

Taking this situation to extremes, we could encounter a lot of confusion when dealing with a file with multiple % characters in its file name. The worst case is, of course, the thoroughly ridiculous situation arising out of attempting to work with a file named %%%%%%%%.%%%, which is a perfectly legal file name. When placing such a file name in a batch file, it would be necessary to refer to it as %%%%%%%%%%%%%%%%.%%%%%%, replacing each occurrence of the % character with a %% combination.

This mild quirk of DOS applies not only to batch files where replacement parameters are used, but to all batch files, whether dummy parameters are used or not. That means that anytime you are using batch files, you must take care to make sure that all the % characters in file names are doubled when used inside a batch file.

It can also happen that the % character is part of a replacement parameter. This occurs when a dummy parameter such as %1 is replaced by a parameter such as the extension .pc%. For example, supposing that we use the batch file we created earlier:

```
rem this is the copyall.bat
format b:
copy a:*.%1 b:
^z
```

If we wanted to format a blank disk in drive B: and copy all the files with the extension .pc% over to the newly created disk, we would issue the command:

```
copyall .pc%
```

In this use of the % character, there is no need to use the double %% representation. The batch command processor handles this situation with no conflict and behaves exactly as would be expected.

Overall, it is best to avoid use of the % character in file names, particularly if you want to use the replaceable parameter capabilities of the batch command processor. Since there are already several characters such as the period and the wildcard characters ? and * that are forbidden for use in file names, it is not so very difficult to add another character to the list—thereby avoiding all confusion.

The replaceable-parameter capability of the batch file command processor brings a level of sophistication and power to DOS that most users never discover. The key to the use of these advanced features is to spot opportunities where they can be used.

The true power of the personal computer lies in its ability to perform many tasks. It can also, in fact, perform the same task in many different ways. No two people will apply their personal computers in the same way, even when confronted with the same problem. One of the major advantages of the PC is that it can handle repetitive tasks without complaining. Coupling this with the fact that computers generally perform this work faster and more reliably than their human counterparts means that they are true productivity tools. The best situation for the use of a computer is therefore a repetitive, tedious task. The real skill of a computer operator is to identify these tasks and use the power of the computer to minimize the tedium associated with them.

Who's on First

Before we finish this chapter there is one more slight idiosyncrasy, not dealt with in the IBM literature, that should be addressed. It is really quite obscure but has some bearing on the average PC user. That is, what happens when you have two files on the disk, each with the same file name, but with the extensions .com, for a regular external DOS command, and .bat for a batch file. To make things more complicated, there is yet another type of external command file; it uses the .exe, for executable, file name extension.

Let's say there are three files on a disk with the names:

```
mytest.com
mytest.exe
mytest.bat
```

when the command

```
mytest
```

is issued, the file mytest.com is executed. The priority scheme says that when a command is issued, DOS first looks for a file by the name specified in the command, having the extension .com. If it finds one, it will execute it as an external command. If it doesn't find it, it will look for a file by the name specified, but with the extension .exe. If neither of these files exists, it will look for a file by the name specified, but with the extension .bat, and pass this file to the batch file processor.

It doesn't matter where the name of the file is physically located in the disk directory. In other words, the order of precedence is not determined by the order in which the files are stored on the disk. In general, it is not good practice to have command and batch files by the same name. It simply leads to confusion.

CHAPTER 9

Mode

Up until now we've seen in detail how to work with almost all the DOS commands in versions 1.0 and 1.1. In this chapter we will take a close look at one of the remaining commands. Needless to say, the further into the subject of DOS we go, the more complex it becomes. Most users of the IBM PC will find that a perfunctory knowledge of DOS will suffice, while others will feel that they may want to grow into their computers and learn all that there is to know.

Consequently, the earlier chapters covered the more important and general commands, while the later ones cover the more obscure and specific commands. In this chapter we will take a look at one of the most obscure of all DOS commands—the **mode** command. Not everyone needs to understand, or even acknowledge, the existence of this command, but as you become more proficient at discovering new uses for your PC, you will undoubtedly run into a situation where you will need to understand it—particularly when it comes time to expand your PC beyond its present capabilities.

*The **Mode** Command*

The **mode** command exists in several different flavors, depending on which version of DOS you have. Version 1.0 of DOS included an initial version of **mode,** but many users reported difficulties in using the command for some specific purposes. Therefore, version 1.1 of DOS sported a new, enhanced **mode** command. The new version supported many new and desirable features, and included everything that was available on the older version. So, we will restrict this discussion to version 1.1 and greater.

Mode is an external DOS command that has been designed specifically for use in configuring peripheral equipment. Peripheral equipment is a general name that is given to any external equipment that can be attached to the PC. Generally it interfaces through one of the card slots inside the PC.

Any of the devices attached to the PC through a slot can be thought of as a peripheral. This, of course, includes memory cards, video interface cards, disk controllers, and the like, although these are so integral to the system that they are seldom referred to as peripherals. The term has come to mean external equipment attached to the PC.

The most general of all peripherals is the printer, although other examples include telephone modems, graphics digitizers (bit pads), analogue controllers, speech synthesizers, mechanical arms, music synthesizers, pen plotters, and joysticks. Usually, the use of the computer for any "real-world" application requires the addition of one, or more, of these peripherals.

Many people quickly discover that the PC can be molded into a very effective word processor simply by the addition of word-processing software and a printer. In fact, many of the popular "dedicated" word processors are actually microcomputers—and internally some of them closely resemble the PC. Therefore, the term *word processor* has become more of a term that describes the position in the market taken by the manufacturer rather than the capabilities of the machine.

Many "word-processor" manufacturers are now offering computational abilities in software as an adjunct to the word-processing software that it was originally shipped with. This is not the result of any new technological breakthrough, but rather a reaction to today's educated consumer market. Similarly, many personal computer manufacturers are offering word-processing software packages for their personal computers, and IBM is no exception.

In order for a word processor to be effective, a printer must be added to the basic computer system. There are essentially two types of printers on the market, the dot-matrix type and the letter-quality type. There are also two methods of interfacing these printers to the PC, through a serial interface or through a parallel interface. The IBM 80 cps printer, which is actually manufactured by Epson, is a dot-matrix parallel printer, whereas most of the letter-quality printers from companies such as NEC and Diablo are serial printers.

The difference between a dot-matrix printer and a letter-quality printer is self-evident, but the difference between a serial interface and a parallel interface is not well understood by the average personal computer user. The difference lies in the number of bits of information that is transmitted at one time.

In a parallel interface the computer sends information across 8 parallel wires, so that it can transmit 8 bits at a time. A serial interface sends information serially, or 1 bit at a time. Obviously, the parallel method is faster. However, the serial method is more common. The reason for this anomaly is simply that few computers utilize a standard parallel interface, whereas most computers have an interface card that allows use of the RS-232C-type serial standard. Also, due to the nature of the circuitry required, serial lines can be run significantly longer than their corresponding parallel cousins—meaning that noisy peripherals can be placed in another room from the computer.

Therefore, many peripheral equipment manufacturers offer the serial-type interface as a means of communication. This allows their equipment to be connected to a large number of different computers. IBM offers what it calls an *asynchronous communications adapter,* which is actually an RS-232C serial interface card. The purpose of this card is obviously to interface the PC to any of the generic peripherals that are available on the open market.

The actual physical hookup is usually trivial since most devices utilize standard connectors, although the software modifications that are necessary to make a serial printer work with DOS are not quite so obvious. DOS is naturally configured to talk to a parallel printer (probably since that is what IBM sells), but a simple command can redirect the printer output to a serial device. This command is part of the **mode** command.

With the initial release of DOS, the syntax model for the **mode** command was:

```
mode [lpt#:] [,n] [,m] [,t]
```

This was later replaced by the somewhat more elaborate command that is a part of DOS version 1.1. The new **mode** command actually has four different and distinct "modes" itself, and is one of the most complex and least understood of all DOS commands.

The first use for the **mode** command is in setting up a printer for different line spacings and characters per line. In this use the command takes the format

```
mode lpt#:[n][,m]
```

where the square brackets enclose optional parameters. The variables are:

#—the printer number (either 1, 2, or 3)
n—the number of characters per line (either 80 or 132)
m—the number of lines per inch (either 6 or 8)

The printer number allows the system to have more than one printer. For example, many people have a dot-matrix parallel printer that can be used for rough drafts of documents or graphics representations, and also a letter-quality printer that can be used for final copies. DOS actually allows up to three such devices, which is really overkill.

Use of the **mode** command for this purpose is actually quite easy. For example, if you wish to change the number of characters per line from 80 to 132, and the line density from 6 lines per inch to 8 lines per inch, you would issue the command:

```
mode lpt1:132,8
```

DOS would then respond with the following messages:

```
Resident portion of mode loaded
Lpt1: not redirected
Lpt1: set for 132
Printer lines per inch set
```

This indicates that all the necessary adjustments have been made—as for the "not redirected" message, we will come back to that a little later. Right now it is inconsequential, because it is telling us that no changes were made.

When you first turn on the PC, the default condition for these parameters is 80 characters per line and 6 lines per inch. You should only use the **mode** command if you wish to change this to some other setting. The IBM 80 cps dot-matrix printer is actually capable of printing in two modes, 80 column and 132 column, and two line densities, 6 lines per inch and 8 lines per inch.

When you issue the **mode** command to change the default setting from 80 characters per line to 132 characters per line, the PC reinitializes the printer and enables it to print in the condensed format. This is particularly handy for printing the sort of wide reports that are normally printed on regular 132-column printer paper on 8½-by-11-inch sheets, for inclusion in a report, or whatever.

Many word processors do not allow text to be output to a printer in a format greater than 80 columns. This capability of DOS and the 80 cps printer allows a convenient way to circumvent such a problem. Since the video display shows only 80 characters across, a word processor would need to be able to scroll horizontally as well as vertically if lines were to be formatted greater than 80 columns.

Included in DOS is a mini line editor that enables a user to enter, and modify, text into the command line interpreter. This is the editor that you would normally use to enter commands in DOS. Very conveniently, this editor also allows up to 128 characters to be entered on a logical line. Of course, the logical line cannot be displayed on a single line on the video display. After 80 characters (actually 78 in most cases since DOS requires 2 characters for its A> prompt), DOS automatically scrolls down to the next line and continues there.

Once you reach the 128th character, DOS will sound the bell and will not accept any other characters to be entered, with the obvious exception of the carriage return character to terminate the entry.

This actually gives the user a very cheap and dirty method of typing letters, since a file can be created on the fly using the

```
copy con: myfile
```

command, and then using a combination of the Ctrl-PrtSc and the

```
type myfile
```

command to dump the contents out to the printer. Either 80- or 132-column formats can be used, although if the 132-column format is selected only 128 characters will be printed per line.

One pitfall that many users encounter occurs when they type characters into a file using **copy con:** and do not enter a carriage return after the eightieth column. DOS will appear to enter a carriage return and line feed, but actually it only appears to do so in order to represent what is being entered on the video screen. No carriage return or line feed is actually entered.

Next, whenever you try to print such a file out in 80-column mode, the printer will print the first 80 columns of the line. It will then do a carriage return, but no line feed. The result will be that it will overprint the first characters on the line with the remaining characters, producing gibberish. If this happens to you, do not despair. Simply change the printer mode to 132 columns.

If you prefer using the printer in 132-column, or condensed-print, mode, as it is known, all of the time, it is probably best to set up your DOS disks with an autoexec.bat file that automatically initializes and adjusts the printer for you whenever you first turn on the system. For example, if you wanted to have the printer come up automatically with the 132-character-per-line and 8-line-per-inch mode, you could create the autoexec.bat file:

```
rem this is the file to initialize the printer
rem for 132 columns per line, 8 lines per inch
mode lpt1:132,8
rem don't forget to get the date and time
date
time
^z
```

As is the case with most DOS commands that require parameters to be entered after the command, it is not necessary to enter all the parameters. However, if the first parameter is not to be changed, but the second one is to be changed from 6 to 8, the command must be entered as in the following:

```
mode lpt1: ,8
```

In this case DOS will reply with the screen messages:

```
lpt1: not redirected
Printer lines per inch set
```

The only difference between this and the reply to the full command used earlier is that it did not make any mention of the "Lpt1: set for 132," which was not necessary since there was no change.

Obviously this format for entering modes is the only way to accurately describe to DOS which parameter it is that you wish to change. If the first parameter is to be changed, but not the second one, it is necessary only to enter the new first parameter. It is not necessary, in this case, to enter a trailing comma, since it is implied. For example, if you wish to change the number of characters per line from 80 to 132, but you do not want to change the number of lines per inch, you only need to enter

```
mode lpt1:132
```

and predictably DOS will return the screen messages:

```
Lpt1: not redirected
Lpt1: set for 132
```

The only error condition that can exist with this version of the **mode** command occurs when you attempt to enter a characters-per-line parameter that is neither 80 nor 132, or when you attempt to enter a lines-per-inch parameter that is not 6 or 8. In such a case, the **mode** command will not return an error message. Neither will it accept the parameter. It will simply not change anything. In fact, if DOS does not accept the illegal parameter, it will simply display the screen message

```
Lpt1: not redirected
```

and nothing else, which indicates that nothing has changed.

A Second Use of ***Mode***

The second use of the **mode** command is as a means of setting up the video display screen. This only works with computers equipped with the IBM color/graphics monitor adapter, and has no effect on units equipped with the monochrome display and printer adapter. The function of the command is to align the edge of the screen so that it can be seen, and to switch between 40 and 80 characters per line on the screen.

Many video monitors and television sets have a particularly hard time in grasping the video signal emitted by a computer such as the PC. One of the results is a poor horizontal hold, resulting in one of the two sides of the screen being somewhat obscured. Since cathode-ray tubes (TV tubes) are curved at the edges, this can result in one or more characters being out of sight at the corners of the screen. When you try to correct this by adjusting the horizontal hold on the monitor or television, sometimes you will lose the picture completely.

The **mode** command, using a different syntax structure, can be used to correct this problem. This essentially makes it into a different command, with a completely different function. The syntax model in this case looks like

```
mode [n] [,m] [,t]
```

where:

n—the number of characters per screen line (either 40 or 80)
m—either r or l (the direction to shift the display)
t—an optional request for a simple test pattern to aid in the alignment of the screen

Of course, the same rules for missing parameters apply to this version of the **mode** command as to the first use that we saw. If parameters are not to be changed, a comma needs to be entered in the command line, unless the only parameter that is being changed is the first one, or both of the first two.

For example, if you want to change the screen mode from 80- to 40-column mode, you should enter the command:

```
mode 40
```

This causes the screen to go blank and all characters to be enlarged in the horizontal direction to twice their normal size. To see the effect, enter the preceding command and then issue a **dir** command. This mode is particularly effective for using the PC with a television and an RF modulator, since most televisions do not have a sufficiently high bandwidth (and hence resolution) to accurately display 80 characters on a line.

The second parameter in this command is either an *r* or an *l*, which stands for right and left. This is a signal for DOS to shift the entire display by a fixed increment one way or the other. For example, if you wish to reset the screen to 80-column mode and shift it to the right, you would enter the following:

```
mode 80,r
```

This would cause the screen to go blank and the entire field of view to be moved over the equivalent of two character positions. If we had left the screen in 40-column mode, it would have moved over by the equivalent of one 40-column character.

If this is not far enough over to the right, we could simply move it over one more by entering:

```
mode ,r
```

Or if it is too far, we could move it back by entering:

```
mode ,l
```

The final parameter is a request for a simple test pattern that can be used for alignment purposes. The test pattern is simply a line of numbers across the top of the display. You request the test pattern by issuing a command something like:

```
mode 80,r,t
```

DOS prints the line of characters—in this case in 80-column mode—and then prompts:

```
Do you see the leftmost 0? (y/n)
```

If the leftmost 0 is clearly visible, press the *y* key. If not, press the *n* and DOS will adjust the screen and continue redisplaying the prompt until you set it just right.

Of course, if you give it the command

```
mode 80,l,t
```

DOS will do exactly the same thing, but will move the display to the left rather than the right.

If you are having alignment problems with your monitor or television, it is worthwhile running through this exercise once to find out how many times you need to move the screen to find its most acceptable position, and then using that information to build a batch file, or an autoexec.bat file, so that it can be reset automatically every time the system is turned on.

For example, if you find that you need to move the screen twice to the right in order to see the whole picture, you could build an autoexec.bat file that would set it up correctly every time. The file would be something like this:

```
rem an autoexec.bat file to set up the monitor
rem turn on 80-column mode and move to the
right
mode 80,r
rem move once more to the right
mode ,r
^z
```

Such a file would certainly make life a lot easier and eliminate a troublesome and potentially fatiguing situation.

The Third Use of **Mode**

The third use of the **mode** command occurs when it is used in conjunction with the IBM asynchronous communications adapter, or the equivalent. As was explained earlier, this type of interface card can be used to drive many different types of peripheral equipment including a serial printer. Since so many different types of equipment can be driven with the serial interface, this particular version of the **mode** command is actually quite complex, in that it encompasses many obscure variables that may not mean much to the beginning user.

The exact syntax model for this version of the **mode** command is

```
mode comn:baud[.parity[,databits[,stopbits[,
p]]]]
```

where

n is the number of the serial interface (either 1 or 2)
baud is a number that defines the speed at which characters will be transmitted and received
parity is either *e* for even, *o* for odd, or *n* for none and is a method of validating data integrity when it is transmitted
databits is either 7 or 8 and defines how characters are being transmitted
stopbits is either 1 or 2 and defines how characters are terminated when being transmitted
p is used as an indicator of whether a serial printer is attached or not

Each of these terms relates directly to general data communications and will be encountered many times when dealing with any type of interface, whether it be to a printer or over a telephone line to a remote host computer. To understand each of them, a superficial understanding of the methods of data communications is helpful.

The problems encountered are best visualized when you relate them to data communications over a telephone line. A telephone line is a good example of a serial-type interface, in that only one thing at a time can happen. There is only one line between any two communications points, so that data must be sent in a serial fashion.

The method that has been standardized, and accepted by the Bell System, is the method whereby bits of information (either zeroes or ones) are converted to specific audio frequencies. These audio frequencies are within the same frequency spectrum and bandwidth as normal voice data. Therefore, anywhere a voice line can go computer data can follow.

The most frequently encountered problems in communicating in this way are having the computer differentiate between normal line noise and deliberately transmitted information, and synchronizing the information at the receiving end. This is easily understood if you imagine yourself typing information into your PC and having it transmitted across a telephone line to another computer. Obviously you don't type every character in an organized and easily timed fashion. How does the remote computer know, then, when you are sending information?

The answer lies in the format in which the information is sent down the line. As we have seen before, alphanumeric characters can be represented by means of ASCII codes or bit patterns. ASCII is used universally, with one glaring exception—IBM. However, the communications protocol that you will most often use will be ASCII.

The problem is best illustrated by way of an example. Suppose we wanted to send the simple string "ABC" across a communications line. The ASCII codes for these characters are:

```
A 1000001
B 1000010
C 1000011
```

As you can see, each of these characters can be represented by a total of 7 bits, or binary digits. To send them down the line, we could simply send out the binary string:

```
100000110000101000011
```

This accurately represents the three characters. However, this doesn't make much sense at the receiving end since that computer doesn't know, and can't tell, where each character representation starts and stops. So, to pass this information across, the concept of the "start bits" and "stop bits" were introduced.

These codes are used to "frame" each character. Most systems use an arrangement where 1 start bit is transmitted, then the character, and then 1 or 2 stop bits. In the latter case, the previous transmission would take on the appearance

```
(start)1000001(stop)(stop)
(start)1000010(stop)(stop)
(start)1000011(stop)(stop)
```

which, of course, is much simpler to understand, and therefore decode. In such a situation we would have 1 start bit, 7 data bits, and 2 stop bits.

Essentially, 10 binary digits, or bits, would be transmitted for each character of information—often called a byte.

The next problem that we run into is differentiating between actual signals and line noise. In many cases it is extremely difficult to make out voice information over the telephone lines. Computers face a similar problem in identifying ones, zeroes, and no information at all. Consequently, many errors can happen, even in the simplest transmission. To guard against these errors, a scheme called *parity* is introduced.

The parity scheme works very simply, and often quite elegantly. It involves having the transmitting device count the number of ones being transmitted for each character. An additional bit is then tacked on to each character. The additional bit is either a one or a zero depending on whether the total count of ones is odd or even.

This eliminates the worst type of transmission error, in which a single bit in a character is not received correctly. Such a simple error, since it is not catastrophic, is very difficult to detect. However, the entire sense of the information that is being transmitted, particularly if numbers are present, can be modified.

There are three types of parity that are used. Even parity adds another bit to each character so that the total number of ones is always even. Odd parity does the opposite and adds a bit so that each character contains an odd number of ones. If the receiving device detects a character that does not conform to this rule, it can signal the controlling software, which can in turn request that the transmitting device retransmit the offending character until it gets it right. No parity means that the upper bit—which is transmitted first—is always set to a one or a zero, and is therefore meaningless and to be ignored at the receiving end.

The last of the strange terms used in the **mode** command is *baud*. Baud is quite simply a numeric indication of the speed at which characters are to be transmitted. For example, the term 300 baud means that 300 total bits are transmitted every second. This can usually be roughly translated into a number of characters per second by a simple rule of thumb. The most popular method of sending information between two devices is to use 1 start bit, 1 stop bit, 1 parity bit, 7 data bits—for a total of 10 bits per character. Therefore, a transmission rate of 300 baud usually translates to 30 characters per second.

When you are entering the baud-rate parameter in this version of the **mode** command, it is necessary only to enter the first two characters. For example, if you are setting it up for 300 baud, simply enter 30. For 9,600 baud enter 96. The baud rates that the **mode** command will accept are 110, 150, 300, 600, 1,200, 2,400, 4,800, and 9,600.

In this particular usage the **mode** command is used to configure a general-purpose serial—asynchronous—interface to a specific piece of peripheral hardware. In general, the add-on equipment will be well documented and will have a table explaining how these parameters are to be set. The last parameter, however, the *p,* is used to indicate that the peripheral equipment being attached to the named serial port is actually a serial printer.

When this parameter is specified, the PC will output information in a special mode. This special mode takes care of what are called "time-out" errors. When a device does not answer a call within a specified time, it is considered an error and control goes back to the computer. Thus, if a peripheral dies in the middle of an operation, the computer will not hang. That is, if a piece of attached equipment fails to operate, then the computer will only wait for a specified time before it goes back into operation.

In the case of a printer, there are times when you will not want the computer to return to normal operation if the device is shut down. For example, if you are using a letter-quality printer and are manually changing sheets of paper between pages, you will not be too happy if the computer aborts the printing operation each time you try to make the change. Specifying a *p* as the final parameter in this version of the **mode** command, alleviates this situation.

However, if you ever find yourself in a situation where you do not want the computer to wait for you—for example, when the printer really does break down—simply press the Ctrl-Break key combination and normal operation will resume.

The Fourth Use of **Mode**

The fourth and final version of the **mode** command brings us to a point where we need to discuss a feature of DOS that sets it apart from other operating systems of its genre—*device independent input/output.* Without getting overly technical, the purpose of this feature is primarily to allow the redirection of input and output streams.

Already, we have seen one interesting example of this feature in the method illustrated to create batch files on the fly by using the command:

```
copy con: myfile.bat
```

What this command accomplished was to redirect the character stream required for the **copy** command from a disk file to the keyboard—with the result that **copy** actually treats the characters typed on the keyboard as though they are a disk file.

In a similar fashion the character stream output that is normally directed to a parallel line printer, such as the IBM 80 cps dot-matrix printer, can be redirected to a serial letter-quality printer attached to the asynchronous communications interface card by use of the command

```
mode lpt#:=comn
```

where

is the number of the line printer (either 1, 2, or 3)
n is the serial port number (either 1 or 2 for the IBM asyncronous card)

Using this command, the letter-quality printer will be initialized and will therefore become the primary output device. In order to redirect the output back to the parallel printer, the command

```
mode lpt1:80,6
```

that we saw earlier should be used.

Well, that pretty much covers the function of the **mode** command. Since it is such an obscure command, much of the detail was eliminated. This was deliberate for two reasons. First, many of the idiosyncrasies of DOS should now be familiar, and as we have seen before rules that apply to one DOS command can usually be applied generally. Second, the **mode** command is not the type of command that should be used as part of the everyday operation of the PC.

In fact, the **mode** command should really only be used when you want to reconfigure your system. This should be done only when the physical configuration changes—whenever you install a new printer or if you add a modem to your system, for example.

By experimenting and reading the manufacturer's documentation, you should be able to determine which version, if any, of the **mode** command is required to reconfigure your system. If you determine that you do indeed need to use the **mode** command, you should build it into a batch file so that you can invoke it with very little fuss. This eliminates the entry of long, involved keystroke sequences just to get started. If it is a permanent alteration that you will need to use all of the time, you should utilize the benefits that can be derived from the autoexec.bat capabilities.

CHAPTER 10

Directory Structures

Over the last nine chapters we've dug deep into the various commands that allow a user to interact with the IBM disk operating system. In fact, we have covered all the DOS version 1 commands—with one exception, the **chkdsk** command. At first, the purpose of this command may seem trivial, and indeed, its primary use is simply to determine how much disk space is still available on a particular disk. However, there are several other uses for this lowly command.

Unfortunately, before the secondary uses of the **chkdsk** command can be adequately understood, a somewhat perfunctory knowledge of the internal structure of the DOS directory system is necessary. So, we are about to open the lid and take a good look at the inner workings of the file management system.

You may recall that earlier, when we were discussing the DOS disk formatting procedure, the concepts of a disk directory and a file allocation table were introduced. At that time, though, these concepts were merely glossed over and explained in somewhat simplistic terms. In this chapter we will see how they actually function and how DOS goes about keeping track of which files are stored on the disk, what type of file it is, where the various components of each file are actually kept, and how free space on the disk is actually allocated for new purposes when DOS, or a user, requests it.

To many people this type of information is very much a requirement of everyday life, and therefore this subject should make interesting reading. To many others, however, it may end up sounding like a modern-day rendition of the famous Abbott and Costello "Who's on first?" routine. It should simply be kept in mind that this type of information is about as necessary for the daily operation of the IBM PC as an understanding of fuel injection design is necessary to drive a car.

Who's on First

As was mentioned when we were discussing the **format** command, when DOS formats a blank disk it writes certain markings onto the disk to distinguish various tracks and sectors, so that it can read and write data to and from the disk in an orderly fashion. It also creates two very important tables: the directory and the file allocation table. These two tables embody DOS's mechanism for keeping track of where each file is stored and how much disk space is available for new files. Both of these tables are located on track 0 on the disk, single sided or double sided.

The directory is, quite literally, a table of contents of a DOS disk. In an earlier chapter we saw how the **dir** command could be used to display information about the various files on a disk. At that time we accepted the fact that the **dir** command was a trivial DOS command that didn't require much thought. Now we'll discover exactly where all that information came from.

The data that the command retrieved from the disk and used to set up the display came from the directory. These data are not, however, all the information that DOS stores about the file, only the stuff that would have any meaning to us mere human types. As you can see (by typing **dir** at the command line interpreter), the typical directory entry looks something like this:

```
Command com 4959 5-07-82 12:00p
```

Obviously, these data represent the file name and file name extension, the length of the file in bytes, the date on which it was created, and the time at which it was created. In addition to this information, DOS stores information about what type of file it is—normal, hidden, or system—which determines whether it will be displayed during the **dir** operation, and keeps a pointer that determines how the directory entry relates to the file allocation table.

On a single-sided disk formatted under DOS version 1, DOS allocates 4 sectors for the directory. Since each sector is 512 bytes long, this allows a total of 2,048 bytes for the directory. These bytes are divided into 64 individual entries, each 32 bytes long. This determines the maximum number of files that can be stored on a single-sided disk.

On a double-sided disk an additional three sectors are allocated to the directory. A quick calculation will show that this additional space permits an additional 48 directory entries, allowing a total of 112 files on a double-sided disk.

Looking at the preceding example of the results of a **dir** command, we can see that there are a total of 27 characters displayed for that particular entry. Since that number is so close to the 32 bytes allocated for each directory entry, you might be tempted to believe that this is actually the format in which DOS stores the directory information. Unfortunately (although not really so) that is far from the truth.

Generally, when computers store information they store it in a way that is not meant for humans to read or even intuitively understand. Instead they store it in a format that makes it relatively easy, and more important, non-time-consuming, for computers to perform the various locate and compare functions that they are most often called upon to do. A quick look at the actual internal format of a DOS directory entry will verify this.

The total length of a DOS directory entry is 32 bytes. The first 8 of these predictably hold the file name. If the file name is less than 8 characters long DOS fills out the remainder with the bytes that represent the space characters. DOS takes great care to ensure that each of the fields in each of the directory entries is at constant fixed offsets from the beginning of the entry.

When DOS searches the directory for a particular file name, it will read each individual entry only up to the first space character. It will ignore all the characters after that. In general, this rule holds true for all DOS parsing, including the parsing of any information entered into the command line interpreter. This is easily demonstrated by trying to create a file with a space character in the file name. The best way to do this is to issue the command:

```
copy con: my_file.bat
```

(Note that the underline character _ represents a blank space.)

Then type:

```
This is a test
^z
```

When you invoke a **dir** command, you will see that the file appears to have been saved as:

```
my.
```

All the characters after the space have been ignored by DOS, including the extension. Since this file now does not have an extension of .bat, it cannot be executed as a batch file, even if you enter a command that duplicates the information that you entered in the command line. Try it and see, by entering:

```
my file.bat
```

DOS will return a "file not found" error message.

DOS determines if a directory entry is in use by first checking to see what the first character in the file name is. If the character is a hexadecimal E5, then DOS knows that that particular entry is not currently in use.

For the uninitiated, hexadecimal is a method of representing the numbers from 0 to 255 in two digits, each of which uses a base sixteen arithmetic. In the older days of programming when software tools were few and far between, it was important, in fact mandatory, that programmers learned to perform simple arithmetic in hexadecimal (or the older octal) notation. The tradition lives on to this day. Although it isn't necessary for a computer user to understand this cryptic arithmetic or how it is used, hexadecimal does present a somewhat elegant method of relating internal computer codes.

E5 could quite easily be translated into the standard decimal representation of 229, but talking about a mystical hexadecimal E5 will make more of an impression on the neighbors and children than talking about an everyday 229.

Back on the track, the next 3 bytes of the directory entry hold the file name extension. As with the file name, all 3 character spaces are filled out with blanks if they are not utilized. Just for an exercise, you can repeat the last example, this time using a file name extension that contains a blank. Again, it can be demonstrated that DOS will only store the name in the directory up to the first occurrence of a space character.

If, for example, you attempt to create a file by the name myfile.b_t (where the underline character represents a space), DOS will simply store it as myfile.b.

Back at the farm, the twelfth byte in each directory entry is called the *attribute* byte and is used to store and recall several properties of a file. As you may know, each byte consists of 8 individual bits, each of which is capable of existing in one of two states—zero or one. Many software designers use these bits as switches, or "flags," to store properties or indicate various states.

The attribute byte can actually be thought of as a bank of eight separate and individual flags, each of which can either be off or on, zero or one. Under DOS version 1 there are only a few states that can exist in an attribute byte, although many of the other states are earmarked for later versions, future expansion, or increased capabilities of the operating system.

If the attribute byte is set to zero—that is, all of the bits are turned off—the file that it is associated with is a normal DOS file. These are the typical files that you see when you issue a **dir** command. They can contain any of the typical information that you normally associate with a file: BASIC programs, batch file information, word-processor data files, spreadsheet models, external DOS commands, etc. Normal files are subject to the normal operation of DOS, such as the **copy** function or the **erase** function.

The first, or "least-significant," bit of the attribute byte currently has no assignment. If it is turned on—which it shouldn't be!—it has no effect on the file.

The second bit is designated as the "hidden file" bit. If a file has an attribute byte with this bit on (in which case the attribute byte would contain a value of 02), it will not appear in a directory listing invoked by the **dir** command. In other words, the file will exist on the disk, and will have a presence in the directory, but certain DOS operations will not be able to find it. These DOS operations include the commands **dir, copy,** and **erase.**

Undoubtedly, utility programs are available that allow the rapid conversion of normal DOS files to and from hidden files. This will permit a fair degree of security for sensitive information that may be kept on a disk that is in use in a public situation. There is no reason why this facility should not be used if it is deemed necessary. It does not harm anything and does add a valuable feature for some applications of DOS disks.

The third bit in the attribute byte is called the "system file" bit. That is, if this bit is turned on, giving the attribute byte a value of 04, then the file is designated as a system file. We have already encountered two system files in an earlier chapter. You may recall that the DOS system itself is stored in several files, two of which, named ibmbio.com and ibmdos.com, are stored on every DOS master disk. These two files are part of the operating system itself, and have been stored in two separate files for the purposes of modularity. However, these files do not appear in the directory listing invoked by a **dir** command. These files have the system file bit set on in their attribute byte.

Any file that is designated as a system file is also immune to the action of the high-level DOS commands such as **dir, copy,** and **erase.** As such, they exhibit the same properties as hidden files. It is reasonable to ask at this point what is the difference between a hidden file and a system file. Well, the answer at this time is that there is essentially no difference, other than the nomenclature. However, future versions of DOS may make extensive use of this distinction.

In actual fact, the two DOS system files just mentioned have their attribute bytes set to 06. That means that they have both the hidden file bit and the system file bit set to on. This apparently does no damage. The files therefore become "hidden system" files.

All the other bits in the attribute byte have no significance in DOS version 1. Turning them on does nothing constructive or destructive. However, do not attempt to play around with these bits. If you have the capability to access these bits through any of the commercially available utilities, stay well away from the attribute byte. Many of these bits are earmarked for future DOS enhancements. Tampering with them at this time may cause unpredictable results, often in the form of disaster, when you try to upgrade to a later version of the operating system.

So far we've accounted for the 8 bytes assigned for the file name, 3 for the extension, and 1 for the attribute byte. The next 10 bytes are not used by DOS at this time. They are, however, reserved for future use. Originally, with DOS version 1.0 there were 12 bytes in this group. However, when DOS version 1.1 was introduced the feature of time-stamping was added.

This new feature required 2 bytes from the pool of free reserved bytes, and is a perfect example of how DOS can expand and make use of reserved spaces. Keep in mind that when the DOS manual says an area is "reserved," that is exactly what it means. Future use of this area is planned.

The 2 time bytes are therefore the next 2 bytes in the directory entry. Every time that DOS is asked to create a new file or update an old one, it retrieves the current system time from the internal clock—the one that you set every time you boot the system—and stores it in the time bytes in the directory. That way each file is "time stamped" each time it is altered.

This feature, if used correctly, can be incredibly useful for people who are writing programs, or where data files are being updated and backed up frequently. It allows the operator to keep track of where the latest version of a particular file is, and is also very handy for the incremental backup of a large hard disk. It is also important for anyone who is handling important information and keeping it on disk to keep the internal system date and time as close to up-to-date as possible.

However, you may recall that when you boot the system or issue the

time command to the command line interpreter, DOS responds with a prompt that looks something like this:

```
Current time is 13:06:19.79
Enter new time:
```

You may be wondering just how DOS manages to cram all those numbers into just two bytes. Well, with 1 8-bit byte to work with, DOS can store a number up to 256, or 2 to the power 8. With 2 bytes to work with, DOS can store a number up to 2 to the power of 16, or 65,536. Since there are 24 hours in a day, 60 minutes in an hour, and 60 seconds in a minute, we have a total of 24 times 60 times 60, or 86,400 seconds in a day. Obviously, then, DOS cannot store the exact time, to the nearest second, in the 2 time bytes.

When DOS creates or modifies a file, it actually rounds the time to the nearest two-second interval and converts that time to an absolute number between 0 and 65,536. The result is then stored in the time bytes. The method by which it converts the time to a number is somewhat elaborate, although quite interesting.

Imagine the 2 8-bit time bytes as a single continuous block of 16 bits. DOS converts the hours portion of the time to a 5-bit binary number and stores it in the upper, or "most-significant," bits of the 16. It then converts the minutes to a 6-bit binary number and stores it in the next 6 most-significant bits. This means that the minutes field is actually distributed between two separate memory locations, since it overlaps the boundary between the 2 time bytes. Three bits are stored in the upper byte and 3 in the lower.

The remaining 5 bits of the time bytes hold a number between 0 and 29, which represents the number of two-second increments. Under this scheme there are no redundant bits and no long conversion formulas that DOS has to run through to convert some cryptic time-storage mechanism into a human recognizable time. The hours component, which is from 0 to 23, fits well in 5 bits; 2 to the power 5, which a 5-bit quantity can group to, represents amounts to 32. The minutes component, which can be from 0 to 59, fits well in 6 bits, which can represent amounts up to 64. The two-second increments, which can number up to 29, also fit well in 5 bits (up to 32).

The following 2 bytes in the directory entry contain a similarly packed code that stores the date on which the file was last written to. In this case the year is stored in the most-significant 7 bits. Seven bits can represent a number up to 128. DOS, however, only uses up to 119. To the number stored here, a constant of 1,980 is added (since there was no commercial DOS before the year 1980), which results in the range from 1980 to 1999. Needless to say, DOS was designed to outlive its usefulness.

The month (1–12) is then stored in the following 4 bits, and the day on the last 5 bits.

You are probably asking yourself, "Why go to all this bother just to store the date and time in two bytes each?" Well, consider if each of these fields were to be expanded to 3 bytes each, one for the hours, minutes, seconds, and the other for year, months, days. This would take an additional 2 bytes for each directory entry—they would now each be 34 bytes long. We could now only fit fifteen directory entries into a disk sector. On a single-sided disk we would lose the capacity to store four files. On a double-sided disk we would lose the capacity to store as many as seven files.

There is still a more important reason than the simple loss of file directory space for cramming both of these fields into 16 bits. Being only 2 bytes long these fields are very easily manipulated by the Intel 8088 microprocessor at the heart of the PC.

You may recall from before you purchased your IBM PC that a major part of the sales pitch stated that the computer was one of the first of the "16-bit" microcomputers to be made available. This 16-bit capability allows the 8088 to perform operations such as comparing two 16-bit numbers at a remarkably high speed. The increase in speed that this affords over the 3-byte method was deemed important by the operating system designers, and is quite an illustrative window into the depth of detail in the design of the operating system.

The following 2 bytes in the directory entry are used as a pointer. They are called the starting cluster number and are used to link a file's directory entry with the disk's file allocation table.

The directory information is DOS's method of keeping track of *what* the files are. The file allocation table continually reminds it *where* the files are. The starting cluster number is the link between the two.

Again, this number is stored with the least-significant byte closest to the beginning of the directory entry. Since this pointer is so integral to the format of the file allocation table, we will defer a detailed discussion about it until we have a clearer picture of the file allocation table.

The final 4 bytes in the directory entry are where DOS keeps track of the length of the file in bytes or characters. The number is stored as two separate 16-bit numbers, with the least-significant number first. Within each number the least-significant byte is stored first. This can make for a rather confusing combination for people who are not used to the hows and whys of programming techniques. This confusion can be avoided by always letting DOS create your files for you—which is how the vast majority will use their PCs—in which case DOS will tackle the problem for you. Aren't computers wonderful.

If, for any reason, this number gets changed so that it does not reflect the accurate length of the file, DOS will have a hard time loading it, and will return the error message:

```
File allocation table bad
```

If the length entry of the file command.com gets messed up, DOS will return the error message

```
Invalid command.com
```

and prompt for the correct disk to be inserted. If either of the hidden system files are damaged, DOS will probably not boot at all. In such a case, simply copy all the valuable files from the damaged disk to a new disk.

Obviously DOS must be capable of handling very large files if it allocates 4 bytes for the file size. Indeed, 4 bytes represent 32 bits. The number 2 to the power of 32 turns out to be a very large number, a somewhat ridiculously high number when compared to the disk capacity of even the largest available hard disk.

This number represents the total number of characters that can exist in a single DOS file. It should become immediately obvious to the more experienced that DOS has been designed to overcome many of the frustrating limitations of older, less-sophisticated operating systems that could not handle particularly large files.

DOS has borrowed this upper theoretical limit for a file from its big brother in the Microsoft family of operating systems, XENIX, which is an enhancement of Bell Labs' famous operating system, UNIX. Much of the expansion of DOS in the future will be in a direction toward XENIX and all of the increases in power that that entails. Already the two operating systems currently in the family can handle all of today's modern storage technology and most probably, with little or no modification, much of the storage technology of the future.

We have seen how DOS simply extended the number of sectors that were allocated to the file directory as it progressed from single-sided to double-sided disks. It is also easy to see how it is just as simple to extend the directory by more sectors to handle even larger mass-storage devices. However, when an extremely large device, such as a large Winchester disk of, say 80 megabytes (80 million bytes) is used, although DOS can handle it adequately, this flat, one-dimensional list of directory entries becomes very unwieldly—for about the same reason as an ancient papyrus scroll is unwieldly when compared to a modern paged book.

XENIX, because of the way in which it handles directories, is highly adept at handling such large devices. This method involves directories contained within other directories, much like files themselves, and the hierarchical file structure that such a concept leads to. The insides of DOS leave this method of structuring a file system quite possible, as we shall see when we take a look at version 2.0.

The File Allocation Table

This all leads to the mysterious file allocation table that has been alluded to several times so far. Before we delve into the mysteries of the FAT, we should summarize what we have learned so far about its partner, the directory.

We know that each file is assigned an entry in a special table, known as the directory. Each directory entry contains information that keeps track of certain unique data pertaining to DOS files. These data include the file name and extension by which the file is stored on the disk, and hence the name that is used to retrieve the data stored in the file. The data also include information that tracks the time and date that the file was created or last written to, so that the most recent version of each file can be ascertained. An attribute byte represents the type of file—limited to a normal file, a hidden file, or a system file. The file length is stored in the directory entry as a number of bytes, or characters. There are also several bytes in each entry that are not used by DOS. These bytes are, however, reserved for future expansion of the operating system.

Finally in each directory entry there are 2 bytes allocated as the starting cluster number. Before we can go any further, we need to take a look at this field and see how it relates to the rest of the directory entry. To do this we should review some of the basics of operating systems.

One of the primary functions of a disk operating system is to manage the transfer of data between the computer's internal memory and the attached peripheral equipment. The most general case of a peripheral that is used to store data is the disk drive.

One of the best examples of this type of management can be seen when you enter the name of an external DOS command at the command line interpreter. DOS retrieves the information from the disk and moves it to a location in memory. It then passes control to the program that it has just loaded, thereby invoking the command.

The actual steps that DOS performs to achieve this relatively trivial result are extremely complex. First, DOS has to "parse" the command to make sure that it is a valid statement. Then, if it is not a recognizable internal command, it must turn on the disk-drive motor and position the disk read/write head over the exact track and sector containing the disk directory.

The directory is scanned to see if the command is stored as an external command, in a .com file. If it is, DOS finds out where on the disk the file is physically located. It then moves the head to that location and proceeds to read the information into memory. It then turns off the disk-drive motor and passes control to the loaded program. This, of course, is an extreme simplification of the actual process, although, as you can see, it is by no means trivial.

All of the complexities of this, the most simple DOS operation, are hidden from the user. All you have to do is type in three or four characters and press the Return key. DOS takes care of all the nasty stuff.

The operation of writing information from memory to a DOS file on a disk is even more complex, although DOS performs this operation many times during the performance of simple commands such as **copy** or **sys.** The write operation is also performed in such nonobvious commands as **erase** and **format.** In **copy,** for example, DOS first goes through the motions of reading information in from a device and then writes it back out to the specified device—most often a disk drive.

The first operation that DOS goes through when it receives a request to write out information to a disk file is to allocate space on the receiving disk for the file. It does this by allocating a section of the disk. Such a section is called a *cluster*. The physical size of a cluster is determined by the type of disk drive that is attached.

For example, when DOS is requested to write information to a single-sided disk drive, it allocates a cluster that is one sector—512 bytes—long. For a double-sided disk drive, a cluster becomes two sectors, or 1,024 bytes, long.

DOS keeps track of which clusters have been allocated by maintaining a table called the file allocation table, or FAT for short. The FAT keeps an entry for each cluster on the disk that indicates whether the cluster is in use or not.

In allocating space for a write request, DOS searches through the FAT until it finds a vacant cluster. It then writes the data to that cluster and marks it as used in the FAT. If more data than one cluster-full are to be written,

DOS will continue through the FAT until it finds the next available cluster. It will continue in this manner until all the information has been written to the file.

Since clusters are two sectors long on a double-sided disk, there is obviously some redundancy, since the remainder, which may be more than a complete sector, cannot be reallocated to another file. However, the advantage of this scheme is that the FAT can be maintained in a very small amount of disk space. When access speed is also considered, this approach seems to be a relatively good trade-off.

In the case of a single-sided disk drive, there are a total of 313 sectors available for file allocation. This number is derived by subtracting the number of sectors that DOS reserves for the boot record, directory, and FAT from the total of 320 sectors that are available in total. These other 7 sectors are always in use by DOS, and therefore are never free for allocation. Therefore, there is no need to have them represented in the FAT, since they can never be made available for file storage. The remaining 313 clusters on a freshly formatted single-sided disk are free for file allocation. These clusters are logically numbered as 2 through 314.

The first two allocation units in the FAT are used to store a code that determines what type of disk drive is in use. Obviously, this information is required by DOS so that it can determine its cluster size. Having this information as the first two entries in the FAT seems like a reasonable approach.

These codes are stored as a 3-byte code, which means that there are a total of 2 to the power of 24 different types of devices that can be interfaced with this method. For a single-sided disk drive the code is FEFFFF. Dual-sided drives are represented by a code of FFFFFF.

Out of the FAT into the Fire

From this information you may have determined that DOS stores two FAT entries in 3 bytes. That is correct. Although it may seem awkward to the nonprogrammer, DOS stores each entry as a 12-bit, or 1.5 byte, number. For the sake of compactness, it crams two of these entries into a 3-byte block. A quick calculation will show that the entire 313 available clusters on a single-sided disk will produce a FAT of 313 × 3/2 bytes, or 470 (since half bytes are meaningless) bytes total. Add to this the 3 bytes that are required to hold the disk-media type code and you can see that the entire FAT fits comfortably within a 512-byte-long sector.

Working backward from the total of 512 bytes available for the FAT, you can quickly deduce that there is really space for 340 entries in a single 512-byte-long sector.

In the case of a double-sided disk, there are actually a few additional two-sector-long clusters available, since the space required to hold the boot record, directory, and FAT is less than double the space required by its single-sided equivalent. Consequently, there are 315 two-sector-long clusters available for allocation on such a disk. Again, the entire FAT fits comfortably in a single 512-byte-long sector.

When DOS first formats a blank disk, it creates the FAT. It then writes the disk-media code into the first two entries, and then zeroes out the remaining entries. Therefore, a free cluster—one that has not been allocated for file use—contains a zero.

When DOS receives a request to write data out to a disk file, it looks through the FAT until it finds the first cluster available for allocation. This will be indicated by the first FAT entry that contains a zero. DOS will then take the number of that FAT entry (from 2 to 314 for single-sided and from 2 to 316 for double-sided disks) and write it into the starting cluster number field of the file's directory entry. In this way, DOS knows where on the disk to retrieve the file.

The information will then be written out to the sector or sectors that are represented by the FAT entry. When that cluster is filled, DOS will proceed by finding the next cluster available for allocation in the FAT. It then writes that cluster's number into the FAT entry for the previously allocated cluster. Complex? Not really, when you look at the situation from the other perspective.

When DOS receives a request to read data from a disk file into memory, it searches through the directory until it finds the entry for the specified file. It performs a few other housekeeping chores such as determining if there is indeed enough memory available to hold the entire contents of the file. Then it looks in the starting cluster number field and retrieves the number of the first cluster that contains the data that it needs.

It then goes to that cluster and reads in the data. Next, it reads the FAT entry for that cluster and retrieves the next cluster number from that entry. It moves to that cluster and simply repeats the operation. It continues in this way until it finds a special code that is used in the FAT for an "end-of-file" marker. When it finds a FAT entry that contains this marker, it knows that there is nothing more to be read in.

Again, this is an oversimplification of the actual process that DOS goes through in reading and writing information to and from a disk, although the description is highly representative of the actual process.

Because of the complexity, an example may well be in order! Let us take a closer look at one of the files on a DOS disk. The file we will look at is the file containing the external DOS command that prompted this entire extravaganza, the **chkdsk** command, stored in the file chkdsk.com. If you have access to one of the various utilities on the market that allow you to examine the contents of each sector on the disk, you may want to look in on the action for yourself.

When you issue a **dir** command, the file chkdsk.com may appear to be the third file on the disk. However, when you examine the directory of the disk by looking at track 0, sector 4, you will find that there are two hidden files that are located at the top of the directory. There are, of course, the hidden system files ibmbio.com and ibmdos.com.

On locating the directory entry for the chkdsk.com file, you will find that the entry contains the following hexadecimal values:

`43 48 4B 44 53 4B 20 20`	(which represent the ASCII characters of the file name)
`C H K D S K _ _`	(_ represents a space)
`43 4F 4D`	(the ASCII characters for the file name extension)
`C O M`	

These values are followed by a null, represented by the value 00. This is, of course, the attribute byte, the file is a normal file, which shows in the directory when a **dir** command is issued.

There follows a string of ten other nulls, which are the reserved bytes in the directory entry. These bytes are not used at this time. Then follow the 2 time bytes

```
00 60
```

(which, if you care to decode, you will find translate to 12:00 P.M.) and the 2 date bytes

```
A7 04
```

(which reduce to the date 5/07/82).

Next follows the starting cluster number, represented by

```
25 00
```

which we will come back to later.

And finally the file length

```
B8 06 00 00
```

which translates to the decimal 1,720. This represents the length of the file in bytes. A quick calculation will reveal that, since there are 512 bytes available for storage on each disk sector, the file chkdsk.com should fill a total of three disk sectors and spill over into a fourth sector.

Going back now to the starting cluster number, we saw that there were two hexadecimal numbers stored there—25 and 00. Since these are stored least-significant byte first, they actually translate to the 16-bit number 0025 (hex), which further translates to the decimal equivalent 37. This reveals that the first sector of the file chkdsk.com is located at cluster number 37.

Since it takes 3 bytes to hold 2 FAT entries, we then take that number and multiply it by 2, and divide by 3; this returns a value of 55.5. The whole part of this number, the 55, represents the offset into the FAT at which we will find the next shred of information about the contents of the file.

At the fifty-fifth and fifty-sixth offsets into the FAT, we retrieve the hexadecimal values of 6F and 02, which form the 16-bit "word" 026F (since words consist of two 8-bit bytes, usually stored with the least-significant byte first).

Since we are dealing with an odd-numbered FAT entry (37), we only want the first one and a half bytes (12 bits) of this value. We are left with the hexadecimal number 026, which is actually the very next FAT entry. DOS would find the second sector of this file's data in cluster number 38 (the equivalent of hex 026).

On examining the next FAT entry, we find the hexadecimal values 27 and 80, which combine to give the word 8027. Since we are dealing with an even-numbered FAT entry, we this time discard the leading half byte to leave us with 027, again the very next entry. DOS would find the third sector of the file's data in cluster number 39.

If we look in FAT entry number 39, we find an 80 and an 02, giving the word 0280. Discarding the low-order half byte, we get a following FAT entry of 28 (hex). Cluster number 28 hex, or 40 decimal, contains the fourth sector of the file's data.

Further investigation shows that at that FAT entry, there are 2 hex bytes, FF and AF, giving the hex word AFFF. Discarding the high-order half byte leaves us with an FFF, DOS's marker for the end of the file.

This scheme is a particularly difficult one for us mere humans to follow.

The computer, however, has a much easier way of understanding it through its logic circuits.

The marker that DOS used as an end-of-file marker in the previous example was the hexadecimal FFF. This is one of eight codes that can be used for this purpose, the others being FF8 through FFE. The other eight codes that begin with an FF, FF0 through FF7, are also reserved by DOS for FAT entry markers for other special purposes.

For example, in version 1.1 of DOS, if a FAT entry contains the code FF7, then the associated cluster has been found to be unusable. In version 1.0 of DOS, bad sectors were allocated to a hidden file named badtrack, and consequently marked as allocated in the FAT. Under the newer version 1.1 scheme, the need to allocate a directory entry for this purpose has been eliminated.

The process of erasing a file from a disk is now quite obvious. It would be a very long and inefficient process for DOS to go out to the disk and physically eradicate the information. Instead, DOS writes the standard erased mark (E5 hexadecimal) onto the first byte of the directory entry, looks up the starting cluster number field in the directory entry, and proceeds to zero out the FAT entries for the file, adding them to the pool of clusters now available for allocation. This way, the next time that DOS receives a write request, it can reallocate the freed sectors and overwrite the data that have been erased.

A deleted file can cause cluster allocation to be nonlinear. Imagine, for example, a disk that contains several files. If one more file is added to this disk, DOS will allocate the next free sectors to hold it. If then an earlier file is deleted, some clusters that are represented by lower numbers in the FAT will be freed for allocation. If the new file is then added to, DOS will allocate the first free cluster from the FAT for this purpose.

This new cluster will not be the next linear cluster in the file's physical layout. Although not a problem, it is a nuisance in that it takes slightly longer for DOS to move the read head around the disk to find the data. This problem was pointed out when we covered the **copy** command. The remedy, as shown earlier, was to copy all the files on the disk onto a new disk. The **copy** procedure realigns all the files on the disk into a physically linear order, allowing them to be loaded or modified marginally faster.

How FAT Is the FAT?

We have seen how a FAT entry can contain a 12-bit binary code that represents the FAT entry for the next cluster. In 12 bits, a number from 0 to

4,095 can be represented. However, the sixteen highest entries are reserved for end-of-file markers and other reserved uses. This leaves a total of 4,080 different FAT entries that the current scheme can make use of. This number is significantly greater than the 315 that can currently be made use of by double-sided disks. Obviously the scheme has been designed to allow FATs that are significantly greater than a single sector in length. If the entire potential of the existing FAT structure could be applied to a device that utilized two-sector-long clusters (1,024 bytes), then DOS's capabilities could be extended to a total of 4,080 × 1,024 bytes, or 4,177,920 bytes.

Although this number may seem astronomically large to those people working with the smaller single-sided disks, it is still not adequate for use with a large Winchester-type hard disk. Obviously, DOS's FAT structure will change as it grows.

Extra FAT

One of the interesting features of DOS is that it always keeps multiple copies of the FAT around. Two copies are kept on each disk—on track 0, sectors 2 and 3. An additional copy of the FAT is maintained in the computer's internal memory. Whenever the status of the disk is altered the disk-resident versions of the FAT are updated. This does not present any objectionable problems, since the process of altering the status of a disk already requires a read or write operation to the disk. Since the disk is already up to speed, DOS may as well update the FATs while it's out there.

Unlike operating systems such as the earlier CP/M, DOS allows the free swapping of disks at all times—with one rather obvious exception. Never remove a disk from a disk drive while information is being written onto it. In fact, it is not good practice to remove a disk from a disk drive whenever the motor is turned on. This could result in the correct file information being written onto the disk, but without updates to the directory and FAT. DOS would not be aware of the new information that has arrived since the last time the directory and FAT were updated.

Problem FAT

There are a couple of ways in which the FAT can get messed up, causing severe headaches for the poor user. Luckily, if the rules of DOS are adhered to, there is no way that these circumstances can occur. However, several "smart" applications programmers have come to the conclusion that they can do the job better by ignoring DOS and doing the housekeeping work by themselves. This approach invariably leads to disaster for the user.

Often, programmers will find "new and more wonderful" ways to do things that take liberties with DOS. However, as DOS grows they find that the liberties that were taken are no longer tolerated. In fact, they may lead to problems.

The two most common problems arise from a program forgetting to update a FAT properly. These problems create what are commonly referred to as "widows" and "orphans," although they are better described as "popular" and "unpopular" FAT entries. A popular FAT entry is the result of an error that creates a situation where more than one file thinks that a FAT entry and its associated cluster belong to it. Obviously, this situation is intolerable. This could arise from having two starting cluster numbers in different directory entries pointing to the same FAT entry, or two FAT chains leading to the same entry. The cluster involved obviously contains data that are relevant to one of the files, but certainly not to more than one. The results are always the same—certain disaster.

The other type of malfunction is an unpopular FAT entry. This type of entry is marked as allocated in the FAT, but does not actually belong to any particular file. Under normal circumstances, there is no way to use the cluster represented by this FAT entry.

Finished? FAT Chance

This now brings us to the point where we started off at the beginning of the chapter. We were discussing the simple DOS external command **chkdsk.** A quick glance at the IBM DOS manual may lead you to believe that this rather innocuous little command is used simply to report on the status of the directory and file allocation table for the specified disk.

The **chkdsk** command does more than report, in a static manner, the status of the directory and FAT; it will actually modify them if it discovers an error. For example, if **chkdsk** discovers a FAT entry containing a number that is too large to represent a physical sector, it will set that allocation block back to its free state, so that it can again be used to store a legitimate file.

Another of **chkdsk**'s interesting efforts is directed toward the freeing of disk-allocation units that are marked as in use in the FAT, but do not belong to any file. Such a set of circumstances can happen accidentally when an applications program does not obey the laws of DOS.

When used on a normal disk, **chkdsk** will return a report like the following:

`160256 bytes total disk space`	(single-sided disk)
`8704 bytes in 2 hidden files`	(system files)
`144384 bytes in 26 user files`	(space taken by user files)
`7168 bytes available on disk`	(free space on disk)
`131072 bytes total memory`	(RAM memory in system)
`118672 bytes free`	(amount of memory available)

The **chkdsk** command may also return a report that states:

```
4096 bytes in bad sectors
```

If it discovers that certain sectors have been marked as damaged, **chkdsk** may also return one or more error messages, each of which indicates the existence of an abnormal situation. The current **chkdsk** error messages include the following:

```
Allocation error for file filename
```

which indicates that an invalid allocation unit number was discovered in the FAT. **Chkdsk** deallocates the offending allocation unit and truncates the file at the end of the previous allocation unit. If the file contained a program, this measure is futile, since it would probably be rendered unusable. If, on the other hand, the file contained data, some data would be saved.

```
xxxxxxxx bytes disk space freed
```

which indicates that allocation units that were marked as used, but not actually used, have been deallocated.

```
Directory error-file: filename
```

which indicates that a directory entry was discovered, but the file was nonexistent. In other words, there were no allocation units allocated to the file. **Chkdsk** removes the bogus file from the directory.

```
Diskette not initialized
```

If **chkdsk** cannot find the directory or FAT, it will assume that the disk has never been initialized (formatted). If this happens with a disk that you know has been formatted, first try to **diskcopy** the disk, and if that fails, try to **copy** the files to a new disk. In most cases, this will most probably not do any good at all—but that's okay, you did make a backup, didn't you?

```
File size error for file filename
```

This error message is returned when **chkdsk** discovers that the size of the file stored in the directory entry does not correlate with the actual size of the file, which it can calculate by counting allocation units. **Chkdsk** will adjust the size of the file contained in the directory entry.

```
Files cross-linked: filename and filename
```

When **chkdsk** sends this error message, it means that it has discovered two directory entries describing the same data block. It is very difficult for a situation like this to arise, as it can only be caused by a blatant error in an applications program. Since it is not a lethal situation, at least as far as the data integrity is concerned, **chkdsk** will not take any action. It will leave it up to you to correct. Such a situation can be corrected quite simply by copying both "files" to two different file names, and then erasing both of the original directory entries.

In addition to these error messages, there are also the usual DOS error messages that may crop up from time to time. These are all self-explanatory and easy to correct.

Thus ends our trek through the **chkdsk** command, and the associated trivia that goes along with it. This should give a better idea of how DOS actually keeps track of all the information that you send out to disk.

CHAPTER 11

DOS File Types

Earlier in this book we touched on the rules for naming files for use with DOS, and we've examined several different types of files very closely—such as autoexec.bat files. We finished the last chapter by looking at how DOS relates the name of the file to its physical whereabouts on the disk. However, we've treated all files as though they were simply "black boxes" that we could store information in. We haven't discriminated between the physical forms of the various types of file.

Information that would be stored in a disk file can be broken down into two primary types—*programs* and *data*. Both programs and data are represented by bytes of information, each byte consisting of 8 bits (zeroes or ones). A single byte of information can represent one of 256 combinations, since 2 to the power 8 is 256. These bytes are commonly expressed as a pair of hexadecimal digits. These digits are the numbers 0–9, plus the characters A,B,C,D,E, and F, representing the numbers 10–15. This is illustrative of how our everyday arithmetic would be if man had been created with three additional fingers on each hand.

A program is a set of instructions that the computer can interpret to perform specific tasks. Computers store programs as sets of these numbers, each combination representing a specific instruction to the microprocessor. Some instructions require more than 1 byte for storage—in fact, the majority do. On the 8088 microprocessor used by the PC, many instructions handle 2 bytes at a time, from which the term 16-bit computer is derived.

Data are simply pieces of information that programs access, manipulate, and store. This type of information can be stored digitally by relating the numbers 0–255 to specific, but *ad hoc* meanings. There are many somewhat arbitrary schemes for storing information on a disk. By far the most common is the ASCII format. ASCII is used almost universally as "the standard" method of representing information digitally. The only serious challenge to the ASCII standard is the EBCDIC (pronounced ebb-see-dick), propagated by none other than IBM itself.

EBCDIC, which stands for Extended Binary-Coded Decimal Interchange Code, is the standard method used to represent data digitally in large IBM mainframe computers. Several years ago there was a raging debate about which of the two methods would become standard. ASCII won out by gaining government and standards committee approval, although IBM did not change its internal systems, since that would have been all but impossible given the magnitude of the job. Luckily, EBCDIC is not used on the IBM PC, where communications with other (non-IBM-supplied) mainframe computers is imperative to the success of the computer.

Actually, the process of converting between ASCII and EBCDIC is a relatively trivial problem for a computer as sophisticated as the PC, so no inherent limit on the capabilities of the machine was imposed by the selection of ASCII.

Many of the most common types of DOS files contain ASCII representations of data. For example, we saw earlier how we could redirect the input and output streams to other than their normal destinations. This led to the concept of typing characters directly from the keyboard into a DOS file—the method we used to create batch files. This type of file contains the ASCII representations of the characters that were typed. The best way to tell if a file contains ASCII information is to type it out on the screen using the **type** command. If the file is readable, it contains ASCII. If it appears as gibberish, it is most probably a program file.

Some files may even appear as a combination of understandable English words interspersed with gibberish when they are typed out. This is because programs store messages that are to appear on the screen in ASCII format, thereby creating a hybrid file containing both program data and ASCII text.

Most of the other types of files contain programs. You may have noticed during an earlier chapter that there are really two distinct types of external command files: those that are stored in .com files and those that are stored in .exe files. These two file types exist for a reason, and have been made to behave as similarly as possible for a reason. It deals with the nature of the Intel 8088 microprocessor that sits at the heart of the PC.

The Intel 8086 family of microprocessors, of which the 8088 and 80286 are members, uses a method of addressing memory locations known as *segmentation,* a concept familiar to those who have worked at the systems level of a mainframe computer. This technique imposes some restrictions on the way programs relate to memory and somewhat artificially limits the amount of memory that can be used at one time. This explains why there are several "magic numbers," such as 64K, associated with the performance of some software. Perhaps a review of the microprocessor architecture will help to illustrate this.

Most PC users are probably aware that the 8088 microprocessor can address up to—the first magic number—a megabyte (approximately 1 million bytes) of memory. The exact number of memory locations that can be used by the microprocessor is the equivalent of 2 to the power of 20, or 1,048,576.

The second magic number that you will encounter is 16; the 8088 is a 16-bit microprocessor. This number is the result of the architecture of the microprocessor which consists of several 16-bit-wide registers. One of the prime functions of these registers is the manipulation of 16-bit numbers for memory-addressing purposes—using numbers as pointers to data tables, for example. Two to the power of 16 (65,536), usually called 64K, is the third magic number.

The 8088 is designed to work with both 8- and 16-bit data, but internally performs 16-bit arithmetic operations. Therefore, when it calculates addresses, it can only work with 16-bit-long addresses. Additional calculations and memory manipulation are necessary to address the larger memory that is available.

Memory is therefore divided into segments of 64K each. The 8088 can work directly with only four of these segments at a time. The predefined uses for the four segments are as "code segment," "data segment," "stack segment," and "extra segment." However, the microcomputer industry at large is still used to writing software for 8-bit architectures. In that world, the entire code, program, stack, and whatever "extra" is in the program are all expected to coexist in just one 64K memory segment. You will find that most of the commercially available programs that can work within a 64K limit have had their roots in the old 8-bit world.

Of course, the decision whether or not to cram all the functions of a computer program into one 64K segment is left entirely to the discretion of the programmer. Although many of the development tools that are available for the PC programmer have the capability of working with the full address space of 1 megabyte, many programmers restrict their programs to a single 64K segment. Why is this?

One of the most convincing arguments for restricting a program to only one 64K segment is that it may be inappropriate for such a program to work in a larger space. The most striking example of this type of program is the BASIC language interpreter supplied with the PC, where programs larger than 64K become extremely unwieldy and very difficult to manage. If a programmer wants to write a program that is larger than 64K, BASIC is probably the wrong language to program it in.

On the other hand, the other language compilers available for the PC all have the ability to work with an increased address space, and are therefore more conducive to the development of larger programs. The decision that a programmer has to make in determining which format his program will take concerns two basic variables—speed and simplicity. Since many single programs can exist in 64K, there is no need to burden the processor with the additional overhead penalty of manipulating a larger address space. The speed-up is noticeable. Also, the programmer only needs to work with a 16-bit address model rather than the more complex 20-bit model. Programming is much simpler.

Since there are then two types of programs (those that work within a single 64K segment and those that use multiple segments), it only seems fair that they be treated differently by the filing system (DOS). As we will see, although this is a technically complex subject, the immediate consequences to the user are minimized by DOS.

During the process of program development under one of the language compilers or the macroassembler, there is a stage called *linking*. This is the process by which different sections of a program may be combined to form a single unit. The net result is what is known as a *run* file. These files are always stored in *.exe* files, for executable. This type of program will usually work with multiple memory segments.

The more popular *.com* files are reserved for programs that do not need to work with multiple segments and are therefore much more compact—under 64K. There are several other differences between the two types of files, as we will see later.

Predictably, there are major differences in the formats by which each of these file types is stored on disk. The actual method of reading and writing the information to and from disk are identical, as are the methods of keeping track of where the data are on the disk. However, the internal structures of the files are quite different. Let's take a look at the various types of files that can exist.

ASCII or Text Files

Text files are the most simple of the DOS file types. The type of information that they contain is rudimentary, usually stored in a format that is compatible with a word processor or text editor. The mini editor, **edlin,** supplied with DOS could quite easily be used to create, examine, or modify a text file. Most text files are compatible with most word processors. This is so because the ASCII standard defines meanings of key combinations beyond the simple alphanumeric keys. The functions that are universal and required by word processors and printers alike, such as a carriage return, a line feed, or a tab advance, are defined in a universal manner. They are referred to as *control characters* and can be accessed through the keyboard by simultaneously pressing the Control key, marked *Ctrl* on the PC keyboard, and the appropriate letter key.

For example, the hexadecimal code 0D, which is the same as the decimal 13, represents a carriage return in ASCII. It is also used to represent the key code for Ctrl-m. If you simultaneously press the Ctrl key and the *m* key on the PC keyboard, you will see that it has exactly the same result as pressing the Return key.

If you press the Ctrl key and the *i* key at the same time, you will see that it has the same effect as pressing the Tab key. Ctrl-i is represented in ASCII by a 09 hexadecimal, 9 decimal, and is the same as the horizontal tab advance code in ASCII. In such a case, where the tab stops are not strictly defined, the PC will assume a default of ten character positions per tab stop. Pressing the ASCII tab advance will probably have different results when used with a commercially available word processor or text editor.

Another important type of information stored in ASCII text files is the source code for a program written on any of the language compilers available for the PC. Although the BASIC interpreter supplied in ROM with the PC uses a special compressed format for storing programs, it also gives the option of loading or storing files in the ASCII format. This makes it easy for such files to be used with generally available programming utilities such as cross-reference generators or program generators, and makes the process of transporting programs written on one computer to another relatively trivial.

Batch files also contain simple ASCII data. In fact, we have already seen an example of ASCII codes at work when we saw how to construct a batch file directly from the keyboard. As you may remember, we always terminate the input of data to such a file by pressing the F6 special function key. This puts a Ctrl-z into the batch file as an end-of-file marker. Ctrl-z is a generally accepted end-of-file marker for most word processors and editors that work with the ASCII file format.

ASCII Record Files

Another type of DOS file in which information is usually stored in the ASCII format is a record file. Usually there is other coded information contained in such a file. This other information is typically *delimiter* information. That is, it usually contains coded markings that are used to separate, or delimit, individual records. The records themselves are usually in ASCII format. Consequently, when such a record file is **typed** out on the console or to a printer, there will usually appear some English words or names, separated by what will appear as gibberish.

This type of file is typically the output of a database management program of some type, such as an accounting application or a name and address file. It is differentiated from a traditional ASCII file in that the information is structured into discrete records, whereas as ASCII file is typically unstructured information such as letters or documents.

.com Files

The .com files are standard DOS external command files that contain nothing but raw machine-language instructions—a memory image of the program. When you enter a name into the DOS command line interpreter, the first thing that DOS does is look on the logged or specified disk drive to see if there is a .com file by that name. If there is, then it will load that file and transfer control to the machine-language instructions.

The loading procedure for a .com file is quite simple. Single-segment programs are always stored in what is known as the code segment of memory. This is the area of memory that is managed through a special register known as the cs, or code segment, register. To load and run this type of program, then, DOS simply builds the appropriate code segment prefix that is required. This sets up the cs register to handle the program once it is loaded. It then directly loads the .com file to the proper part of memory and passes control to it. The program is now loaded and running. Complex? Don't worry about it. You don't need to understand the complete workings of an electronic fuel injection system to drive to work in the morning.

.exe Files

The .exe files, as we saw earlier, are used to store program data that have not been "fixed up" to handle the segmentation problems. These are typically programs that work with multiple segments of memory and are consequently more difficult to load and run than simple .com programs. Consequently, when an .exe file is loaded, there is some initial processing and shuffling done before control can be passed to the machine-language program that it contains.

At the beginning of each .exe file, there is a signature number that identifies the file type. Immediately after that there comes a series of numbers known as a control header. This information tells DOS a number of factors that it needs to correctly process the information in the file. These factors include the number of bytes actually used in the last sector of the file and the number of 512-byte segments in the file. From this information DOS can quickly determine the actual length of the program contained in the file.

One of the major functions in loading and running an .exe file is the posting of various modules to their correct positions in memory and setting up the appropriate registers accordingly. To facilitate this, there is what is called a relocation table. The number of entries contained in this relocation table is passed to DOS through the control header. Following these are a number of largely technical descriptors that aid DOS in first loading the file, and then directing it, or relocating it, to its correct memory location or in some cases several locations.

During the load process, DOS will read portions of the .exe file into memory, and use them to determine what to do with other parts of the file. As complex as this may seem, many of the actual details are handled transparently by both the linker at link time and by DOS at load time, so that all the user has to do is give DOS the name of the file that is to be loaded and run—DOS does the rest.

On the DOS master disk is a utility program that can be used to convert certain .exe files into the .com format. This process speeds up both the programs' loading and execution. The loading is faster, since DOS does not have to analyze tables and dispatch or relocate several program modules, and the execution of the program is faster, since there is no need for the program to go through the overhead of working with multiple segments.

Of course, any program that is to be converted from an .exe file to a .com file must first be convertible—that is, there are a few simple conditions that must first be met. Obviously, the most important consideration is that the program must be able to fit into and work within a single 64K segment.

The utility that is used to convert the .exe file to the .com format is called **exe2bin.com.** The *bin* part is short for binary, since a .com program is simply the binary image of a program as it would exist in memory. The command format for using the **exe2bin** utility is similar to the other DOS commands we have seen. In general, it is

```
exe2bin filespec filespec
```

where the first *filespec* determines the "source" file—the .exe file that is to be converted—and the second *filespec* determines the "output" file—the new file that is to be created.

There are several other simple rules associated with this command. For example, since the source file must be in the .exe format, there is no need to enter the file name extension. It will automatically default to .exe.

The output file name extension will also default—in this case to .bin. The .bin extension is assigned, since there are some cases where DOS can convert the source file to the appropriate file format, but the command processor will not be able to load and run the file as it would a normal .com file. To understand why this is, we need a complete understanding of machine-level programming, which will not be assumed at this time.

On some occasions, when an .exe file is run through the **exe2bin** utility, a very important register value, known as the code segment instruction pointer, will be missing. The utility will therefore need to prompt the user for a "fix-up" value. This value corresponds to the memory segment at which the program is to be loaded. The type of file created by this process is not directly runnable under the command processor. It would normally be loaded and run under the control of another program. This technique is used for applications such as overlaying programs.

In most cases, however, the **exe2bin** utility will provide a clean conversion. The prerequisite is that the code segment pointer and the instruction pointer are set so that the program will load into the lowest portion of available memory. That is, it must reside in the very first code segment—defined by 0000—and have a hexadecimal offset into the segment of 0100 (decimal 256). The very lowest 256 bytes of memory are reserved for DOS. Immediately above these locations is where a .com file would be loaded and run. When a file has been processed through the **exe2bin** utility and can meet these requirements, it can then be converted to a simple .com file. This, of course, is done by renaming the file to the appropriate name, and specifying the .com extension.

If, in the course of its use, the **exe2bin** utility discovers either that the source file has the code segment instruction pointer specified incorrectly, or that the file requires more than a single memory segment in order to run, it will print the error message

```
File cannot be converted
```

and abort the process.

Nonstandard DOS Files

The types of files that we have discussed include only the structures that are standard under DOS. It is also possible for a programmer or software designer to design and implement his or her own file structure under DOS. There are few limitations. The advantage to staying with the standard DOS file formats is that the files can be manipulated by the standard DOS utilities and the data that the file contains can be shared or accessed by other programs running under DOS.

The most significant of the nonstandard DOS files are the files that contain uncopyable programs. Some software manufacturers have come up with methods of modifying files so that they cannot be copied using the standard DOS utilities, **copy** and **diskcopy**. This prevents the user from making an unlimited number of copies of the file. Usually this method is reserved for the type of program that is susceptible to software piracy.

Protected files are usually modified in some way so that they can be run under the standard DOS, but cannot be copied. The methods of doing this are usually proprietary to the software vendor for obvious reasons, and are beyond the scope of this discussion. For programmers who want to have their files protected by such a method, DOS does supply several variables that can be modified, such as the physical size of a sector. It should be kept in mind that such methods limit the usefulness of DOS, and should only be used if absolutely necessary.

PART II

DOS Versions 2 and 3

CHAPTER 12

Introducing DOS Versions 2.0 and 3.0

Early in 1983 IBM announced version 2.0 of DOS, an upgrade that added many new capabilities and complemented the newly announced IBM XT—the fixed-disk-equipped version of the PC. Many of the upgrades were logical extensions of the earlier versions of DOS, while many others were new features. Those readers who are using DOS versions 2 or 3 should also read the first part of this book, DOS version 1, since most of the features of that version are also available in DOS versions 2 and 3.

NOTE: It is strongly recommended that if you have not yet moved up to DOS version 2 or higher, then you should do so immediately. Otherwise you may not be able to get the most from your PC.

In 1984, IBM announced the PC-AT, and with it, DOS version 3.0. What became clear immediately from this announcement is that DOS version 2 is definitely the base version for all PC users. DOS version 3.0 is simply a version of DOS version 2 with transparent extensions to handle the new high-density disk drives.

If you own IBM PCs that do not use the ninety-six-track-per-inch high-density floppies, there is absolutely no need to switch to DOS version 3.0. DOS version 3.0 users can read the rest of this text and substitute version 2 for version 3—the DOS that runs on their machines is externally identical to DOS version 2.

Meanwhile, IBM has also released DOS version 2.1, which incorporates several minor "fixes" to correct problems with the earlier DOS version 2.0. Since they are functionally identical, they will both be referred to as DOS version 2.

The Difference between Version 1 and Version 2

The first thing that people will notice when they look at the package that DOS version 2 comes in is that it is bigger than DOS version 1. As soon as they open the manual, they will find that it is also significantly different from DOS versions 1.0 and 1.1. IBM is obviously not content with simply accepting the PC as the "state of the art" and leaving it at that. A portent of better things to come? The difference between the last release of DOS (version 1.1) and this one (version 2.0) is quite staggering compared to the difference between the prior two releases (version 1.0 to version 1.1).

In fact, there probably has never been a piece of popular system software that has changed as quickly and dramatically as DOS. From version 1.0 to version 2.0, the space of slightly over a year, DOS has gone through more changes and improvements, for example, than CP/M has in all of its history. We are left with the task of determining if these changes are for the better. Of course, many of the enhancements in DOS version 2 are features designed to work with many of the new hardware items announced—such as the IBM hard disk, or fixed disk, as it is called.

A quick look at the general 16-bit computer market will show the reasons for the changes in DOS. When the PC was first introduced in August 1981, it was effectively the first major introduction of a 16-bit personal computer system. As such, there was a considerable lack of software available for it, since it took time for the software community to adapt to the new environment. Much of the software that was made available for the PC—mainly by IBM at first, but gradually by other independent software vendors—was at first considered adequate for the machine. Much of this software had its roots in the older 8-bit world and was simply a feature-for-feature translation onto the PC.

As times goes on, we discover more and more uses that the computer can be put to. More demanding tasks can be considered the domain of the computer and new, more powerful concepts can be introduced. Many of the limits in complexity and performance that once seemed insurmountable fall as software becomes more and more mature. This progression was seen in earlier mass-market microcomputers, such as the Apple II, where the quality of software steadily grew. Today there are several programs available that would not have been considered possible three years ago.

Much of the early PC software simply emulated the performance and features of earlier incarnations. DOS, in its earliest version, is one of the best examples of this. Initially it was compared by those "in the know" with the 8-bit CP/M operating system.

Admittedly, DOS did overcome many of the limitations of CP/M and was restructured so that many of the intolerable "features" of CP/M were replaced with those with more acceptable performance characteristics. However, a consideration of CP/M basic design philosophy in DOS is obvious.

In its new version, DOS goes far beyond the capabilities of any of the older 8-bit systems. In many ways, it is no longer even fair to compare it with CP/M, since few of the features that had their genesis in that generation of operating systems remain.

DOS now comes closer to many of the minicomputer operating systems that have become popular—with the major exception that minicomputer operating systems tend to be designed to simultaneously handle more than one user at a time, whereas the PC is designed specifically as a single-user machine.

Since the vendor for DOS, Microsoft Corporation, is also the vendor for the very powerful XENIX multiuser operating system, it is probably fair to assume that DOS is gradually becoming a single-user version of XENIX. In fact, many of the new features of DOS version 2 point in that direction. In addition, IBM's announcement of the XENIX operating system as the multiuser operating system on the PC-AT would seem to substantiate this.

Before we go into depth about any of the new commands in DOS, it would be better to paint a quick picture of the major differences between the two main versions of the operating system—version 1 and version 2. Here, then, is a quick summary of the major features of DOS version 2.

Tree-Structured Directories

The first, and most obvious, feature that users of DOS version 2 will encounter is the new hierarchical directory structure. This new addition is designed to overcome a feature of DOS that quickly runs out of steam when the PC is used with a fixed disk.

In the past IBM did not acknowledge the existence of a fixed disk, but with the introduction of its own system, it becomes obvious that DOS must be made to work with it. As we have seen in earlier chapters, there is a small, finite number of files that can be stored on a disk. This number is determined by the amount of disk space available, which is directly proportional to the amount of storage space allocated to the directory.

On a floppy-disk-based system, it is quite convenient to work with a single directory, since the number of files that can fit onto a floppy disk is really quite limited—64 for a single-sided disk and 112 for a dual-sided disk. However, when a fixed disk is attached to the PC, the number of files that can be stored is increased dramatically—to several thousand if you extrapolate according to storage space available.

There are two major problems with storing so many files in a single directory the way DOS version 1 does. You can imagine how frustrating it would be if every time you issued a **dir** command, you had to sit for several minutes as all of the files on the disk whisked by on the screen. The situation becomes more intolerable when you try to limit the number of files that are to be displayed on the screen by issuing a **dir** command with an argument containing wildcards, and still the list quickly scrolls off the top of the screen.

The other major problem relates to the access time for DOS to read to or write from a file. If all the files were accessed through a single directory, DOS would have to search through a list of several thousand names and disk addresses each time it wanted to access the disk. Although this is an acceptable access method when working with limited-storage floppy disks, the result would be a very slow operating system when used with a fixed disk.

The solution is to break the system down into multiple directories and allow the user to construct a custom directory system, according to his or her needs. These directories are related to each other in a hierarchical fashion, often called a "tree structure."

Under this structure there exists the very bottom directory of the system, called the "root directory." This directory looks very much like the simple single directory that was available under DOS version 1. However, instead of containing a simple list of files, each directory entry can either be a normal DOS file or the name of another directory—or more accurately a "subdirectory." So, branching out from the root directory can be several other directories, each of which can likewise contain files or other subdirectories. This allows the user to break up file space by function, rather than having all the files stuck in a single directory.

Like the standard single directory of DOS version 1, the root directory on a floppy disk can hold either 64 or 112 entries, depending on the disk drives used. On the fixed disk the number of entries that can be contained in the root directory depends on how the disk space is allocated. This is a somewhat complex mechanism that we will take a closer look at in a later chapter.

The link between two connected directories is known as a "path." The user can travel up and down the tree by specifying a "path name." Along with these new capabilities come several new utility commands designed to move between directories and up and down the tree structure. There are also new commands to create and remove directories.

This gives the impression of having several disks in the drive at once. Obviously, this has some sort of bearing on the filespec that we have all come to know and love. Since there can now exist two or more files with the same name on the same disk (not in the same directory, though), the only way to discriminate between them is to show the path from the root to the appropriate directory—the path name. Now the filespec for a particular file not only has to include the drive designation and the name of the file, but it also must include the path that DOS needs to take through the tree to find the file.

Under DOS version 1 we were introduced to the concept of a *default drive,* also called the working drive, logged drive, or current drive—the drive that would be accessed if you did not specifically tell DOS which drive to work with. Under DOS version 2 we now have the analogous concept of a *default directory,* also called the working directory, logged directory, or current directory.

Background Printing

Perhaps the most handy of the new features added to DOS is the ability to queue documents for printing in background mode. This means that while the printer is busy printing the documents, the computer is available for use, so that you have better control over the peripheral hardware facilities. The result is quite impressive, particularly when using a highly interactive program. The PC will send characters to the printer between keystrokes.

IBM does not push this feature to any prominence in the DOS version 2 manual, although it does represent a significant advance for DOS. This feature does not mean that DOS has become a full multitasking operating system, or, to use one of the industry buzzwords, a *concurrent* operating system, since such capabilities do not make much sense considering the styles of software that are available for the PC. However, this capability can be extended to any specially configured task, meaning that one day we will have other background tasking capabilities built into DOS. Good examples of these are background communications and electronic mail facilities.

The background print capability takes the shape of a new external DOS command called **print,** which can be used to queue up to ten disk files for printing. Since DOS version 2 features better I/O redirection capabilities, the implications of this background printing capability can be extended to other tasks quite easily.

Fixed Disk Support

Of course, one of the major reasons for the release of DOS version 2 is so that the PC can now officially work with a fixed disk drive. DOS version 2 will support one or more fixed disks. Each of these fixed disks can be partitioned into separate areas for those who have to work with operating systems other than DOS.

Volume Names

Another new feature of DOS is its ability to identify disks by name—a *volume* name. Assigned to the disk when it is formatted, this name is always visible when a directory of the disk is listed. This provides a handy method of keeping track of which disk is which, so that the user is always sure of writing information onto the proper disk. Of course, this volume name is available to applications programs so that they can check that the user has inserted the proper disk in the disk drive, a safety feature that will further increase the reliability of applications running under DOS.

Installable Device Drivers

A feature that may not strike you as particularly wonderful, but will gradually become more and more important, is DOS's new ability to configure and install device drivers at boot time. To many users this will sound somewhat complex, since the term *device driver* has not been used before with DOS. A device driver is a software routine used to control a specific peripheral attached to the computer. It is logically placed between the operating system and the device itself and presents a standard method for applications programs to operate the device without any special software included in the application.

Many new peripherals will either have to emulate an IBM-supplied device, in which case they can use the device drivers built into the system, or they will come with a separate device driver. This feature, although technical sounding, has been added to aid the novice in configuring and reconfiguring the system. This process is typically the result of installing a new piece of hardware, such as a printer or a fixed disk.

With DOS version 1 the installation of the device driver was left up to the hardware manufacturer—typically, the manufacturer would ship a "patch" with the equipment. This patch would modify DOS so that it could work with the new device. Fixed disk manufacturers, for example, would ship a converted BASIC input/output system (BIOS) interface containing the appropriate device drivers needed to operate their hardware. This new BIOS interface would replace the one supplied in the earlier DOS by IBM.

This practice worked quite well until you needed to install more than one "foreign" device. Many times the result would be a conflict between the two peripherals. One peripheral could be operated, providing that the other was not. This situation arose because there was no convention for peripheral manufacturers to follow when writing a device driver and the drivers would compete for memory or interrupt control.

The solution was to separate out all the driver components into individual modules and give users control over which modules are used in their computers, making it a relatively trivial task for even a novice to modify or add to the configuration. This greatly simplifies the task of peripheral manufacturers, who instead of having to ship a patch for DOS, limiting the usefulness of their product, simply ship a device driver that you can install yourself.

By modifying a special file that exists on the DOS version 2 master disk, you can now configure your system to work with the new device—without having to put up with some kluged together, second-hand DOS that may or may not work with other devices.

The new file that is included on the DOS disk to handle this process is called config.sys. It is a simple ASCII file and can therefore be modified either by the **edlin** file editor or by any DOS-compatible word processor or text editor. Since it is an ASCII file, it can also be listed on the screen using the **type** command.

New, More Compact Disk Format

With DOS version 2 there also comes a new disk format—along with all the benefits and disadvantages that that entails. The benefits are obvious: 12 percent more storage on a disk with little or no cost. DOS version 2 will allow a single-sided disk that could previously store 163,840 characters to now store up to 184,320 characters. Similarly, a double-sided disk that could store 327,680 characters under DOS version 1 can now store up to 368,640. The disadvantages are not quite so obvious. They arise from the fact that we now have twice as many disk formats we have to deal with.

Luckily, many of the disadvantages have been made transparent, since DOS version 2 has been designed to automatically adjust, wherever possible, to the particular disk format that it discovers on a disk, each time that it reads or writes. For those who were using DOS versions 1.0 or 1.1, new features in the **copy** routine allow the routine copying of files from the old format onto the new format.

The additional storage space that has magically appeared on those once easily filled disks is due to the fact that DOS now formats each track with one additional sector. Instead of eight sectors of 512 bytes each, DOS version 2 allows nine sectors of 512 bytes each. There is, as always, a slight overhead associated with the new format, so that the increase in available disk space is not all free. Though, when we take a closer look as the new format in the following chapters, we'll find that DOS version 2 manages the newly found disk space so economically that this overhead is almost insignificant.

Improved Batch Mode

As if the existing batch-mode commands in DOS version 1 were not enough, DOS version 2 comes standard with additional power in the batch mode by including **if** constructs. Now, within a batch file (.bat), there exists the ability to define lines by labels—names assigned to each command line. The command processor can be made to **goto** a specified label depending on whether some condition is met or not, in much the same manner as nonstructured languages, such as BASIC.

The number of replaceable parameters that can be used in a batch file has also been increased, and another new construct (**for**) has been added. These new abilities make DOS even more functional than before for anyone doing repetitive tasks, such as the usual edit-compile-debug-edit cycle used in programming.

Improved I/O Redirection

In the area of input/ouput redirection, DOS version 2 differs significantly from version 1. Input and output can now be redirected among devices by indicating special characters on the command line. Since this can be done at any time, it allows for temporary redirection—a handy tool for debugging. In this area DOS has become much more like its big brother XENIX, borrowing many of the UNIX-like concepts such as *pipes* and *filters*.

Intermediate forms of input and output can be processed by several XENIX-like filters (e.g., **sort**) before being piped to a final destination. An example of this type of usage would be to issue the **dir** command, **sort** the directory listing, and send the output to a file. This entire process can now be done with one single DOS command. As complex as they sound, these new capabilities are extremely useful and will be explained in depth in later chapters.

One particularly useful capability that I/O redirection opens up is the ability to store the output from a program in a disk file, by simply redirecting the output that would normally go to the screen. This gives the creative programmer a very powerful tool for debugging programs. The converse of this feature is the ability to store the input to a program in a file and redirect the input away from the keyboard to the disk file. This can be thought of as yet another type of batch operation, this time at the applications program level rather than the operating system level.

The new pipe and filter capabilities of DOS will eventually attract the attention of applications software developers and allow them to create new and better concepts in their software designs. Many of these will remove a burden from the user by automating some task that was previously handled manually.

ANSI Escape-Sequence Cursor Positioning

Another important new addition for all the "techies" out there is DOS's ability to support the American National Standards Institute's ANSI 3.64-1979 and the International Standards Organization's ISO 6429 specifications for terminal cursor addressing. These standards describe the manner in which a nondescript terminal may be attached to an operating system and operated correctly.

Essentially the same standard, both the ANSI and ISO standards describe ways to position the cursor and set certain terminal attributes by sending serial strings of characters to the terminal. Since these strings all begin with the ASCII Escape character, they have become known as the ANSI Escape sequences.

This ability allows software to be written for any type of compatible computer, regardless of its terminal characteristics, and makes the software developer's job of reaching as many vendors' computer systems as possible with the minimum amount of redundant work a little easier. It also allows the different letters of the alphabet to be reassigned to different keys on the keyboard, a use that will only be exercised in some extreme cases, although it may have some utility when applied to the special function keys.

To the casual user, unless you have a remote terminal attached to your PC—a rare occurrence at best—this new facility will not directly affect you, although it will provide a much needed utility to software developers interested in having their products operate on other MS-DOS computers.

The ability to work with Escape sequences is a feature that can be dynamically installed into your system by placing a reference in the config.sys configuration file to a special extended screen and keyboard-control device driver that is supplied on the DOS version 2 master disk.

Upward Compatibility

One of the major drawbacks in advancing software technology in the way that DOS has been advanced is that much of the time software developed on the older operating system is not compatible with the operating system that is replacing it. DOS successfully addresses these issues and offers a path to move older software onto the new system.

However, some of the programs written for DOS version 1 will not run under DOS version 2. This is not due to some inadequacy of DOS, but to liberties many programmers have taken with DOS version 1. Technically speaking, any program that does not work within the supported framework of DOS version 1 is not guaranteed to work with DOS version 2. This category includes those programs that do not make, or worse bypass, the proper operating system calls, or make direct BIOS calls. Also, due to changes in the way the file allocation table is handled, some programs that directly manipulate the FAT may not work.

With all of the new additions and capabilities in DOS version 2, there is obviously some penalty. Indeed, DOS does burn up considerably more user memory than it did before. IBM recommends that the system running DOS version 2 be equipped with a minimum of 64K memory, and 128K if used with a fixed disk.

Some programs do not use multiple memory segments, leaving them too large to be loaded and to be run under DOS version 2. This does not seem to be too severe a price to pay for the additional capabilities, since, after all, the low cost of RAM memory is one of the realities of today's technology that makes 16-bit systems feasible.

In the DOS version 2 manual there is an appendix that refers to problems created with individual programs supplied by IBM. If you are using software that was supplied by an independent software vendor other than IBM, you should obtain information on upgrading to DOS version 2 either from the retailer who sold you the software or directly from the manufacturer. Needless to say, any of the programs written in the IBM-supplied languages should work without modification.

Command Summary

Since there are so many enhancements to the system in version 2, it is probably appropriate that we list the important commands and see how they have changed between the two versions.

Internal Commands

The list of internal DOS commands has increased, primarily because of the new hierarchical directory structure. This rise in capability, however, is more than directly proportional to the additional requirements in memory. The following is a quick list of the commands that are memory resident in DOS version 2.

dir	minor differences over DOS version 1 command
rename	same as before
erase	same as before, except for enhancements to manage paths
type	same as before, except for enhancements to manage paths
copy	same as before, except for enhancements to manage paths
date	same as before
time	same as before
ver	new command to print DOS version number

chdir	new command to change the current directory of a specified drive to a new directory
mkdir	new command used to create a new directory or subdirectory
rmdir	new command used to delete an existing directory, along with all of its contents
break	new command used by programmers to turn on and off the checks for a Ctrl-c typed on the keyboard
verify	new command that can turn on and off the facility to verify all data after a disk write
path	new command used to set the command search path through the directories (this command is one of the most important of the new DOS commands and will be covered extensively in later chapters)
vol	new command to print the volume identification name of the specified disk on the screen
ctty	new command to select the standard input and output devices
set	new command to set the environment by defining and aliasing strings that can be recognized and processed by the command line interpreter

Batch Mode Commands

The batch operations of DOS, as powerful as they were before, have been enhanced tenfold in version 2. With the addition of conditional testing, a little intelligence has been added to the system. DOS itself can now determine if certain conditions exist and act accordingly if they do.

rem	same as before
pause	same as before
echo	new command to enable or suppress the printing of commands on the screen during the processing of a batch file
goto	new command for use with labeled lines in a batch file; can be used to transfer control to a specific line in a batch file depending on some test
shift	new command that cleverly allows the user to have more than the ten previously allowed replaceable parameters; it works by shifting replaceable parameters so that there are never more than ten active at one time

if	new command used to conditionally invoke commands based on the condition of some test; this construct considerably enhances the functionality of the entire batch processor
for	new command used to set up sequential processing in batch files; it sequentially binds a replaceable parameter to a command and executes it
cls	new command that allows batch files to clear the video display

External DOS Commands

As with DOS version 1, any machine-readable file that uses the extension .com or .exe is considered to be an external command. Many of the existing DOS external commands will thus work without modification because of it. Therefore, this list will consider only those commands where changes have occurred between the two versions.

format	same as before, except for new switches that have been added to allow for the formatting of disks in either DOS version 1 or DOS version 2 format; also handles the assigning of volume names for disk identification (the actual formatting process is different in DOS version 2, since the the physical layout of the sectors has changed)
chkdsk	same as before, except for new switches
edlin	same as before—invokes mini file editor
debug	same as before—invokes debugger, which has been enhanced
sys	same as before
diskcopy	same as before
diskcomp	same as before
mode	same as before, with minor modifications
assign	new command to instruct DOS to use a different drive from the one that was specified
backup	new command for fixed disk users to copy files from fixed disk to floppy
restore	new command that does the opposite of backup
tree	new command to display all the directory paths on the specified disk; can also be used to display files on more than one directory

recover	new command to reconstruct damaged disk directories from the FAT; removes any bad sectors from files so that the data are not totally lost
print	new command that allows files to be printed in "background" while the computer remains free for the operation of other programs
exe2bin	same as before
prompt	new command that allows the user or an applications program to set the system prompt

Special New Features

filters	there are several filters included with DOS version 2; all of these are new features
more	new filter command that reads data from the standard input device and passes them one screenful at a time to the standard output device; it sends out the message "**--more--**" between screens and pauses until a key is pressed
sort	new filter command that sorts data coming in from the standard input device and routes the sorted information to the standard output device
piping of standard input and output	this facility allows data being output from one program or command to be used as the input to another; data are temporarily held in a disk file with a special name
config.sys	this file contains special configuration information that DOS uses each time it is booted; it contains all the information for installable device drivers, RAM drive settings, etc.

Summary

As you can see the changes are not trivial. They amount to a complete overhaul of the operating system, adding many new features and streamlining many of the existing features.

The obvious move toward XENIX makes it attractive to applications software developers, in that moving software between the two operating systems is greatly simplified. Hopefully, it will result in even more software being made available for the PC, as well as in the migration of much PC software up to the XENIX world.

CHAPTER 13

Hierarchical Directories

As we saw in the last chapter there are many facilities in DOS version 2.0 that were not there before. Probably the most exotic and undoubtedly one of the most functional of these is the ability to construct customized hierarchical directories on each disk. This new feature allows better use of large disk-storage devices and more efficient distribution of storage space between different users or for different tasks.

DOS is not unique in having this ability. Indeed it is one of the hallmarks of the UNIX operating system for minicomputers, and more appropriately, the Microsoft commercial version of UNIX for microcomputers, XENIX. DOS, however, is the first popular mass-market microcomputer operating system to have such a capability.

Under DOS version 2 the ability to break down a large disk drive into several components is now an option. You can construct several directories on a single drive—regardless of the size of that drive. The size of each of these logical devices is entirely up to you—it is not fixed.

As always, the best way to look at this new and somewhat novel situation is by example. Suppose that you use your PC for word processing, database management, and as a remote terminal on an information network, and suppose that it is connected to a Winchester-type hard disk. If all the word-processing files, all the database management files, all the communications files, and all the DOS command files were lumped together in a single directory, the situation would be chaotic at best. DOS version 2.0 allows you to create several different directories—in this case, by function.

At the very top level there is a master directory that allows access to any of the functional directories. This top directory is commonly called the "root directory," a reference to the so-called tree structure of the directory system. In our example the root directory will not contain any DOS files, but will instead contain four subdirectories—one for each of the functional categories that we have split our files into.

Quite simply we have created a tree that looks like this:

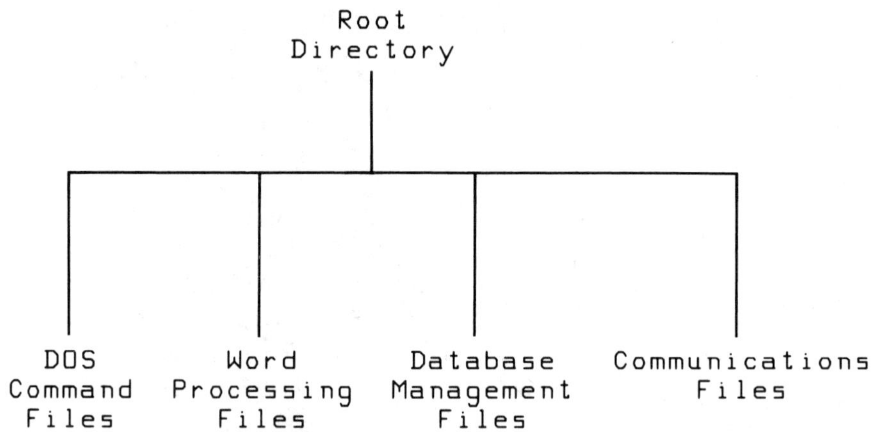

Each of the subdirectories must be given a name. The names for the subdirectories follow exactly the same rules as the names for standard DOS files. In other words, a directory can be given a name of up to eight characters, followed by a three-character extension separated from the name by a period—exactly the same as a file name and extension. Also, as with file names it is best to give directories names that are meaningful. Directory names should be selected to reflect the nature of the contents. They should also be short, since you will find that you may have to type them many times. In our example we are going to give the four subdirectories the names system, wp, db, and term.

Since we are creating a relatively simple directory structure, the names we have selected for the subdirectories do not have extensions. As with file names there is no absolute requirement that directory names have extensions. Directory name extensions come in very handy whenever the directory structure gets more complex—for example, when there are several people using the system and each is performing similar tasks. In a situation like this, the task names can then define the main body of the directory names, and the extensions can identify the owner of the directory.

Once these subdirectories have been created (we'll step through the actual creative process later), a listing of the root directory (still by use of the internal **dir** command) will produce the following:

```
    Volume in drive B has no ID
    Directory of B:\

COMMAND COM   17503     1-28-83   5:23p
SYSTEM       <DIR>      2-21-83   3:15p
WP           <DIR>      2-21-83   4:10p
DB           <DIR>      2-21-83   4:35p
TERM         <DIR>      2-21-83   4:50p
    5 File(s)   150528 bytes free
```

DOS clearly marks those directory items that are themselves subdirectories by placing the word **DIR** between less than and greater than signs, and tagging it on after the directory name.

If we actually log on to one of the subdirectories, we will see the contents of that subdirectory. Suppose, for the moment, that we have the *WordStar* program as our word-processing program, and we have placed all the *WordStar* files in the subdirectory wp. If we log on to wp and issue the **dir** command, we may see something like this:

```
    Volume in drive B has no ID
    Directory of B:\wp

.            <DIR>      2-21-83   4:10p
..           <DIR>      2-21-83   4:10p
WS        COM   20864   1-01-80  12:04a
WSOVLY1   OVR   41216  11-15-82
WSOVLY2   OVR   28160  11-15-82
    5 File(s)  59904 bytes free
```

As you can see, all the *WordStar* files are located in the same directory. The other two entries that appear to be directories, represented by the single and double periods, will be explained a little later. At the moment they may be considered part of the overhead required to maintain a hierarchical directory structure.

Now, if we have, say, three classes of documents that we want to maintain under *WordStar*—memos, letters, and program listings—after a while these files could again become too numerous to list on the screen with the **dir** command. So, we create three more directories, each of which is a subdirectory of the wp subdirectory—one for each class of file, named memos, letters, and programs. When this is done, the wp subdirectory now appears as:

```
         Volume in drive B has no ID
         Directory of B:\wp
.               <DIR>         2-21-83   4:10p
..              <DIR>         2-21-83   4:10p
WS          COM    20864      1-01-80  12:04a
WSOVLY1     OVR    41216     11-15-82
WSOVLY2     OVR    28160     11-15-82
LETTERS     WS  <DIR>         2-21-83   5:51p
MEMOS       WS  <DIR>         2-21-83   5:53p
PROGRAMS    WS  <DIR>         2-21-83   5:54p
         6 File(s)      58880 bytes free
```

We now have a hierarchical file structure that is logically laid out as:

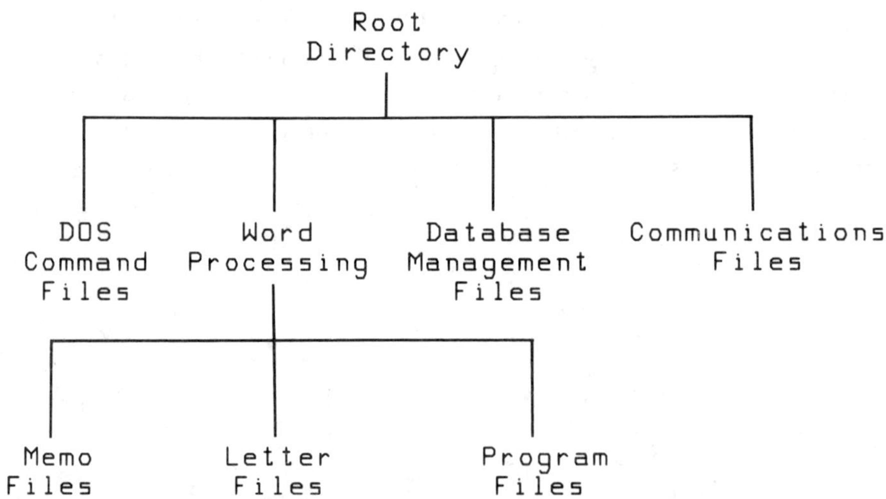

The nesting of directories could go on and on, getting more and more complex with each iteration. The trick in constructing a directory hierarchy is to find the balance between functionality and complexity—that balance will change for each PC installation, depending on the particular demands of the task that the computer is being used for.

Multiple Directories for Multiple Users

Another good use of hierarchical directories is for installations where more than one user accesses the PC. It may be, for example, that the PC is used in an office, usually by a manager, but sometimes also by a secretary, and occasionally by a bookkeeper. Each user can have a subdirectory in the root directory, and his or her own separate hierarchy of directories under it—which helps to keep the file system structured and uncluttered.

In this situation the directory hierarchy might look something like this:

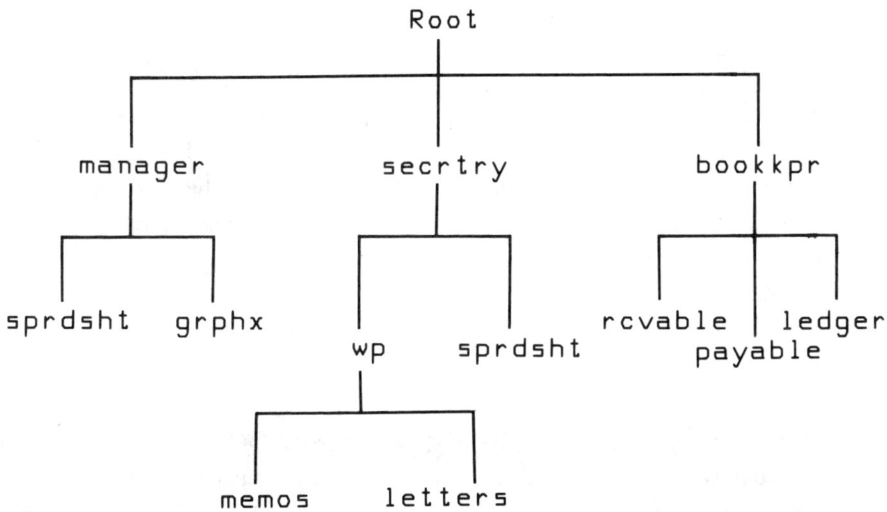

Notice that there are two directories with the name *sprdsht,* one being used by the manager and one by the secretary to store their spreadsheet models. How does the system tell the two directories apart? If we tell it to store a file in a particular directory, how does it know which directory we mean?

The answer lies in the path name—the path through the directory structure starting at the root that would be traversed in order to find the correct directory.

Path names are strings of directory names separated by the backslash character (\). For example, the path names of the two like-named directories in our example are represented by:

```
\manager\sprdsht
```

and

```
\secrtry\sprdsht
```

respectively. The difference between the two path names is obviously the beginning part *\manager* in one and *\secrtry* in the other. This indicates the difference in the paths required to reach the two directories from the root, and differentiates the two.

The path name can be thought of as an extension of the file name that we learned to love under DOS version 1. Where DOS version 1 required a drive designator and a file name to identify a file, DOS version 2 and beyond will require (at least) a drive designator, a path name, and a file name.

New Commands for New File Structure

Now that we have seen how directory structures look, and how they can be used, we should examine the new DOS commands that have been added to aid in the creation and manipulation of these directories. The first, and most constructive, of these new commands is the **mkdir** command, used to create new directories.

The **Mkdir** Command

The **mkdir** command is (conveniently) an internal DOS command. It was made internal so that you wouldn't have to copy it onto whatever directory you wanted to create. **Mkdir,** like several other DOS commands, has a pseudonym—in this case, the short **md** command. As you become more familiar with the system, you'll find it convenient to move to the short forms, but when you're first learning new DOS commands you should stick to the full name, since it's more representative. For the purpose of this text, we'll continue to use the full names.

If we look at the example we used earlier, you'll see that we had four subdirectories branching off the root. These subdirectories were assigned as one for system files, one for word-processing files, one for database files, and one for communications files. These subdirectories can all be created using the **mkdir** command.

Before these directories can be created, we must assume that the new disk has been formatted using the DOS version 2 **format** command. Under DOS version 2, **format** automatically creates the root directory—in much the same way as it creates the sole directory in DOS version 1.

Once the disk has been formatted, we can create a new directory simply by typing

```
mkdir dirname
```

where *dirname* is the name that you want to assign to the directory. DOS will then spin the disk for a few seconds as it creates the necessary structures. When you next issue the **dir** command, you'll see that the new directory has been created and given the name that you assigned to it. It will be indicated in the directory listing by a <DIR>. It's that easy!

By way of an example we can create a new directory called level1 under the root directory of a newly formatted disk. This is done by first formatting a blank disk and then entering the command:

```
mkdir level1
```

Before we create the directory, our **dir** listing might look like this:

```
         Volume in drive B has no ID
         Directory of B:\

         File not found
```

If we then go ahead and create the new directory, out listing will look like this:

```
         Volume in drive B has no ID
         Directory of B:\

LEVEL1          <DIR>        2-21-83    7:32p
         1 File(s)    174592 bytes free
```

The **Chdir** Command

Once you've created a new subdirectory, you are still left in the directory that you started in. In order to move to the new directory, you use the next new command—**chdir. Chdir** is another internal DOS command that is used to change the current, or working, directory. This supplies the means to move up, down, and around the hierarchical directory system.

In this example, you would enter the command

```
chdir level1
```

to move down the hierarchy to the directory that you've just created. As soon as you move to the new directory, take a look at the directory listing with the **dir** command. You should see something like the following:

```
      Volume in drive B has no ID
      Directory of B:\level1

 .            <DIR>       2-21-83    7:32p
 ..           <DIR>       2-21-83    7:32p
      2 File(s)    174592 bytes free
```

The first thing you should notice is that the **dir** command only lists the contents of the current directory. It doesn't show the files that we left in the parent directory.

You should also notice the "Directory of" message that appears at the head of the listing. When we were at the root directory, this message simply said "Directory of B:\." In the next level of the hierarchy, the message reads "Directory of B:\level1." This shows us the path name of the current directory.

If we go another step further in building the hierarchy, we'll see another example of this. To do so, we'll create another level of the hierarchy by creating another new directory. This time we'll create it while we're in the \level1 directory, so that it's really a sub-subdirectory. While in the \level1 directory, type:

```
mkdir level2
```

Then look at the results by typing **dir** and listing the current directory. You should see something like this:

```
      Volume in drive B has no ID
      Directory of B:\level1

 .            <DIR>       2-21-83    7:32p
 ..           <DIR>       2-21-83    7:32p
 LEVEL2       <DIR>       2-21-83    7:42p
      3 File(s)    174080 bytes free
```

We've just created another level in the directory structure and can move down to the new level by typing:

```
chdir level2
```

List the new directory by typing **dir.** The screen should show:

```
        Volume in drive B has no ID
        Directory of B:\level1\level2
.               <DIR>      2-21-83   7:42p
..              <DIR>      2-21-83   7:42p
        2 File(s)    174080 bytes free
```

If we go yet again one level deeper and create a new directory called level3, move down to that directory, and list it out, we might see:

```
        Volume in drive B has no ID
        Directory of B:\level1\level2\level3
.               <DIR>    2-21-83    7:50p
..              <DIR>    2-21-83    7:50p
        2 File(s) 173568 bytes free
```

and so on.

The conclusions that we can draw from this meaningful little exercise are quite clear. When you issue the **dir** command under DOS version 2.0, you don't necessarily see all the files on the disk. You only see a listing of the files on the current directory. If there are any files on any directory that have the <DIR> marker appended to them, then there are other directories on the disk.

Any commands that are issued to DOS that have some sort of file-dependent action associated with them will work only with the files in the working directory. At first this seems like it's actually a step backward from the way it was before, since we've lost some of the universality of many of the functions of DOS. This isn't the case, although the creation of such directories is a convenience that makes most sense to users who have very large capacity disk drives, such as Winchester-type hard disks. Before we can adequately make a case for or against creating a hierarchical disk-directory structure, we should take a look at some of the other utilities that allow greater flexibility in working with a tree structure, particularly those functions that allow us to move rapidly from one directory to another.

Moving in the Hierarchy

Before starting, we should set some confusing semantics to rest. We've already been introduced to the concept of a tree structure. We've also seen that, as in real trees, there is a root. However, in our tree, the root is at the top and the subdirectories are below—creating an inverted tree. Consequently, when we talk about moving down through the hierarchy, we mean that we're moving away from the root directory—and hence further into the directory structure. When we move up, we'll be moving toward the root.

With that said, let's go back and take a look at the example we've been working with. We've created a very simple hierarchy that can be represented by the following diagram:

```
root            (\)
 |
\level1         (\level1)
 |
\level2         (\level1\level2)
 |
\level3         (\level1\level2\level3)
```

We've also seen that we can move down through the hierarchy one step at a time with the **chdir** command. Predictably, we can go much further and faster by using this command in other ways.

Whenever a new directory is created, DOS version 2 creates two files—designed by the . <DIR> and the . . <DIR>—and places them in the directory. The purpose of these two files is to assist in the process of traveling up and down the tree structure.

The first of the two periods is simply DOS's shorthand for the current, or working, directory—the directory on to which the system is currently logged. If you need to enter a DOS command that accesses the current directory, there is no need to enter the entire path name. Simply use the shorthand method. In general, however, this is a somewhat useless practice.

The other abbreviation, . ., is used to indicate the parent directory of the current directory. The parent directory is the directory that is immediately above the current directory. In our example the directory \level1\level2 is the parent directory of \level1\level2 \level3 and the directory \level1 is the parent of \level1\level2.

The . . abbreviation is particularly useful for moving up a level in the hierarchy. For example, if we were currently logged on to the directory \level1\level2\level3 and entered the command

```
dir ..
```

we'd get a listing of the directory \level1\level2, and if we issued the command

```
chdir ..
```

we'd immediately pop up to the parent directory—\level1\level2. If we entered the same command again—conveniently by pressing the F3 special function key—we'd pop up to the directory \level1.

In addition to using the **chdir** command with these abbreviations, we can also use it with a complete specification for a path name. This allows us to specify an *absolute* destination, rather than a *relative* destination. For example, if we were in the directory \level1\level2\level3 and wanted to move up two levels to the \level1 directory, we could enter the single command:

```
chdir \level1
```

If we wanted to back out completely to the top level (the root), we could enter the command

```
chdir \
```

which would have the effect of directing us to the directory \, the shorthand name for the root directory.

To demonstrate a somewhat more elaborate use of the **chdir** command, try creating a directory structure with the following form:

```
                 root
                   |
      -------------------------------
      |                             |
   level 1                       other1
      |                             |
   level 2                       other2
      |                             |
   level 3                       other3
```

When you've done that, move all the way to one of the extremities, for example by typing

```
chdir \level1\level2\level3
```

and then try to move randomly around the tree by use of the **chdir** command in conjunction with a full path name. For example, try

```
chdir \other1\other2\other3
```

and verify that you have indeed moved to the correct directory by getting a directory listing with the **dir** command.

There is one other rule that you should be aware of when moving around directories with the **chdir** command. What happens when you specify a path name that does not begin with the backslash character? If you were in the directory \level1 and entered the command

```
chdir level2\level3
```

you would still move to the appropriate directory. If you enter a path name that does not begin with a backslash character, DOS will assume that you want to make a move *relative* to the current directory. This only makes sense when you want to move deeper into the hierarchy along the path that you're already on.

If you begin a path name with a backslash, DOS assumes that you are specifying an *absolute* path name—one that begins at the root directory.

When DOS is given a relative path name (not starting with a \), it creates the absolute path name by adding the specified path name to the absolute path name of the current working directory.

To illustrate this, place yourself in the directory named \level1 and enter the command:

```
chdir level2\level3
```

Verify that you end up in the directory \level1\level2\level3—a relative move. Next, return to the \level1 directory by entering

```
chdir \level1
```

and then enter the command

```
chdir other1\other2\other3
```

You should get the error message "invalid directory." This is so because DOS was looking for a relative offset from the current directory. In other words, it made an attempt to find the directory that lay along the hypothetical, and in this case nonexistent, path name:

```
\level1\other1\other2\other3
```

Relative path names are useful if you're in a directory and want to move down the hierarchy one or more levels. It eliminates the need to enter the entire path name. Only the relative offset need be entered. For example, if you were in the directory \level1 and wanted to move to the directory \level1\level2\level3, instead of having to enter

```
chdir \level1\level2\level3
```

you would enter the slightly more simple

```
chdir level2\level3
```

The **chdir** command has another useful and interesting capability. The bare-bones version of the command

```
chdir
```

prints the full path name of the current working directory. For example:

```
B:\level1\level2\level3
```

Tree-structured directories, although very useful when used with large storage devices, do incur a certain penalty in both storage-requirement overhead and file access times. Every time you create a new directory, you are adding to the complexity of the filing system. However, there are also many unexpected benefits that can be derived from the intelligent use of hierarchical file systems.

By allowing you to structure the directory system according to your individual needs, DOS version 2 has opened new frontiers in data storage for small computers.

Working with the Hierarchical File System

With a little forethought on how the tree structure of the directory system is arranged, DOS version 2 can be a system for the user that's actually made to work for the user—an uncommon situation when applied to operating systems.

It is usually best to group disk files in directories according to their contents. For example, a directory substructure could be created to manage three different types of word-processor files. The parent directory could hold the files that actually contain the word processor itself, while three subdirectories could be created to hold different types of files created by the word processor. This could be structured as a directory for files containing letter-type correspondence, another directory for files containing internal memos, and a third directory for files containing program listings.

Suppose that you were working with a directory structure substantially like that just described and had spent the entire workday creating a new program, using the word processor as a file editor. The new program would consist of a source code listing spread across several files—all of which are stored in the subdirectory created especially to hold program listings. Under DOS version 2 it is now very simple to log on to that subdirectory and back up only the files in that directory onto a floppy disk.

As usual, the best way to illustrate this new concept is to actually do it, and analyze each of the steps involved. The exercise that we will undertake is to create a directory structure that can be represented by the following diagram:

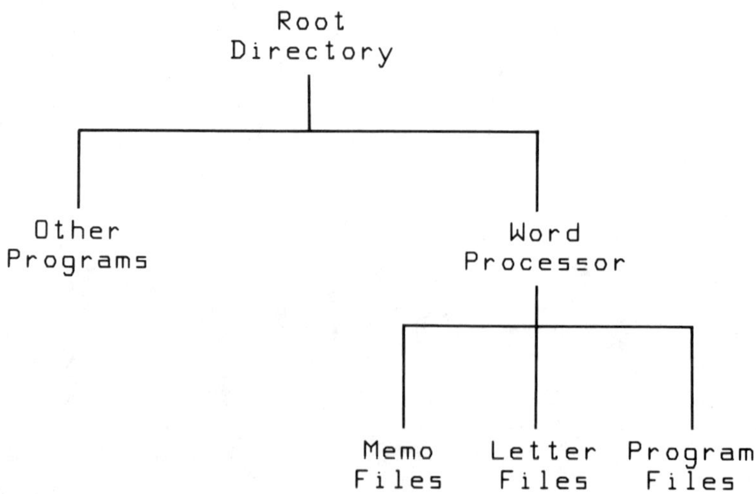

Let's assume that the program listings that we've just completed are all in the directory with the path name \wp\programs and have been given the names code1.src, code2.src, code3.src, code4.src, and menu.cod. Assume that the last file, menu.cod, is a file that was created a long time ago for use in another program and was given a name according to a different set of naming conventions. This deliberately complicates matters when attempting to use DOS's wildcard character methods of copying files with the **copy** utility.

Let's step through the process of creating this directory structure—an exercise that should reinforce the understanding of tree-structured directories—and then see for ourselves how DOS's new abilities make file manipulation much more interesting.

First, format two blank diskettes using DOS version 2's **format** command. At this point don't worry about the changes made to the **format** command between DOS version 1 and version 2. Simply use the default version of the command (**format b:**) and DOS will automatically sense the type of disk drives that you have and format the blank diskette accordingly. If you have a single-sided disk drive, DOS will format the diskette for single-sided operation, and if you have a double-sided drive, DOS will create a double-sided diskette.

When you've formatted both disks, place one in drive A: and the other in drive B:, and then log on to drive B: in the usual manner. The following procedure describes step by step how to create a directory structure on the disk in drive B: similar to that described previously. When that's done, we can play with some dummy files we create and see how the structure can be put to work for us.

The formatting process creates the top, or root, directory on each of the disks. When you first place a disk in a disk drive, you will automatically log on to this directory, and will stay there until you tell DOS that you want to move to another directory. Use a **dir** command to see the root directory. You should see something like this:

```
Volume in drive B has no label
Directory of B:\

File not found
```

This is the usual blank root directory DOS version 2.0 creates when it formats a disk. You can now create two subdirectories on this disk—one to hold a word processor and the other as a general-purpose directory for other programs we may want on this disk. These directories are to be called wp and other. To create them, simply enter the following:

```
mkdir other     (creates, or makes, a new subdirectory called other)

mkdir wp        (creates another subdirectory called wp)
```

Now, when you use the **dir** command, you should see that DOS has created two subdirectories on the root directory. The new root directory listing might look like this:

```
         Volume in drive B has no label
         Directory of B:\

OTHER          <DIR>       3-02-83   12:41a
WP             <DIR>       3-02-83   12:41a
         2 File(s)     165376 bytes free
```

Now you should create the three further subdirectories under the subdirectory wp. There are actually two ways that you can create these subdirectories, and by way of illustration, we will use both.

The first method is to issue another **mkdir** command from the root directory. Obviously, though, we need to specify the path name for the new directory or DOS will simply create a new subdirectory on the root directory, which is not what we want. In this case we need to create a subdirectory called letters under the subdirectory called wp. The new path name for this directory would therefore be \wp\letters.

Since you are already logged on to the root directory (signified by a single \), you could simply enter the command:

```
mkdir wp\letters
```

This would cause DOS to create the subdirectory letters under the subdirectory wp. To verify that that indeed is the case, move down the hierarchy one level to the wp subdirectory by entering:

```
chdir wp
```

Then issue a **dir** command. You should be able to verify that indeed a new subdirectory was created. The directory listing should look like this:

```
         Volume in drive B has no label
         Directory of B:\wp

.              <DIR>       3-02-83   12:41a
..             <DIR>       3-02-83   12:41a
LETTERS        <DIR>       3-02-83   12:43a
         3 File(s)     165376 bytes free
```

As you can see DOS has created the new subdirectory letters under the path name \wp\letters. The other two standard overhead directory files, . and . ., have also been created.

The second method of creating a subdirectory is to first log on to the parent and then issue a **mkdir** command using a relative path name as we saw earlier. If you are logged on to the \wp subdirectory—which is to be the parent of the next subdirectory to be created—you can create the second subdirectory by entering:

```
mkdir memos
```

Again, the disk will spin and DOS will create a second subdirectory. A quick look at the directory will verify this:

```
          Volume in drive B has no label
          Directory of B:\wp
.               <DIR>       3-02-83   12:41a
..              <DIR>       3-02-83   12:41a
LETTERS         <DIR>       3-02-83   12:43a
MEMOS           <DIR>       3-02-83   12:44a
          4 File(s)     165376 bytes free
```

So far, two out of the three subdirectories have been created. In the creation of the third subdirectory, programs, we will reinforce the difference between relative path names and absolute path names. The way to do this is to log on to the other subdirectory that you created earlier and create the new subdirectory from there.

To do this, first back out from the /wp subdirectory and move up to the root. Enter the command:

```
chdir ..
```

This pops you up to the parent directory—in this case, the root. From here you can log on to the other subdirectory by entering:

```
chdir other
```

You are now logged on to the directory with the path name \other. However, from here you need to create a directory with the path name \wp\programs without changing your position on the tree.

To do this, you must use the **mkdir** command with an absolute path name. When DOS is given an absolute path name, it resets itself to the root and follows the path from there. In this example you would enter the command:

```
mkdir \wp\programs
```

When you've done this, you should move directly to the \wp directory by using a **chdir** command with an absolute path name and see the results of your handiwork:

```
chdir \wp
```

(absolute path name causes DOS to go directly to \wp)

```
dir

         Volume in drive B has no label
         Directory of B:\wp

.                <DIR>       3-02-83   12:41a
..               <DIR>       3-02-83   12:41a
LETTERS          <DIR>       3-02-83   12:43a
MEMOS            <DIR>       3-02-83   12:44a
PROGRAMS         <DIR>       3-02-83   12:45a
         5 File(s)     165376 bytes free
```

At this point you have created the entire directory structure needed for our exercise. All that is left is to create some dummy files on the directories so that we can play with them.

The first set of files are to put onto the \wp\programs subdirectory, so you must log on to that first:

```
chdir programs
```

A quick directory listing should prove that other than the overhead files created by DOS, the directory is empty. However, you will soon rectify that. You should create several dummy files that are to represent the source code files discussed earlier. To do this, you'll make use of the old standby command **copy con:** *filename.*

First create a dummy file called code1.src by entering:

```
copy con: code1.src
```

Then just bang out some junk on the keyboard into the file. When you've entered several lines of characters, press the F6 special function key to enter the end-of-file marker and close the file. You can then use the **copy** command to copy this dummy file several times to create the illusion of having the other files on the directory. When you're done, your new directory listing should look something like this:

```
         Volume in drive B has no label
         Directory of B:\wp\programs
.              <DIR>        3-02-83  12:41a
..             <DIR>        3-02-83  12:41a
CODE1     SRC         117   3-02-83  12:46a
CODE2     SRC         117   3-02-83  12:46a
CODE3     SRC         117   3-02-83  12:46a
CODE4     SRC         117   3-02-83  12:46a
MENU      COD         117   3-02-83  12:46a
         7 File(s)    165376 bytes free
```

The next thing you should do is to copy the dummy file from the directory \wp\programs onto its parent directory \wp and use it to represent the file that contains the word processor itself. The generic form of the **copy** command when used in cases such as this can be represented by the format:

```
copy d:pathname\filename d:pathname\filename
```

Notice that in DOS version 2.0, the entire path name is separated by the file name not by a : but by a \, since the actual file name is considered part of the full path name. The path name, of course, need not be entered if it is the same as the default (current) path name.

On the other hand, though, you are allowed to enter either an absolute path name or a relative path name where one is called for. Therefore, in this case if you are to copy the dummy file with the path name \wp\programs:code1.src onto a file with the path name \wp:word.com, there are several forms of the **copy** command that you can use. The first is the obvious

```
copy \wp\programs\code1.src \wp\word.com
```

which is the absolute version of the command.

In this case all of the information is in absolute format, so DOS knows exactly what is required, regardless of where it is currently logged in the tree structure. Consequently, this form of the command can be used at any time, regardless of hierarchical position.

The second form of the **copy** command that can be used is:

```
copy code1.src \wp\word.com
```

In this form of the command the first argument is a relative argument. This is so because there is no absolute path name specified—the argument does not begin with a \. The file name alone has been specified, so DOS assumes that the file is located on the currently logged directory. The second argument is an absolute path name and presents no problems.

The third version of the **copy** command that can be used is the one in which both arguments are relative offsets. It would take the form:

```
copy code1.src ..\word.com
```

In this case the symbol . . means the parent directory. A logical extension of this says that if you had wanted to copy the file code1.src onto the root directory, then there are two ways you could do it. Either of the following two statements would accomplish the goal:

```
copy code1.src \
```

or

```
copy code1.src ..\..
```

In the latter case each of the double period symbols means back up one directory level.

In neither case was the destination file name specified. As with DOS version 1, unless otherwise specified, the newly created file is given the same name. However, if you remember, when working with DOS version 1, it was not possible to have a file existing twice on the same disk with the same file name. With DOS version 2, however, the same file names can be used—as long as they are in different directories. What is not permitted is for two files to have the same path name and file name.

At this point you should have created a hierarchical directory structure similar to that described earlier. Now you can see the effect of some of the standard commands from DOS version 1 when used in a hierarchical file structure. You've already seen how to use the **copy** and **dir** commands, and the changes that they have undergone between versions. Now let's dig a little deeper and expose some more interesting rules that we'll have to learn to live with under DOS version 2 and beyond.

First, log on to the disk in drive A: and just for fun create a new directory called test.

```
mkdir test
```

Then log onto it.

```
chdir test
```

When that's done make sure your current directory on B: is \wp\programs. You can check this by typing **dir b:** and verifying the path name. If your current directory on B: is not \wp\programs and you want to change it without logging on to drive B:, you can enter:

```
chdir b:\wp\programs
```

This form of the command allows you to change directories on an inactive drive without having to log on to it first. B:'s current directory will be set to \wp\programs, and the logged drive will not be changed.

Your active directory in drive A: should be \test and in drive B: it should be \wp\programs. Next switch the two disks. Physically remove them and replace them in the opposite drives. Take a look and see which directories are logged on to.

Whenever DOS version 2.0 finds that there has been a change in a disk drive, it resets its position in the tree to the root. Take a look at the directory by entering **dir b:**. Notice that you are given a listing of the root directory.

Remove the disk from drive B: and place it back in drive A:. List the directory contents again and you should see that in drive A: you are still logged on to \test.

Now replace the disk that you originally removed from drive B:. As you may remember, when you last looked at this disk, you were logged on to \wp\programs. Since the disk has been removed and replaced, we should now be logged back on to the root directory.

This simple exercise should help clarify tree-structured directories. But let's play around some more and find out how things work. Take the disk on which you created the dummy files and hierarchy and place it in drive A:. Then place the DOS version 2 disk in drive B:.

Suppose that you wanted to copy the diskcopy.com file from the DOS master disk and place it on your play disk. Supposing also that you wanted to place it in the directory \other, so that it would have the path name \other\diskcopy.com.

Again, there are a couple of different ways to do this. You could simply change the current directory of drive A: to the \other directory and then issue a **copy** command:

```
chdir \other    (sets the default directory on A: to \other)
copy b:diskcopy.com a:
```

The **copy** command in this case does not have a target directory specified for the file. Consequently, it will be written onto the currently logged directory—\other.

There is an easier method of copying the file, and that is to specify an absolute path name for it on the target disk. In this case there would be no need for the default directory on drive A: to be changed. All of this could be done by entering the following command:

```
copy b:diskcopy.com \other
```

You can then verify that the process was successful by looking at the directory listing of the \other directory. Again, this can be done by entering:

```
dir \other
```

Now you can use the **diskcopy** command to copy the entire disk that you have just created. To do this, remove the DOS master disk from drive B: and replace it with the other formatted disk that was created earlier. Then make sure that you are logged on to drive A:. You should reset the position on the tree to the root directory on drive A:. This can be done by entering:

```
chdir \
```

Even though you know that the **diskcopy** command is not located on the root directory, issue the command:

```
diskcopy a: b:
```

Predictably, you get the "Bad command or file name" error message. As you can see, a hierarchical file structure can easily become very clumsy if it is not set up correctly.

The **Path** Command

Wouldn't it be tedious if you were working on the \wp directory and had all of your DOS utility programs stored on the \other directory. Every time you wanted to exit the word processor and use a utility program, you would have to change directories. After a half dozen or so times it would become very tedious indeed.

Fortunately, DOS provides a very simple mechanism for coping with this situation. This takes the form of another new DOS version 2 command—the **path** command. Quite simply, the **path** command is used to tell DOS on which paths it should search for a file if it is not found on the current directory. In our example, we would tell DOS that if it is looking for a file and cannot find it on the current directory, it should look in the \other directory.

This is done by entering the command

```
path \other
```

which tells DOS that if it does not find the specified file on whatever directory it is working on, then attempt to find it on the path \other.

Now attempt to run the **diskcopy** program by entering the command again. This time the command will be found and the disk can be copied. Go ahead and make a backup copy of the play disk and make sure for yourself that the directory hierarchy is preserved on the duplicate.

As you can see the function of the **diskcopy** routine is the same under DOS version 2 as it was in earlier versions. A complete mirror image of the source disk was created. For the moment, though, let's go back and play with the interesting **path** command.

Log back on to drive A: and replace the disk in drive B: with the DOS master disk again. Make sure that on drive A: you are logged on to the root directory and create another new directory called test. Then copy the chkdsk.com file from the DOS master disk to the newly created directory. This can be done by entering:

```
copy b:chkdsk.com \test
```

Next, to make matters more complicated log on to the \wp\programs directory on drive A: and issue the **chkdsk** command. Again, you'll get a "Bad command or file name" error message. This is not a problem, though, now that you've discovered the **path** command. All you have to do is set the path to \test:

```
path \test
```

Now if you enter the **chkdsk** command, DOS will be able to find the chkdsk.com file. It is interesting to note the output format of the DOS version 2 **chkdsk** command. It should look something like this:

```
179712   bytes total disk space
3072     bytes in 6 directories
10752    bytes in 8 user files
9216     bytes in bad sectors
156672   bytes available on disk

131072   bytes total memory
104224   bytes free
```

As you can see there are some slight differences in the report. DOS version 2 reports on the overhead used for the directories themselves. We'll come back to this later and find out what the numbers mean.

When you're finished with the **chkdsk** command, reissue the **diskcopy** command. Obviously, since you've changed the search path that DOS looks for files to \test, you've lost immediate access to **diskcopy,** which is in the \other directory. Wouldn't it be nice to be able to set multiple search paths on a disk? Well, DOS has that capability. All have to do is specify a list of different path names that you would want to be searched. In this case the command would be:

```
path \other;\test
```

The individual path names that you allocate must be separated in the list by the semicolon. Path names can also consist of disk-drive identifiers (a:, b:, etc). Consequently, several search paths can be set on more than one disk. Therefore, if you're using a fixed drive and also several floppy disks, you can create an entry in your autoexec.bat file used at boot time to identify all the directories containing utility programs or batch files, so that you don't have to move around the tree to find the appropriate files.

One of the other interesting features of the **path** command is its ability to identify the currently selected paths. To do this, simply enter the word **path** with no arguments. DOS will show the paths that are currently selected.

Now back to our initial exercise—incrementally backing up directories.

As our story goes, you've been working all day in the directory \wp\programs. The names that were selected for the files you've created do not lend themselves to being copied by the wildcard character method. DOS version 2, however, has some interesting features in store for us when we look at the concept of treating directories as files.

One of these nice features is the ability to copy all the files in a directory simply by copying the directory itself. In our example you would do this by logging on to the root directory and issuing the standard **copy** command. Instead of inserting a file name, however, you use the path name of the directory containing the files.

Try this by logging on to the root directory and issuing the following command:

```
Copy \wp\programs b:
```

DOS will respond by going into the programs directory and copying each of the files that are located there. You should see messages come across the screen substantially like the following:

```
copy \wp\programs b:
A:\WP\PROGRAMS\CODE1.SRC
A:\WP\PROGRAMS\CODE2.SRC
A:\WP\PROGRAMS\CODE3.SRC
A:\WP\PROGRAMS\CODE4.SRC
A:\WP\PROGRAMS\MENU.COD
```

You might also notice that DOS places each of the copied files into the directory on which it is currently logged on drive B:. This follows the normal set of default rules to which DOS adheres. If you had wanted to make sure that the copied files were all placed in a specific directory on the target disk, you could simply have specified the name of the directory into which you wanted the files copied.

Since you have two disks with the same hierarchical directory structures, you would want to copy the files to their counterpart directories on the target disk. To do this, enter the command:

```
copy \wp\programs b:\wp\programs
```

Hopefully, this exercise will have served to explain many of the intricacies of tree structures and many of the new rules that have been added to DOS to manage them.

*The **Tree** Command*

So far, we've seen how to construct and manipulate hierarchical directories, and how their very existence has extended the naming convention we use for files by introducing paths and path names. We've constructed a simple tree-structured directory system and played around with it in a simple exercise. In doing so you've probably recognized the fact that it could be very easy to get lost in a complex tree structure.

In an attempt to simplify the mapping of a complex directory structure, DOS version 2 had added the **tree** command. **Tree** is an external command that can be used to create a "map" of a hierarchical directory structure. To illustrate the **tree** command, we'll run it against a slightly more complex version of the simple hierarchical directory structure that we created earlier. A structural diagram of the tree would look like the following:

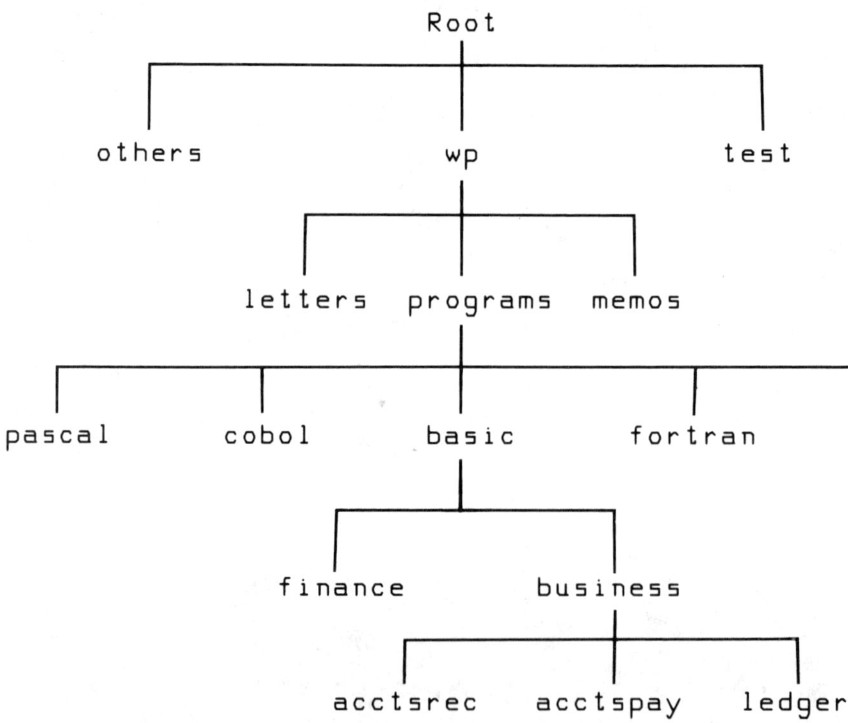

For the sake of simplicity in this exercise, only one of the paths has been expanded, since it can serve to demonstrate the capabilities of the **tree**

command. Under this structure, the longest path that we can traverse would be to one of the three directories under

```
\wp\programs\basic\business\dirname
```

five levels below the root directory. With such a directory structure, the **tree** command would produce a report that would supply all the information needed to construct the hierarchical diagram.

With the DOS version 2 master disk in drive A: and a disk with the foregoing directory structure on it in drive B:, the **tree** command would produce the following report:

```
tree b:
DIRECTORY PATH LISTING FOR VOLUME ???????????
Path: \WP
Sub-directories:  LETTERS
                  MEMOS
                  PROGRAMS
Path: \WP\LETTERS
Sub-directories:  None
Path: \WP\MEMOS
Sub-directories:  None
Path: \WP\PROGRAMS
Sub-directories:  BASIC
                  COBOL
                  PASCAL
                  FORTRAN
                  C
Path: \WP\PROGRAMS\BASIC
Sub-directories:  BUSINESS
                  FINANCE
Path: \WP\PROGRAMS\BASIC\BUSINESS
Sub-directories:  ACCTSREC
                  ACCTSPAY
                  GENLEDGR
Path: \WP\PROGRAMS\BASIC\BUSINESS\ACCTSREC
Sub-directories:  None
Path: \WP\PROGRAMS\BASIC\BUSINESS\ACCTSPAY
Sub-directories:  None
Path: \WP\PROGRAMS\BASIC\BUSINESS\GENLEDGR
Sub-directories:  None
Path: \WP\PROGRAMS\BASIC\FINANCE
Sub-directories:  None
Path: \WP\PROGRAMS\COBOL
Sub-directories:  None
```

```
Path: \WP\PROGRAMS\PASCAL
Sub-directories:   None
Path: \WP\PROGRAMS\FORTRAN
Sub-directories:   None
Path: \WP\PROGRAMS\C
Sub-directories:   None
Path: \OTHERS
Sub-directories:   None
Path: \TEST
Sub-directories:   None
```

As you can see the report is somewhat long. However, when a directory structure becomes so complex that it gets out of control, the **tree** command will supply all the information that you would need to logically construct a diagram of the underlying hierarchy. Hopefully, it is a command that you'll never have to use, but when it is needed, it is there.

There is one switch that can be applied to the **tree** command—the /f switch. When this is used, **tree** will include all of the *files* in each directory in the report. It does this by adding a *Files:* category in each directory map. In our sample directory structure, when it comes to the \wp\programs directory description, it would print the following:

```
Path: \wp\programs

Sub-directories:   BASIC
                   COBOL
                   PASCAL
                   FORTRAN
                   C

Files:             CODE1  .SRC
                   CODE2  .SRC
                   CODE3  .SRC
                   CODE4  .SRC
                   MENU  .COD
```

For anyone constructing a complex hierarchial directory structure on a hard disk, it's a good idea to run the **tree** command at regular intervals. It should be run with the printer turned on (Ctrl-p) so that a hardcopy can be stored. If you ever forget in which directory a file is stored, or what the path name is to retrieve that file, the listing will prove valuable.

*The **Rmdir** Command*

Now that we've learned how to construct a complex tree-structured directory, it's about time that we did exactly the opposite and pulled one apart. DOS has another new command that lets us do that quite easily—**rmdir,** to remove a directory. **Rmdir** is an internal DOS version 2 command that works as the antithesis of the **mkdir** command. The major difference between the two is that **rmdir** will not allow you to remove a directory when that directory contains one or more files or subdirectories. Like its counterparts, **rmdir** also has a short form—**rd.**

Before a directory can be removed from a hierarchy, *it must be at the end of a path and not contain any files or subdirectories*. If it does contain anything that would be lost by the removal of the directory, DOS will not permit the operation. Given the alarming ease with which stored computer data can be erased, this approach is refreshing. If you attempt to remove a directory that is either not empty or not at the termination of a limb, DOS will return the standard error message:

```
Invalid path, not directory,
or directory not empty
```

As with the **mkdir** and **chdir** commands, the **rmdir** command will accept either relative or absolute path names for the directory. Hopefully, most users who decide to construct a tree-structured directory system will not have to use the **rmdir** command, having taken care to reason out the design of the tree before beginning construction.

There is one important shortcoming of the system that should be noted. The **rename** command cannot be applied to directories. Therefore, once a directory is named, it cannot be modified by other than drastic measures. If you ever make a mistake in typing a **mkdir** command line, you may have to use **rmdir** to correct it.

The other drawback of tree-structured directories is that a directory takes up a fixed amount of overhead from the disk system. A quick experiment on a blank disk will show that when you create a new directory, DOS extracts a mere 512 bytes from the space available on a disk. Although this overhead does not amount to much on a hard disk, a complex directory structure on a floppy-based system will quickly tally up into something more meaningful.

The general rules for the use of tree-structured directories therefore seem to be the following:

1. Use them only when you are working with a hard disk, since they don't really buy much utility on a floppy system.
2. Keep the tree structure to as few levels of hierarchy as is reasonable, so that it is difficult to get lost in the limbs.
3. Keep the names of directories as short as possible, since you will have to type them in over and over again.

CHAPTER 14

The New Format

With tree-structured directories behind us, we can now take a closer look at some of the new versions of the commands we were introduced to under DOS versions 1.0 and 1.1. Several of these have been radically enhanced under DOS version 2. The first, and most important, command that we should examine is the new version of the **format** command.

The functions of the command—to format blank disks for use with DOS—of course remains the same. However, there are several new options that have been added. If you remember from our discussion of **format** under DOS version 1, the general format of the command is

```
format d: (switches)
```

where *d:* represents the drive containing the target disk to be formatted, and the switches determine which, if any, of the formatting options are to be selected. Under DOS version 2, the most significant changes are in the plethora of switches that are now available.

One of the most useful of these switches is the /1 switch, which will force DOS version 2 to create a single-sided disk, even though the disk drive may have double-sided capabilities. This is particularly useful for all those lucky people who have more than one IBM PC. When the default version of **format** is issued, DOS checks to see which type of disk drive is at the target location. If it finds a double-sided disk drive, it will merrily format the disk as a double-sided disk. Using the **/1** switch, you can override this default and create a single-sided disk. For obvious reasons, it is not possible to do the opposite and create a double-sided disk on a single-sided disk drive.

Another new switch that can be used with **format** is the **/8** switch. This switch tells DOS to format the target disk as an eight-sector-per-track disk—i.e., one that is compatible with earlier versions of DOS. As you may remember, DOS version 2 has the added capability of storing 12 percent more on a disk than earlier incarnations. It does this by creating nine sectors on a track, which is one more than earlier versions of DOS were capable of. When DOS reads a disk, it first determines if the disk is eight or nine sectors per track, and then automatically adjusts. This transparency makes life very easy, and overcomes many of the headaches that usually accompany an operating system where disk formats take more than one form.

When you want to create a disk that has only eight sectors per track—for example, if you want to send a file to someone by mailing a disk and don't know whether that person has purchased DOS version 2—you can take advantage of the format transparency by formatting the disk with the **/8** switch set.

One of the other useful switches in the **format** command is the **/b** switch. This is a special switch that has been created for commercial software vendors and fills much of the same need as the **/8** switch. When the **/b** switch is used, DOS will format the target disk as an eight-sector disk. It will then mark several of the sectors as used in the file allocation table. These are the sectors that will normally contain the DOS system files ibmbio.com and ibmdos.com.

With these sectors reserved, you can write the system files onto the disk using the **sys** command. When the **/b** switch is used, the resultant disk can have *any* of the DOS versions written onto it. Disks prepared without the use of the **/b** switch can only become masters when the DOS version 2 (or later) of the **sys** command is used.

This switch is recommended for anyone creating a disk for distribution as a commercial software product. Since DOS is a copyrighted product (owned by IBM and Microsoft both), it is illegal to sell a disk that contains a copy of DOS. The use of the **/b** switch creates a disk that all owners of DOS can use by simply writing a copy of their operating system on it.

As with DOS versions 1.0 and 1.1, the **/s** switch can be used to create a master disk. The operation of the **format** command under the **/s** switch has not changed.

The most original of the new **format** switches is the **/v** switch. Use of this switch tells DOS that you want to assign a *volume name* to the disk. DOS writes this name onto a specified location of the disk and during a **dir** command will display the volume name that you assigned to the disk. This provides a convenient electronic method of labeling and cataloging disks.

The procedure is really quite simple. Select the **/v** switch when you format a disk:

```
format b:/v
```

When DOS has finished formatting the disk, it will prompt:

```
Volume label (11 characters, enter for none)?
```

Type in the name that you want encoded on the disk. There are (inevitably) a set of rules that govern the allocation of disk volume names. Fortunately, the characters that are legal for use in file names are legal for use in volume names.

The allocated volume name will appear at the top of any directory listings of the disk, regardless of the position in the tree-structured directory system. For example, a disk formatted with the volume name *datadisk* will produce a directory listing with the following heading:

```
Volume in drive B is DATADISK
Directory of B:\

File not found
```

Whereas if the same disk had been formatted without the use of the **/v** switch, we would have had the message:

```
Volume in drive B has no label
Directory of B:\

File not found
```

This switch allows the electronic labeling of disks, so that if ever the paper label is removed, a quick identification is possible. Also, since the volume name is stored on the disk itself, it is possible for applications programs to use this facility to check that it is reading or writing information to or from the appropriate disk, further eliminating the chance of error.

Formatting hard disks is accomplished in exactly the same fashion as formatting a floppy disk. The major difference is that since a hard disk covers so much area, formatting it is quite a radical thing to do. Great care should be taken when using the **format** command in a hard-disk environment. IBM's hard disks are shipped preformatted and do not need to be reformatted by DOS. When you use the **format** command with a hard disk, it will simply check the areas of the disk that are assigned as DOS segments. *It will not reformat them.*

As with any of the other DOS commands that use switches, **format** can be used with multiple switches set at the same time. For example, to create a master disk that would have a volume label assigned to it, the command

```
format b:/s/v
```

would be used. Some quick thought will tell you that there are inconsistencies in the switches used with **format,** so that there are some combinations of switches that are illegal. For example, use of the **/b** switch with the **/s** switch would be a contradiction. Also, the **/v** switch cannot be used with the **/b** switch.

*The **Diskcopy** Command*

With multiple disk formats available, there is an obvious problem with the **diskcopy** command. This problem arises when you attempt to copy a disk formatted for nine sectors onto a disk formatted with eight sectors. Obviously, it cannot be done, since the source disk could feasibly contain more data than the target disk could hold.

For similar reasons, it would be impossible to **diskcopy** a double-sided disk onto a single-sided disk. When the new version of the **diskcopy** command senses that there is a difference in the formats of the source and target disks, it will automatically reformat the target disk to be the same as the source. This promptly cures any complex problems that could arise by using **diskcopy.** In addition, switch /1 has been added so that you can now force only one side to be copied if you want.

One of the interesting by-products of this procedure is that there is no need to format the disk onto which the source disk is being copied. DOS will sense that the format is wrong on the virgin disk and format it before copying. To show that it has not found the correct format, DOS will display the message:

```
Formatting while copying
```

It will also display the regular message detailing how many sides and sectors per track it has found on the source disk.

*The **Chkdsk** Command*

One of the major beneficiaries in the change from DOS version 1 to DOS version 2 has been the **chkdsk** command. The new version of **chkdsk** takes the form:

```
chkdsk filespec/f/v
```

When a filespec parameter is specified, **chkdsk** will list the distribution of the specified file on the disk after it generates its usual report. The command and the most usual form of the report will look something like this:

```
chkdsk b:*.*

179712  bytes total disk space
10752   bytes in two user files
168960  bytes available on disk

131072  bytes total memory
106496  bytes free

All specified file(s) are contiguous.
```

The statement that all the specified files are contiguous means that they occupy contiguous space on the disk. This is an indication that the files have not become fragmented. You may remember that fragmentation occurs when you successively erase files from a disk, freeing up space, and then write new files onto it. The files then become distributed somewhat randomly.

This is caused by the manner in which DOS allocates disk space. The first free segment is allocated as required. If you erase a file from a disk, the space that it was occupying becomes free. Since it will most likely be space in the middle of the disk not at the end, the next time a file is created and DOS needs some space it will allocate the space that was previously owned by the deleted file. If the new file is larger than the file that was deleted, DOS will then allocate at least two contiguous blocks of disk space for the file—the space freed by the deletion and new virgin space at the end of the used space.

If **chkdsk** finds that a file is spread across several sections of a disk because of fragmentation, it will report it by saying something like the following:

```
B:Article.bak
contains 2 non-contiguous blocks.
```

If the **chkdsk** command reports many noncontiguous files on your disk, you should clean it up by copying all the files on the disk to a new disk. Noncontiguous files are not in themselves bad or dangerous; they simply slow down the reading and writing procedures used by DOS, since they cannot be read from or written to as one large block. When the **copy** command is used to transfer noncontiguous files to a new disk, it will remedy the situation by writing the files in contiguous blocks.

You should note the effect of tree-structured directories on the effect and use of many of the DOS version 2 commands, including **chkdsk**. Any command that contains an ambiguous file specification—one containing the wildcard characters * and/or ?—will operate only on the currently logged directory, unless otherwise specified. It will ignore any files stored in other directories.

One of the other major changes in DOS version 2 of **chkdsk** is that it will no longer automatically correct errors found in the file allocation table as it did before. This is presumably because some users found that strange or unusual file structures could be damaged by indiscriminate use of the old version of **chkdsk**.

Instead, we now have the **/f** switch (for fix). If the **/f** switch is not applied, **chkdsk** will work like it always did, reporting on any inconsistencies that are found in the file allocation table and directory. However, it will not actually write any changes that have to be made back onto the disk unless the **/f** switch has been set.

The other switch, **/v**, simply invokes a special version of **chkdsk** that reports more information, such as the addition of a directory on the disk. It will also print more information about any errors that it encounters. The normal procedure for using the **chkdsk** command would therefore be simply to use the general form of the command. If errors in the file structure are found, you should rerun the command with the **/v** switch specified. This will report more information on the errors that are encountered. Finally, if you determine that the errors could be destructive—such as two files sharing a common block in the file allocation table—you should rerun the command with the **/f** switch selected and clear up any errors.

If **chkdsk** finds any lost clusters on a disk—that is, clusters that are marked as used in the file allocation table but are not associated with any files—and if the **/f** switch has been specified, it gives you the option of bundling them together and creating a special group of files out of them.

These special files will be placed in the root directory of the specified volume and will be given the names filexxxx.ckh, where xxxx represents a sequential number 0000 to 9999.

The purpose of placing these lost clusters into special files is so that the contents can be checked to see if they contain valuable information before the clusters are freed for normal use. Since they are regular files, the contents can be viewed via the **type** command. If they are found to contain valuable information, it has not been lost. If the contents are simply junk, the clusters can be freed for use by simply deleting the files.

One of the other useful features of DOS version 2 is the ability to "pipe" the output of a command to a file. This is particularly useful for commands such as **chkdsk.** Essentially, piping is simply an extension of the input/output redirection that is possible with DOS, although it is elegant enough to offer real power to even a first-time user. We'll learn more of these concepts in the next chapter.

CHAPTER 15

I/O Redirection

At this point in our journey through the mysteries of DOS, we have reached a particularly interesting juncture. We are now ready to take a look at some of the advanced features. In the last chapter it was mentioned that we would be looking at the concept of "pipes." Before we delve into that feature, we need to understand a little more about one of the most basic features of DOS—one that we have not yet explored—the facility to *redirect input and output*.

I/O redirection, as it is called, is simply the ability to interchange devices through the operating system. As with many of the features of DOS version 2, I/O redirection is a popular feature of larger computer operating systems, particularly the UNIX operating system for minicomputers. Of course, the feature can also be found in the XENIX operating system from Microsoft.

Several times in earlier chapters, we used a simple example of I/O redirection, although it was not described as such. In the normal, or default, state of affairs the PC is set up as a "console." That is, the operating system always assumes that the input comes from the keyboard and the output is displayed on the video screen. There are, however, several other input and output devices. The disk drives and the various types of printers are good examples of I/O devices. Under DOS several of these devices are designated as standard and are treated specially. They are given special names by which they can be called. The example we have used in the past is the simple **copy con:**

example that we regularly use for creating "on the fly" files such as batch files and other small and sundry file-creation tasks.

The devices that are considered special are the following:

Device	Name	Stands for
keyboard	con:	console
screen	con:	console
asynchronous port #1	com1:	communications port #1
	or aux:	auxiliary device
asynchronous port #2	com 2:	communications port #2
parallel port #1	lpt1:	line printer #1
	or prn:	printer
parallel port #2	lpt2:	line printer #2
parallel port #3	lpt3:	line printer #3
dummy device	nul:	null device

The names that are associated with each of these devices are reserved words under DOS. That means you cannot create a file with the same name as any of these device names. The nice thing about them is that you can apply any DOS command to a device in exactly the same way as you apply it to a file name.

The **copy con:** example that we've been using tells DOS to treat the **con:** device (in this case the keyboard) as the source file for the command, and to **copy** the contents of this file (as it is created) onto the designated target disk file. Just as easily we could have designated another standard device, as opposed to a disk file, as the target for the command.

For fun, and as an illustrative example, you may want to set up your PC as a simple electronic "memory typewriter." To do this, you simply use the **copy** command to tell DOS to copy the contents of the "console file" to the "printer file." This can be done by entering the command:

```
copy con: lpt1:
```

This command works in much the same way as the **copy con:** example, with the exception that now when you press the F6 special function key, the characters that you have entered into the "console file" and that appear on the screen will be sent to the "printer file" and be printed on paper. Although this facility does not exactly turn DOS into a word processor, it does a good job of illustrating the function of special devices and how they can be used and interchanged.

A second example of the use of standard devices in a DOS command is the alternate method of viewing disk files. Normally we would use the **type** command to view the contents of a file. If we wanted to print them out, we would turn on the printer with a Ctrl-p from the command line. However, using standard devices we can achieve the same results using the **copy** command. To view the contents of a file on the screen, we could tell DOS to:

```
copy filename con:
```

This sends the contents of the designated file to the screen part of the console standard device. You should note from these examples that the console device (**con:**) is used to specify both the screen and the keyboard. This is easily maintained because each of these devices is unidirectional by nature. The keyboard is only an input device and the screen is only an output device. This includes any of the nonstandard uses of these devices, such as a light-pen as an input device on the screen, since in these cases the screen is still used as an output device. When you use the device name **con:** in a command or a field that implies input, you are referring to the keyboard. Likewise, when you use it in an output command or field, then you direct the output to the screen.

If you wanted to direct output to the printer connected to the standard printer port, you could use a version of the preceding command that directed the output to the device. In this case the command would be:

```
copy con: lpt1:
```

In a similar fashion, output can be directed to or from any of the standard devices. It would be just as easy to send a file out a communications port using the

```
copy filename com1:
```

command, or retrieve a file coming over a modem attached to communications port #2 using the

```
copy com2: filename
```

command. These standard device names can be used in the place of a file name in any of the DOS commands that make sense. For example, you would not attempt to **diskcopy** a disk to the screen or use the **sys** command on the printer. Conceptually, they can only work with file-oriented commands, such as **copy**, that make sense.

One interesting example of how I/O redirection can be used is in the situation where a word-processing program is part of a multiprinter configuration. With some word processors it is not possible to send a file that you want to be printed to a serial printer attached to the asynchronous communications port, nor is it possible to send it to a second or third attached parallel printer. DOS supplies a solution to this dilemma.

The answer is simply to use the "print to a file" command, if it is available in the word processor, to send the output, in the same ASCII format that it would be sent to a printer, to a disk file rather than to the printer. Once the ASCII file has been stored in a disk file, it can be copied to whatever device is designated as the target, thereby offering a simple and low-cost solution to a complex problem.

The **nul:** device is the only standard device that does not equate to a readily available piece of hardware. It is for use in testing and debugging situations by programmers. For example, a programmer can be writing a program that contains code for driving an output device, such as a printer. Usually this type of output device tends to be very slow compared to the normal operating speed of a computer. By substituting the **nul:** standard device for the slow real device, programmers can greatly speed up their development and debugging efforts.

When the **nul:** standard device is used as an input device, it simply generates an end-of-file marker as soon as it is accessed, effectively bypassing the input stage. If it is called as an output device, it simulates all the actions of receiving output, although no data are ever sent. Therefore, it can be thought of as a high-speed debugging device which programmers and support personnel can use to get their jobs done better and faster.

Another interesting use for the **nul:** device is as a diagnostic tool to determine whether there is a problem with a piece of software, or if the problem is caused by a malfunctioning piece of hardware. The suspect device is simply replaced by the **nul:** device, and if the software runs without a hitch, that indicates a problem with the hardware device that was bypassed. If the effect is the same with or without the **nul:** device, that indicates the problem is most likely with the software. This is an interesting little trick that anyone involved in either supporting or servicing hardware or software on the PC should learn to use.

It is particularly important to note that you should never use the name of a standard device that you do not actually have attached to your PC—with the obvious exception of the **nul:** device. As the IBM manual points out the results could be "unpredictable." On the other hand, it is perfectly safe to use a real standard device name anywhere you would normally use a file name.

Since it is treated as a file by DOS, you cannot do any damage by using it in this way.

If you accidentally attempt to use a standard device name with a DOS command that normally operates on files, but which does not make sense in this use, DOS will probably return either the "file not found" or the "illegal parameter" error message. An example of this is attempting to erase the console by the command:

```
erase con:
```

In fact the only command that really makes sense for use with standard device names is **copy**, although on rare occasions the **comp** command may be used to compare the input from two devices. They do, however, present a good example of how input and output can be redirected from one device to another very simply.

Back on the mainstream again, we find that DOS goes a giant step further by allowing what is known as dynamic I/O redirection. This means that any input or output stream can be temporarily directed or redirected to just about anywhere that makes sense. This redirection can be made to happen simply by typing an easy-to-remember command on the command line.

The most immediate consequences of I/O redirection are that a DOS command, or any other program for that matter, can receive its input from a source other than the keyboard, usually either a standard device or a disk file, but not limited to those, and its output can be directed to any other target. Output redirection is the most obvious of the two forms, so let's take a look at what this entails first.

The most obvious use of output redirection is in sending the output that would normally have gone to the screen to a disk file instead. This is a facility that is very useful in software development and debugging, since it allows all output to be captured for review. The general format of the redirection command is simply:

```
command >d:path\filename
```

Here, *command* represents a standard DOS command or program, > is the redirection symbol that tells DOS not to send the standard output from the command to the screen but instead to the file or whatever device is described by the following parameters. In the form shown it is redirected to a file along a specified path, but it could be to any target that is described by a file name, including a standard device.

As an example of the most trivial use of output redirection, we can see that the output of a simple DOS command, such as the **dir** command, could be sent to a disk file or printer rather than to the screen. To redirect it to a file, the command

```
dir >filename
```

could be issued. Instead of generating a directory listing on the screen, as it normally would, the output of the **dir** command is redirected (the result of the > symbol) to the designated file, in this case called *filename*. Any valid file name can be used, as can a valid standard device name, such as **prn**, which would direct the output to a file or standard device. If you use the redirection to a file, you can then examine the contents of the file with the **type** command.

This facility is useful for any type of systems-related work. For example, if there was some trouble with a program and the operator was not located in the same vicinity as the programmer, the output of the program could be redirected to a modem connected to one of the asynchronous ports. The service people at the other end of the line could examine the output of the program and diagnose the problem.

Another interesting and immediately useful feature of output redirection is that reports generated by a spreadsheet could be sent to a disk file for later formatting and dressing up with a word processor, or for inclusion in a longer report.

One of the major problems with trying to use I/O redirection with some commercially available programs is that some of these try to bypass the input/output mechanisms of the operation system and attempt to work directly with the hardware. This makes using the facilities of DOS impossible and is a strong argument for programmers to stick to the rules laid down by the operating system.

When an output redirection command is entered, DOS will first check to see if the designated file exists. If it does not, DOS will create it. If it already exists, DOS will overwrite it by resetting the write pointer to the beginning of the file before it writes the information out to it. So, as with any process that creates new files, you should be careful how you use it.

Obviously, then, there is some sort of need for a version of the output redirection that does not destroy an already existing file but instead appends the output to the end of the file. DOS does have that capability. You simply use two > symbols instead of one.

For example, in a situation where you want a disk file to be appended with a directory listing on a regular basis, you would use the command

```
Dir >>filename
```

which will cause the new directory listing to be added on to the end of the designated file if it exists. In this case DOS sets the write pointer to the end of the file before it writes information to it, thereby appending new data to the end of the file. If the file doesn't exist, it will be created, as it normally would be before data are written out to it. Obviously, it does not make particular sense to try to append information to a standard device file.

Of course, the use of output redirection can be extended to any program that runs under DOS and uses the input/output facilities of the operating system. The best way to illustrate this is by using one of the sample BASIC programs that appears on the DOS master disk. On that disk there is a BASIC program that generates a mortgage schedule called mortgage.bas. This is the program that we will play around with to demonstrate the power of output redirection.

First, you should format a blank disk and copy the files basic.com and mortgage.bas onto it. Then log on to that disk and enter the following command:

```
basic mortgage >mort.txt
```

This command tells DOS to invoke the disk version of the BASIC interpreter and then run the BASIC program contained in the file mortgage.bas. The output of that file is to be redirected to another file called mort.txt.

When you issue this command, the program will run as it normally would (with minor aberrations), although every once in a while the disk will spin. Run through the program and prepare several mortgage schedules, then exit the program and return to the operating system by typing **system.**

You should notice that the file mort.txt has indeed been created. If you examine the contents of the file by using **type,** you will see a complete record of the program run. Every character that was normally sent out only to the video screen has been captured in the disk file and can be reviewed.

This simple demonstration should serve as a guide to how you can create a file of the output of any legitimate program running under DOS. Once the file has been created, it is available for further processing by a word processor or text editor.

On the other side of the coin from output redirection is the ability to redirect input, a feature that is very powerful, but not quite as obvious as output redirection. Essentially the corollary to output redirection, input redirection allows a source other than the keyboard to be specified as the input device. This feature is particularly useful in certain situations, such as when a second terminal is attached to the PC, either directly to a serial port or remotely through a modem connected to a serial port. In this case the source of input would be defined as the standard device through which the terminal was attached.

The < symbol is used for input being directed to a DOS command or program. Therefore, the command directing input to come from the remote terminal would be:

```
command <com1:
```

This assigns the terminal hooked up to the first asynchronous, or serial, port to be the input device for the program command.

The preceding is the most obvious usage of input redirection. However, there is another, far more exotic use for it—having input come from a disk file. This provides a very interesting method of processing information stored in disk files, since the information can be passed very simply to a processing program simply by having it defined as the source of input to a DOS command or any other DOS program. As with many of the more complex features of DOS, this concept is best described by way of an example or two.

The first example is very simplistic and does not present a situation where realistic use can be made of input redirection; it simply serves as a guide to the concept. For this example, we are going to use the **format** command. When you normally use **format,** in its very simplest form you enter a command like

```
format b:
```

to tell DOS to format the blank disk in drive B:. DOS then retrieves the code for the **format** command from the disk in drive A: and issues a prompt that says:

```
Insert new diskette for drive B:
and strike any key when ready
```

DOS then pauses and waits for the user to press a key. Whenever a key is pressed, it proceeds to format the blank disk. When it has finished, it prints its standard report explaining the format of the disk and how space has been allocated. It then issues the prompt

```
Format another (y/n)?
```

and waits for either the *y* key or the *n* key to be pressed.

Now, if we examine what exactly the interaction between the user and the computer really amounted to, you will find that the first prompt was answered by pressing any key—let us assume Return was pressed. Then either a *y* or an *n* was pressed as a response to the second prompt.

If we wanted to format the disk twice just for fun (dumb, but don't worry about it) and then exit the **format** command and return to the operating system, we would press the following keys in sequence: Return, *y*, Return, *n*. If we were to create a file that contained these keystrokes and redirected the input to that file, we would essentially have created a process that would automatically format a disk twice.

Of course, the way we enter such a simple file into DOS is by way of directing output to a standard device by means of the

```
copy con: test
```

command. We then press Return, *y*, Return, *n*, and finally the F6 key and Return to close the file. Now we would invoke the **format** command and redirect the input to the file that we just prepared and named test.

The command would take the form:

```
format b:<test
```

The input to the command would now come from the test file instead of the keyboard.

Without stopping, DOS will forge ahead and format the disk twice, since it doesn't have to wait for keyboard input. This feature is very powerful and when combined with other DOS features, such as batch files with replaceable parameters, can lead to arbitrarily complex situations. However, the true power of such a system cannot really be demonstrated until again we use it with a normal program running under DOS, just as we did with the mortgage program.

With this example we are going to use not only DOS, but a very simple little program written in the PC's inherent BASIC interpreter. Although we are using a BASIC program to illustrate this feature, it does not mean that you need a knowledge of BASIC to run DOS. It is simply for illustration and the complexity will be kept to a minimum for those who do not know BASIC, or those who do not want to know BASIC. The BASIC statements that are used are the most simple input and output statements.

The BASIC program that we are going to use is a simple little program that collects four people's names entered from the keyboard and stores them in a small array. The listing is as follows:

```
10 cls: dim n$(4)
20 for I = 1 to 4
30 input n$(I)
40 next I : print : print
50 print "The four names are:" : print
60 for I = 1 to 4
70 print n$(I)
80 next I
90 end
```

The object of the program is simply to collect four names and then print them out in the order in which they were entered. It is a good idea to actually enter this little program, as we'll be using it in another more complex example later.

To enter a BASIC program from the operating system, it is first necessary to load the BASIC interpreter. To do this, simply type **basic** from the command line. You are now in the BASIC editor. Type in the program and when you are done, test it out by typing **run.** When you're sure that there are no errors in the program, save it to disk by typing:

```
save "names"
```

Then press Return. To return to the operating system, type **system.**

You've just created a BASIC program that should be stored on your disk under the name names.bas. In order to run the program directly from the operating system, you would enter the command

```
basic names
```

on the command line. Try it out and make sure it works.

Once you know that it works take a close look at the interaction between the operator and the program. The input to the program consists of four names, each terminated by a carriage return. So, if we were to create a file containing four names and define it as the source of input for the BASIC program, then the process would be automated.

Back to our old faithful **copy con:** to create a file called list. Enter four names, each terminated by a carriage return. Then close the file with the

F6 Return combination and you're ready to demonstrate input redirection. To do so, enter the command

```
basic names <list
```

and note the results. The BASIC program did not halt to wait for input from the keyboard, but instead read the contents of the list file that we created. It read the file exactly as it would have read the keyboard—one character at a time until it found a Return, then on to the next command. One interesting side effect of having the input specified as a file is that when the BASIC program has finished, control is returned directly to the operating system—there is no need to enter the **system** command from BASIC.

Finally, we are going to do something one level more complex. We are going to use this little BASIC program with all of its input and output redirected. The input will be from the file named list that we created earlier, and all the output will be directed to a file called report. To do this, enter the command:

```
basic names <list >report
```

This form of the command instructs DOS to load the BASIC interpreter from disk, then run the BASIC program called names. However, the responses required for input are stored in the file called list, which will be used as the source of input rather than the keyboard, and the output has been redirected to a new disk file called report.

When you examine the file named report, you will see that it is a complete transaction record of exactly what happened on the screen. This demonstrates an excellent method of tracking down problems in a program by capturing the output for further examination. It also speeds up and allows a facility to automate the testing of new programs as they are developed.

The uses for I/O redirection are many. As well as the simple direction of standard input and output streams between different physical devices connected to the system, there is the whole new world (at least for microcomputers) of software I/O redirection. Since system software typically leads applications software development by quite a long time, it will be some time before we see applications software that takes advantage of its capabilities. When it arrives, it will add yet another dimension to the PC's abilities.

One of the fallouts of DOS's I/O redirection is that it can simulate the piping capabilities of XENIX—which was the subject that initially brought us to this discussion. That is exactly what the next chapter is all about.

CHAPTER 16

Pipes and Filters

As promised in the last two chapters, we will finally cover the powerful concepts underlying the features of "pipes" and "filters." These features, first made available with DOS version 2.0, are derived, like hierarchical file structures and input/output redirection, from the UNIX operating system. They are somewhat unique in the realm of microcomputer operating systems, having no functional equivalent in either of the other single-user operating systems available for the PC (CP/M-86 and the UCSD p-System). However, even though they may represent new concepts to many of you, particularly first-time users of computers, they are really quite easy to understand and hence to use.

Both pipes and filters behave in much the same way as their real-life analogies in, for example, a plumbing system. Pipes are traditionally used to pass liquid from one place to another. In DOS, pipes are used to pass data from one command to another, while filters treat the data that pass through them.

When applied to the world of microcomputers, a filter is simply a command that takes input from a source, performs some sort of action on the data stream that the input comprises, and sends it out to some predefined destination. Filters are simply DOS commands that have both an input and an output component.

This can be contrasted with other DOS commands that do not require a source of input such as the **dir** command. When the **dir** command is invoked, it will perform its function without any other source of input from the keyboard. Its output will be sent to the screen by default, unless the output is deliberately redirected.

A pipe, or pipeline as it is also called, is simply the joining of two DOS commands or programs. Pipes provide the mechanism whereby the output of one DOS command can be sent, or piped, to the input of a second DOS command. In this way, DOS commands can be strung together to create other DOS commands to fill a particular need. Users can thereby customize their working environments to cater more to their own likes or dislikes.

Let's take a hypothetical example of the use of pipes and filters. Suppose we had a problem for the computer to solve that involved scanning a file of vendors for a particular item, extracting all the vendors that are in the Los Angeles area, sorting them based on the price they charge for the particular item we are looking for, and printing the list. Normally this would be accomplished by breaking down the process into discrete steps and then writing programs to handle each individual step.

The final solution might involve the following steps:

1. Write a program that filters through the file and extracts only those vendors who are in the Los Angeles area.
2. Take the output of step (1) and create a temporary file for later processing. The file would be a subset of the master file but would contain only those vendors who are in Los Angeles.
3. Write a program to sort the previously created temporary file by the cost for the item we are looking for.
4. Take the output of step (3) and create a temporary file for later processing. The file would contain a list of all the vendors for the item in Los Angeles, ranked by the price for which they sell the item we are looking for.
5. Print the temporary file that we created in step (4).

This approach can be summarized by the first diagram on the next page:

To reach the solution to our problem we have three individual and distinct steps, coupled with the creation of two temporary files. If we apply the proper terminology, we have actually "filtered" the original master file, extracting all the vendors in the Los Angeles area, "piped" the results (via temporary file #1) to a second process that "filters" the data, sorting them in a particular order and placing the results in temporary file #2, and finally processed the data in that file by "piping" them to a command that prints the contents of the file.

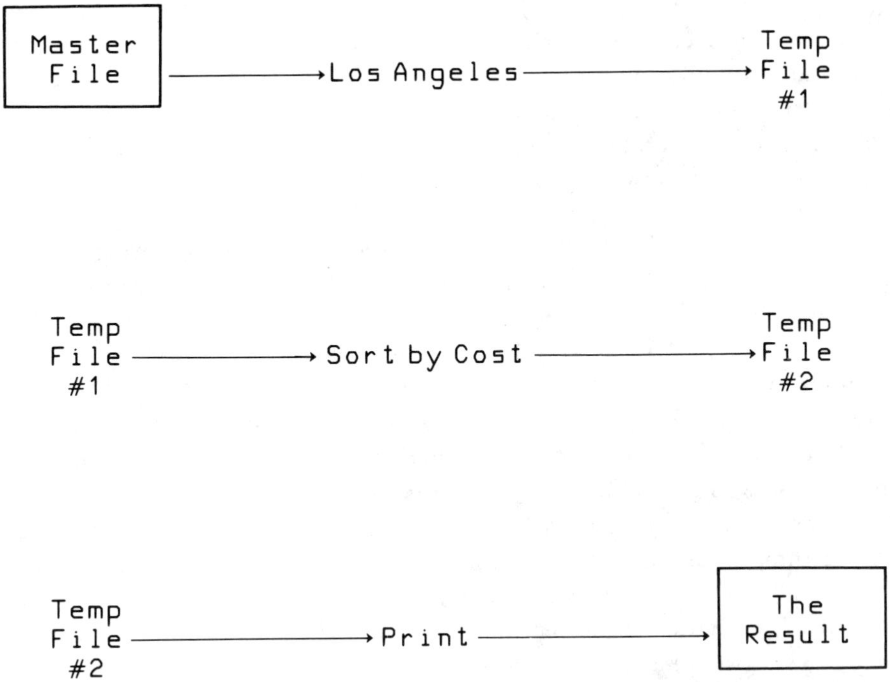

It can therefore be reduced to the following conceptual diagram:

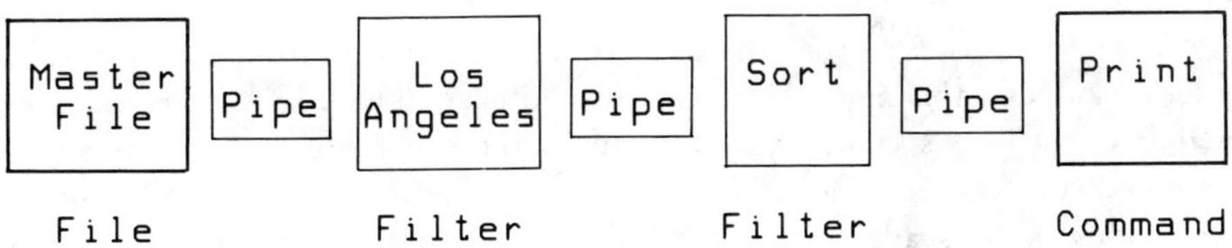

Each of the individual processes can be thought of as a filter, while each of the temporary files can be thought of as a pipe. From this we can reach a definition for each of the two.

A pipe is a mechanism that can transfer the output of one process to the input of another. A filter is a process that acts on the data that are input to it and modifies them.

Through pipes and filters the processing of data can be accomplished by a single DOS command. Complex as it sounds it is really quite easy. However, the IBM DOS manual covers the entire subject in only about three pages, and covers only the very basic uses for the features involved. As you would expect, pipes and filters are a natural extension of the I/O redirection capabilities we have been playing with in the past few chapters. When they are used in conjunction with other I/O redirection capabilities, they represent a new and powerful way of processing data from within DOS, without having to resort to a programming language.

Before we get in too deeply, let's digress for a moment and lay some of the groundwork that will help in understanding where these new features come from and how they are applied. In the XENIX operating system there exists the concept of the *shell*. The shell is the part of the operating system that the user sees and interacts with. It also describes the environment that the user is working in.

Of course, XENIX is a multiuser operating system derived from minicomputer operating systems and by definition has to be considerably more powerful and therefore more complex for the user than DOS. XENIX users quickly discover that the shell can be used as a very powerful programming language, as well as a simple command line interpreter.

DOS actually is structured quite similarly to XENIX, in that the unit that we think of as the command line interpreter is a separate module stored on the disk in the file named command.com. The file is read into memory at boot time (when the operating system is first read from the disk into the computer's memory) and is incorporated into DOS.

With the structure of DOS, the command line interpreter can be replaced with a special customized program that any competent programmer could write. In this way, a programmer can create a shell customized for a particular application so that the user would be sheltered from the operating system. To DOS, this new custom shell would have to look like command.com in the way it passes commands through to the operating system. As such, command.com can be thought of as a shell, not quite in the same league as the various shells available under XENIX, but powerful enough in its own right to be useful.

Shell programming is accomplished by stringing together groups of DOS commands, with the output of one command piped to the input of another. In this manner DOS commands can be made arbitrarily complex.

When we were looking at the function of I/O redirection, we were introduced to the concepts of standard input and standard output. Standard input is the source device from which input is obtained for a DOS command. The default for standard input is, of course, the keyboard (**con:** device). Standard output is the destination device to which all output is directed. The default for standard output is the video screen (**con:** device).

As we saw when we looked at I/O redirection, all devices attached to DOS can be treated as simple files. By changing the source of data for a command, we can redirect the input from a file, rather than from the keyboard.

Most DOS commands, like the **dir** example that was mentioned earlier, simply use the standard output facility. Filter commands are commands that accept their input as standard input and write their output to the standard output. This, of course, is different from regular DOS commands where special sources of input and output that are local and applicable to that particular command are defined within the command itself.

For example, the **copy** command uses a specified file as its source of input, and another file as its target for output. The standard input and output devices do not play an integral part in the process. To complicate matters, the standard input and output devices can be made to work with the **copy** command through redirection, but the regular mode of operation does not involve these devices for other than error messages and prompts.

To illustrate the use of a filter, let's take a look at a filter command that is easy to understand and constitutes a very desirable feature—the **sort** command. **Sort** works by analyzing an input stream coming in as standard input, sorting the contents, and writing the sorted information out as standard output. This takes the form:

Standard Input → filter → Standard Output

Using redirection, you can change the source of standard input and the destination of standard output. However, for now let's take a look at the use of a filter command as a stand-alone, interactive DOS command invoked through the command line.

Slip a copy of your DOS master disk into the disk drive and enter the command **sort.** Since the **sort** code is stored in the file sort.exe, DOS will load it and execute it just as though it were a regular DOS command.

When it is in place, DOS will display its usual prompt to show that it is expecting some characters to be typed as input. The best way to illustrate the use of the **sort** command is simply to enter a half-dozen names, each on its own line. As usual, when the keyboard is being treated as an input file, it is necessary to end the file with the standard DOS end-of-file marker, Ctrl-z, which can be entered with the F6 special function key.

When you send the **sort** command an end-of-file marker, it will sort the names that you've entered and list them back out on the screen in sorted order. Try it and see. Your screen should look something like the following:

```
sort
Piggy
Gonzo
Scooter
Bert
Ernie
Kermit
^z

Bert
Ernie
Gonzo
Kermit
Piggy
Scooter
```

The **sort** command has filtered the input coming from the standard input device, in this case the keyboard, sorted it in alphabetic order, and output it on the standard output device, which in this case is the screen.

Sort sorts on a line-by-line basis. That means it will sort the items based primarily on the first character on the line. It will sort the items depending on the ASCII values for the characters, and where there are two items that have the same first character, it will continue the sort based on the second character, and so on. If there are two items that have the same fifty characters at the beginning, but have different fifty-first characters, then the fifty-first character will determine the sorting order.

Since **sort** is a full 8-bit ASCII-based sort, it will differentiate between upper- and lowercase characters. This means that it will sort all of the uppercase alphabet before any of the lowercase alphabet. A simple example will illustrate this. Let's tell DOS to sort the first three individual characters of the alphabet in both their uppercase and lowercase forms. To do this, enter the following exactly as you see it:

```
sort
B
b
a
A
C
c
^z
```

DOS should respond by printing the sorted list as follows:

```
A
B
C
a
b
c
```

As you can see, this is not the straightforward lexicographical sort that most people would imagine. It is somewhat counterintuitive and awkward, but easy to live with as long as the data that it is working on are in a consistent case format.

Now, let's take the example we were working on one step further. We'll take the names entered on the keyboard, sort them, and write the results to a file on the disk. To do this, we would simply redirect the standard output from the screen to a named file using the conventions that we learned earlier for redirecting output—that is, the > symbol before the target file name. For example, to redirect the sorted list that we entered at the keyboard to a file named list, we would enter the following:

```
sort >list
Piggy
Gonzo
Scooter
Bert
Ernie
Kermit
^z
```

When we are done, as signified by the Ctrl-z end-of-file marker, DOS will open the file named list and write the sorted names into it. Look inside the file with the **type** command and see for yourself.

Of course, we can go yet one step further and redirect DOS so that it takes a file as its source of standard input and another file as its target for standard output. This is done by using the standard input redirection symbol < before the source file name. To demonstrate this, first create a file called names using the **copy con:** command. Then have DOS sort it to another file called list. To do this, you should enter the following:

```
copy con: names
Piggy
Gonzo
Ernie
Kermit
```

```
Scooter
Bert
^z

sort <names >list

type list
Bert
Ernie
Gonzo
Kermit
Piggy
Scooter
```

Sort is one of three filter command programs shipped with DOS version 2.0. The other filter commands are **find** and **more.** Each of these commands has a simple use and serves to demonstrate the functionality of filter commands.

The second filter in the series, **find,** simply looks for occurrences of specified strings in a file. This can be easily demonstrated by having DOS find any occurrences of the letter *i* in the file we created for the last example, list. Enter the command

```
find "i" list
```

and DOS will respond with the output to the screen:

```
--------- list
Ernie
Kermit
Piggy
```

As you have probably realized by now, the **find** filter command is line oriented. That means it will find and pass any complete line that contains the string of characters that we specify—in our example, the single character *i*.

Find has a convenient built-in slot for the user to change the source of standard input to the command. However, like any other filter command, it can be just as well applied to the interactive mode of use, where it takes its input from the keyboard and outputs the modified data to the standard output device. This can be demonstrated by entering the command

```
find "i"
```

on the command line. When you then type lines of text at the keyboard, the

find filter will analyze each line and print those lines containing the string *i* one additional time. This can be made minimally useful when you also redirect the output.

If, for whatever reason, you wanted each line that contained the letter *i* to be sent to the printer as well as the screen, you could enter the command

```
find "i" >prn
```

in which case everything that you enter on the keyboard will be echoed on the screen, but each line that has one or more occurrences of the letter *i* will also be sent to the printer. Alternatively, a regular file name could be used instead of the special **prn** reserved name to log any occurrences of a string being entered into a file.

The third filter command, **more,** is quite trivial in its operation, in that its function is simply to halt the output to the screen (standard output) when the screen is filled. It will then prompt for a key to be pressed before it will continue outputting. This command is particularly nice if you want to look at the contents of a long file, one that will take more than one screen to display. We will come back to these filters in a while and take a closer look at them.

With the **find** filter, the **sort** filter, and using the I/O redirection facilities, we now have all the capabilities required to tackle the task we set for ourselves at the beginning of this chapter—extracting Los Angeles vendors from a file, sorting them in a particular order, and printing them out.

To work out this exercise, it will be necessary to enter a short table into a DOS file using the **copy con:** command, or, preferably, using any editor capable of producing standard ASCII text files, such as the **edlin** mini editor supplied with DOS. The table should be entered exactly as it is shown, beginning each line in the first column. Note that where there are multiple spaces in the table, you should actually enter all the spaces independently. Do not use the Tab key. Terminate each line with a carriage return and terminate the file with a Ctrl-z (F6) end-of-file marker.

```
copy con: table
Vendor                    City           Cost

International Corp        Los Angeles    123.44
Fortnum International     Chicago        101.99
Drury Imports             Los Angeles    102.55
Applied Systems           Los Angeles     95.00
Maxwell Widgets           Los Angeles    104.15
```

```
Widgets Inc                  New York         104.15
Allied Widget                Los Angeles       99.88
Smith Inc                    San Francisco    101.85
^z
```

When you've entered the table, you should reconsider the problem and the steps to the solution that were mentioned earlier.

First, the file named table should be filtered by the **find** command, and only those items that contain the string "Los Angeles" should be selected. A temporary file should be created to hold these items. Assuming that the temporary file is given the name temp1, it should be easy to see that the command to make this happen would be

```
find "Los Angeles" table >temp1
```

which says "find all of the items in the file named table in which the string Los Angeles occurs and instead of printing the results on the screen, as the **find** command would normally default to, send them to a temporary file named temp1."

When you've done this and the PC finishes the job, you should check to verify that DOS has indeed created the file named temp1. If you then **type** the contents of this file onto the screen, you will see that it contains the following:

```
type temp1
---------- table
International Corp        Los Angeles     123.44
Drury Imports             Los Angeles     102.55
Applied Systems           Los Angeles      95.00
Maxwell Widgets           Los Angeles     104.15
Allied Widget             Los Angeles      99.88
```

The **find** filter has eliminated all the items in the file that did not contain the string Los Angeles, exactly as we had planned.

The second step is to take the contents of the temporary file temp1 and sort it using the **sort** filter. However, if we just simply run the contents of the file through **sort,** it will sort the file alphabetically instead of numerically in the column that we want. Try it and see for yourself. Enter the command

```
sort <temp1 >temp2
```

which will take the contents of the file temp1 and sort it alphabetically into the file temp2. The results will be as follows:

```
type temp2
--------- table
Allied Widget            Los Angeles     99.88
Applied Systems          Los Angeles     95.00
Drury Imports            Los Angeles    102.55
International Corp       Los Angeles    123.44
Maxwell Widgets          Los Angeles    104.15
```

As you can see, **sort** has changed the order in which the items are listed based on the ASCII collating sequence, which, since each of our items begins with a capital letter, will be alphabetical.

This is not quite the result we are looking for. We would like to see the items sorted in order of cost, rather than alphabetically. The trick to this one is to define the starting column number on which the sort will operate.

In our example, the cost field in each item starts on either the fortieth or forty-first column, depending on whether the cost is above or below 100. This problem can be solved simply by sorting on the fortieth column, since a blank space will be sorted before a 1; the ASCII value for a space character is lower than the ASCII value for the 1 character.

To perform this little trick, you need to include a switch in the **sort** command when it is issued. The switch that we'll use in our example is the **/+n** switch that tells DOS to start the sort on the *nth* column of each item line.

This leads us to the final command format:

```
sort /+40 <temp1 >temp2
```

When you type out the contents of the file temp2 onto the screen, you will see that this has exactly the desired effect.

```
type temp2
--------- table
Applied Systems          Los Angeles     95.00
Allied Widget            Los Angeles     99.88
Drury Imports            Los Angeles    102.55
Maxwell Widgets          Los Angeles    104.15
International Corp       Los Angeles    123.44
```

By sending the contents of the file temp2 to the printer—copying it to the device **prn:**—we can accomplish the third and last stage of our task. So, it would appear that we have a solution to the problem that we outlined earlier. The commands, when they are all stacked next to each other, would look like this:

```
find "Los Angeles" table >temp1
sort /+40 <temp1 >temp2
copy temp2 prn:
```

To simplify the process into a single system we could always prepare a batch file containing these commands. We could even go a step further and use a replaceable parameter for the string that we are looking for, providing, of course, that the string does not contain a space character, since replaceable parameters cannot pass spaces. In other words, we could use it to find vendors in Chicago or Angeles or York, but not Los Angeles or New York. In this case, the batch file would contain the following:

```
copy con: mytest.bat
find "%1" table >temp1
sort /+40 <temp1 >temp2
copy temp2 prn
^z
```

Then, when the command

```
mytest Angeles
```

is submitted, the same report will result.

This little exercise shows how powerful the DOS shell can become when it is used for simple file processing. However, there is yet one more capability that when added to the preceding capabilities takes DOS another step further—pipes. Piping allows the standard output from one DOS command to be routed as the standard input of another DOS command, instead of being sent to the screen.

The classic example of piping is to use the **sort** filter to sort the output of the **dir** command. Of course, this can be done using what we have already learned by simply entering the following sequence of commands:

```
dir >temp3
sort <temp3
```

This will have the effect of printing a list on the screen of all the files in the directory, sorted alphabetically.

However, we have created a temporary file again and now have so many on our disk that they are beginning to get a bit difficult to manage. They also take up disk space, which, although minimal in this simple example, could rapidly get out of hand under more complex circumstances.

The piping feature of DOS allows us to accomplish the same result as the foregoing without all the fuss of having to name and create a temporary file, and having to delete it when we're done. In fact, we can send the output of the **dir** command directly to the input of the **sort** command. This is done by piping with the command

```
dir | sort
```

where the | character is used to denote a pipeline from the output of one command to the input of another.

In executing this command, DOS will automatically take care of creating the intermediate temporary files for us. When it has finished with them, it will discard them. Although this command has some minimal use when used with the DOS master disk, since there are so many files on the disk, it would be very nice if we could further pipe the output of the **sort** filter into the **find** filter, to find all the files created on a certain date. This can be done quite easily by entering:

```
dir | sort | find " 3-08-83"
```

If this selects and passes so many directory entries that it casually scrolls off the top of the screen, you could always send the output of the entire process to the **more** filter, causing it to halt after each screenful. In its longest form, then, the command would become

```
dir | sort | find " 3-08-83" | more
```

which would invoke the **dir** command, sort the output, eliminate all the lines in the sorted directory listing that do not contain the date 3-08-83 (note that a space was left before the date string so that it could not be confused by dates like 13-08-83 and 23-08-83, both of which contain the string "3-08-83") and send the modified sorted list out one screenful at a time, pausing until a key is pressed after each screenful.

In light of this example, let's go back and take a look at the original example—finding vendors in Los Angeles—that we were using earlier. As you should remember, we left it as a series of individual commands, each served by one or two temporary files. The entire problem was reduced to the following:

```
find "Los Angeles" table >temp1
sort /+40 <temp1 >temp2
copy temp2 prn
```

Using pipes, the problem can now be restructured to something considerably more simple. It is very similar, in fact, to the simple directory sorting and finding example we just dealt with.

The approach you should take this time would be to use the **find** filter to find all occurrences of the string "Los Angeles," pipe the output of the **find** filter to the input of the **sort** filter, which will structure the items into their proper order, and redirect the output of the **sort** filter to the printer instead of a file. Quite simply, the command would take on the form:

```
find "Los Angeles" table | sort /+40 >prn
```

Using the capabilities of both pipes and filters together, you can immediately see that we have reduced the entire problem to a single command on the command line. Again, if this is a facility that you expect to use often, it could be stored as a batch file with a replaceable parameter instead of the string "Los Angeles."

This type of solution is really only beneficial when applied to files that already exist. Obviously, it would be pointless to require the user to enter the table that we entered manually every time he or she wanted to update the list. Therefore, this type of processing is only appropriate for a system where files already exist.

Because of the positional peculiarities of the **find** command, the type of file that it can work on is also limited. Since each field in a record must be in the same position in every record, it is only feasible for this system to work with fixed field length and fixed record length files—which are actually fairly heavily used in the real world—and text files.

Of course, many database management and personal-filing systems already have such a capability built in. DOS's abilities to compete against these dedicated systems is limited, and it is certainly not meant to replace them. However, it offers an extremely flexible tool for prototyping more complex systems and generating "on-the-fly" reports.

In the rest of this chapter, we'll expand on what we started, and dig a little deeper into the subject of pipes and filters. Combining the features that we've just seen demonstrated with the features inherent in I/O redirection and batch commands, we will see how to create whole new commands out of the existing set that is normally supplied with DOS.

To begin with, we should elaborate on many of the features of the filter commands, **sort, find,** and **more,** that were simply glossed over earlier.

A filter command is defined as a DOS command that accepts standard or redirected input, modifies it or acts on it in some way, and sends output to a standard or redirected output. Filter commands are all external DOS commands, so before they can be used, they must be resident on the disk system. The three filters that are supplied with DOS, as well as being functional in their own right, also serve as excellent examples for those who want to create their own customized filters.

*The **Sort** Filter*

The **sort** filter, as we saw earlier, performs a line-oriented 8-bit ASCII sequence sort on a specified input file, or it can be used interactively with the keyboard entry if no input file is specified. In its default condition it will sort from lowest to highest, placing all the lines that begin with *A* first and all the lines beginning with *B* after that. It also has a pair of switches associated with it, one of which, the **/+n** switch, we saw in use earlier. This switch allows the sort to proceed from a character position other than the beginning of the line. In the example we used earlier, we began the sort in the fortieth column. This was done by using the command

```
sort /+40 <stdin >stdout
```

where *stdin* and *stdout* represent the source and destination for standard input and standard output.

The second switch associated with the **sort** command is the **/r** switch, which has the effect of reversing the sort order, sorting from the greatest to the least in the standard ASCII collating sequence.

When using the **sort** filter on nontext files, or even files that appear to contain text but also have other nonprinting characters buried within them, you should exercise caution. The ASCII character sequence allocates a code number between 0 and 255 to each character. The standard ASCII table begins with several nonprinting characters such as the Bel character, which when printed on the PC's screen causes the speaker to beep. Bel, for example, is an ASCII 7 character. Before any of the alphabetic characters are reached in the ASCII table, there are many of the punctuation characters that can be entered directly from the keyboard.

The numbers 0 through 9 also appear before the letters of the alphabet, with number 0 having an ASCII value of 48 and the number 9 having a value of 57. The actual alphabet begins with the uppercase set A–Z, which has the ASCII values 65 through 90. There then follows some more punctuation characters, and the lowercase alphabet, having ASCII values 97 through 122.

The upper 128 values in the PC's character set are allocated to the extended ASCII nonstandard characters, which include the foreign alphabetic characters and graphics character sets that are in the PC's character ROM. The **sort** filter is capable of working with any file containing either the regular ASCII character set or the extended set.

The upper limit on the file size that **sort** can work with is 63K. If you attempt to sort a file that is larger than this limit, you will be given an error message that says:

```
Sort: insufficient memory
```

The ***Find*** *Filter*

The **find** filter, as we saw earlier, is a utility command that can be used to identify a specified string in each item in a file. The output of the **find** command contains only those items in which there was one or more occurrence of the specified string. In the example we used earlier, we had **find** locate and pass all the items in a file that contained the string "Los Angeles." **Find** also has some other capabilities that allow it to be used in differing circumstances. These take the form of switches to the command.

The first of these switches is the **/v** switch, which causes **find** to have exactly the opposite result from its default result. That is, it will pass all the items that *do not* contain the specified string. For instance, in our earlier example if we had wanted **find** to locate and pass only those records that did not contain the string "Los Angeles," we would have included the **/v** switch, in which case the command would have become:

```
find /v "Los Angeles" table
```

This would result in the following:

```
--------- table
Vendor                    City           Cost

Fortnum International     Chicago        101.99
Widgets Inc               New York       104.15
Smith Inc                 San Francisco  101.85
```

You can eliminate many items in a file by filtering the file several times through the **find** filter. For example, if you wanted to locate all the vendors in the example file that are not located in either Chicago or New York, you could run the file through the **find** filter and eliminate all the items that contain the string "Chicago," and then pipe the output of that process back to the **find** filter and have it eliminate all the records containing the string "New York." The command to do this would look like

```
find /v "Chicago" table | find /v "New York"
```

which would result in the following report on the screen:

```
--------- table
Vendor                  City           Cost

International Corp      Los Angeles    123.44
Drury Imports           Los Angeles    102.55
Applied Systems         Los Angeles     95.00
Maxwell Widgets         Los Angeles    104.15
Allied Widget           Los Angeles     99.88
Smith Inc               San Francisco  101.85
```

In fact, we could pipe the results from one operation back through the same filter as often as is necessary to pare the file down to whatever set of information we need. If, for example, we wanted to eliminate the header line and the blank line under it from our report, we could refilter it and pass only those lines that contain the decimal point:

```
find /v "Chicago" table | find /v "New York"
| find "."
```

This will generate a file containing the following:

```
International Corp      Los Angeles    123.44
Drury Imports           Los Angeles    102.55
```

```
Applied Systems         Los Angeles         95.00
Maxwell Widgets         Los Angeles        104.15
Allied Widget           Los Angeles         99.88
Smith Inc               San Francisco      101.85
```

Notice that when the **find** filter has its input piped from another process, it is not necessary to specify the source of input, since it defaults to the standard input, which is where all piped data come from.

The second switch that can be applied to the **find** command is the /c switch, which suppresses all output to the standard output and instead writes a count of the matching items.

For example, it is apparent from the example that six items met the selection criteria we specified. If we were to modify the command that resulted in that report so that instead of actually printing the items that passed the selection, it only printed the number of items that passed, we would get the following:

```
find /v "Chicago table | find /v "New York" |
find /c "."
```

The final **find** has the /c switch set. The result will be that the number 6 will be printed on the screen, or redirected to a file if one is specified. This is useful if you have a very large file that you want to examine. Instead of having to wait while all the items are printed on the screen, you can be immediately informed how many items you have pared the selection down to.

The third switch used with the **find** filter is the /n switch, which is used to display the relative line number of each matching item. This means that it will tack on a number at the beginning of each line that it qualifies. The number will represent the line number in the input file from which the selected item was derived.

For example, if we were to use the following command on our original table, we would get these results:

```
find /n "Chicago" table

-------- table
[4]Fortnum International     Chicago    101.99
```

The [4] represents the line number in the original file—table—that the line item was taken from. Notice that blank lines are significant when it comes to line numbering.

This feature is useful as a quick-and-dirty method of finding which lines in a file match a certain selection. The line numbers that are generated can then be used with a text editor to edit the lines involved.

One final feature of the **find** command that is particularly useful is its ability to operate on a list of files as well as on one single file. The way to do this is simply to include a list of the files that you want it to operate on in the command line. The syntactic version of this would therefore be

```
find "string" file1 file2 file3 . . .
```

This is best demonstrated by first taking the table file that we built earlier and breaking it into several smaller files. This should be done as follows:

```
find "Los Angeles" table >table1
find "New York" table >table2
find "Chicago" table >table3
find "San Francisco" table >table4
```

This has the effect of creating four subfiles, each of which should contain a list of vendors in the specified city.

Now, if we wanted to create a list of all the items that contain the letter *i,* we could specify the entire list of subfiles that we have just created. The result would be as follows:

```
find "i" table1 table2 table3 table4
-------- table1
International Corp        Los Angeles      123.44
Applied Systems           Los Angeles       95.00
Maxwell Widgets           Los Angeles      104.15
Allied Widget             Los Angeles       99.88
-------- table2
Fortnum International     Chicago          101.99
-------- table3
Widgets Inc               New York         104.15
-------- table4
Smith Inc                 San Francisco    101.85
```

This example serves to illustrate why the source file is indicated in each report—that is, the "-------- table1" part. In a report like this where there are several source files involved, it is always beneficial to know where the record comes from. If you wanted to remove these headers, you could simply pipe the output of this command back through the **find** filter and remove them.

One subject that should be mentioned while we are looking at the multiple source-file use of the **find** command is that wildcard file name characters, * and ?, are not permitted—which is unfortunate. In other words, the command

```
find "i" table?
```

is illegal and will result in the error message:

```
Find: file not found table?
```

This brings us to another important property of DOS that is closely related to the concepts of standard input and standard output. Let's illustrate it through the use of an example similar to the one we used earlier. Suppose we enter a list of files as sources of input for the **find** command and we accidentally enter the name of a file that doesn't exist. What will happen? Let's examine it and see. Enter the following:

```
find "i" table1 tabel2 table3
```

Note the spelling error in the second file name. As we would expect, DOS will generate a screen report with an embedded error message as follows:

```
-------- table1
International Corp     Los Angeles   123.44
Applied Systems        Los Angeles    95.00
Maxwell Widgets        Los Angeles   104.15
Allied Widget          Los Angeles    99.88
Find: file not found tabel2

-------- table 3
Widgets Inc            New York      104.15
```

If we were using the **find** filter to produce some sort of subfile for use with another program, this error message could very well get in the way of further processing. Luckily, DOS does not print this error message to the standard output device, but only sends it to the screen. This means that if we were to redirect the output of the last command to a file instead of to the screen, the error message would not be written to the file but instead would go directly to the screen.

This feature is somewhat similar to the *diagnostic output* (sometimes called *standard error*) feature of UNIX/XENIX. It has two beneficial attributes. The first is that our file does not get messed up by having an error message written to it. The second is that we don't have to wait until processing is finished to discover that an error was encountered. We can immediately reissue the corrected command and get the correct results.

*The **More** Filter*

The **more** filter, as we saw earlier, is a trivial filter that simply stops the output to the screen after each screenful. It will then print the prompt "---more---" on the screen and wait for a key to be pressed before it will continue. This, in fact, describes the entire operation of the **more** filter. It has no switches or options associated with it.

There are two ways to use the **more** command, each of which produces the same result. You can use it directly as a command or pipe the output of another command, such as **type,** to it:

```
type myfile.txt | more
```

Or:

```
more <myfile.txt
```

Each achieves the same result.

Making Your Own Filters

Now that you've seen the power of filters, there remains the exciting possibility of creating your own. It is, in fact, quite easy to design custom filters, since the BASIC language (version 2.0 and greater) supports the concepts of standard input and standard output, as well as I/O redirection. In fact, any program that works through DOS to talk to the hardware will support these features.

Programs that bypass DOS and interface directly to the hardware for their I/O will obviously not work. In fact, the effects of trying to redirect I/O using a program that does not support DOS can be dangerous, since the results can be unpredictable.

BASIC itself is structured as a DOS command, so it is entirely possible to create filter commands by using the interactive mode of BASIC directly from DOS. To demonstrate this feature, first prepare a file called nums that contains the following information:

```
copy con: nums
Print 3*5
^z
```

This file can then be used as the input to the BASIC command line editor in the interactive mode. To do this, simply enter the command

```
basic <nums
```

which tells DOS to load the BASIC interpreter portion from disk and then to direct the input to the interpreter from the file that we just created. The result will be the following:

```
OK
print 3*5
15

A>
```

Before the interpreter was started, the screen was blanked, which always happens when you start BASIC. Then the standard prompt that BASIC uses to show that it is in interactive mode, *OK,* is displayed. Input is then redirected to the file called nums, which enters the *print 3*5* line.

BASIC, which cannot differentiate between data entered through the keyboard and data entered through input being redirected from a disk file, will calculate the result, print it out, and then return to the operating system. We have just redirected input through the BASIC interpreter in its interactive mode. However, it is just as possible to use BASIC in its deferred mode by writing a BASIC program and calling it from DOS. Try the following example:

```
copy con: nums
4
6
^z
basic
```

```
OK
10 input a
20 input b
30 print a * b
40 end
save "mult"
OK
system
basic mult <nums
? 4
? 6
24
```

In this example we first create a file called nums that contains the numbers 4 and 6, each on a separate line. We then load the BASIC interpreter and write a little BASIC program that, when run, requests that two numbers be entered through the BASIC **input** statement. It will then multiply the two numbers together and print the result on the screen.

When we've finished writing this program, we save it under the name mult—BASIC will automatically attach the file name extension of .bas to signify that it is a BASIC program file for use with the interpreter. When that is done, we can return to DOS by giving the BASIC command **system.**

Finally, we can run the program from DOS by entering the **basic mult <nums** command, which will load the BASIC interpreter, load the BASIC program mult, and run it with its input redirected to the file nums. When it has finished its run, it will return to DOS.

This demonstrates how BASIC programs can be used in the deferred mode with redirected input. Now, you should remember that a filter is simply a DOS command that accepts its input from the standard input and sends its output to the standard output, or, when I/O redirection is applied, it will modify its source or target as specified. Therefore, it should be quite simple to create a custom filter by simply writing it in BASIC.

As usual, there is an example that we can use to illustrate this process. In many programming applications it is desirable to work with files in which each line has a line number associated with it. This makes it easy to locate lines from a text editor. The following BASIC program will read lines in from the keyboard and print them out on the screen with line numbers assigned to them. However, it makes more sense for it to be used as a filter from DOS.

```
10 on error goto 70
20 linenum = 1
```

```
30 print linenum;": ";
40 input "", a$
50 linenum = linenum + 1
60 goto 30
70 end
```

The **on error** statement in line 10 is simply a cheap-and-dirty way of detecting the end of a file when the program is used as a filter. If we then save this file by entering

```
save "linenum"
```

we can later invoke it as a DOS command with its input and output redirected. To do this, though, it is best to have a file that can be used with it. For the lack of a better example, you can always run through it the table file that we created earlier. The command and resulting output would be:

```
basic linenum <table
1: Vendor                  City            Cost
2:
3: International Corp      Los Angeles     123.44
4: Fortnum International   Chicago         101.99
5: Drury Imports           Los Angeles     102.55
6: Applied Systems         Los Angeles      95.00
7: Maxwell Widgets         Los Angeles     104.15
8: Widgets Inc             New York        104.15
9: Allied Widget           Los Angeles      99.88
10: Smith Inc              San Francisco   101.85
11:
```

If you want to create a separate file containing this information, it is just as easy to redirect the output to another file. This procedure would look something like

```
basic linenum <table >newtable
```

where *newtable* is the name of the new file we have created to hold the line-numbered information.

A DOS filter command like the one we have just created can be given a new name by storing the invocation command in a batch file and then using it as a regular DOS command. For example, we could store the command

```
basic linenum
```

in a batch file called num.bat and then treat it like any other filter command. The preceding command would therefore become:

```
num <table >newtable
```

In this form, the new command looks and feels much more like a regular DOS command, although, since the BASIC interpreter is involved, it will operate considerably slower than other DOS commands. Still, it is much more intuitive for an unsophisticated user to use and remember. It can also act as a filter to which data are piped from another command. For example, we can achieve the same result of tacking line numbers on at the beginning of each logical line by first using **type** on the file with the output piped to the **num** command. The output of the **num** command would be redirected to a new file.

Even though all the demonstrations so far have used different source and target files, it is actually just as easy to redirect the output of a command to the same file from which input is being drawn, thereby replacing the file, although this is not a recommended practice. In other words, it is perfectly feasible to use a command like

```
num <table >table
```

although if you want to attempt this, you should first make a backup of the original file table.

In order to do this, DOS reads all the information out of the source file and then bulk processes it through to the target file. It does so by creating temporary files where necessary, and using any excess memory wherever practical. Piping works in exactly the same way. In fact, there is a very convenient method of showing the process at work, by essentially having the computer catch itself in the act. By doing so we will be able to derive information about exactly how DOS manages pipes and filters. The trick is to issue the **dir** command while a pipe is in existence.

The way to do this is to issue the command sequence required to sort the directory listing and print it on the screen. Of course, this is:

```
dir | sort
```

When this command is issued on a blank disk, you will be very surprised to find that at the time that DOS went to look at the directory listing, there were actually two files present. They have the names %pipe1.$$$ and %pipe2.$$$.

DOS actually creates these temporary files as it needs them and allocates names in the sequence as appropriate. If you list the directory again, after the piping is completed, you will find that the files have vanished. DOS automatically removes them when it finds them no longer necessary.

Of course, it is always dangerous to use a filter command that erases the file from which data are being extracted. Although in many cases this can be done without any harm, it can lead to an aborted operation that halts after the source file has been deleted and before the target file has been created, thereby destroying the data. Practices such as these are very dangerous and should be avoided by the naive user.

Summary

I/O redirection is one of the most important and most useful of all the DOS version 2 facilities. Its capabilities are unique to the world of single-user operating systems. When logically extended to pipes and filters, it offers a level of operating system functionality matched only by much larger and consequently more expensive operating systems such as XENIX and UNIX.

Since no two microcomputers are used for exactly the same function, every user will see a different way of using these new and powerful capabilities. The system is extensible, in that new commands consisting of hybrids of existing commands can be created; therefore, there is logically no limit to the functionality that can be derived from such a system.

One of the most touted features of Bell Labs' UNIX operating system for minicomputers is that the family of users creating software under UNIX has created a vast library of extended operating system commands. This library has become so extensive that it is now somewhat trivial to create vastly complex commands from the library of available commands. Over time, DOS will have such a library associated with it, too.

In this light, it has become increasingly obvious that any programs written for use under DOS must have their input and output handled by the operating system rather than by making illegal (but faster) calls to the hardware, which is a common programming trick. If a program uses the standard input as its source of input and the standard output as the target, it can simply be treated as a standard DOS filter command. Users can then custom design their own programs by stringing together various building blocks to create arbitrarily complex programs for whatever purpose.

Of course, there are some programs that do not lend themselves to such use. Since there is, as yet, no standard in existence for passing graphics parameters from one program to the next at the operating system level, programs utilizing graphics cannot be used as filters, although data can still be piped to and from them through the standard input and output. One day there will also be a way to pass other types of data, including graphics and voice information, in a standard format between various programs. To be prepared for such an eventuality, you are encouraged to practice by making use of the input/output redirection facilities currently available in DOS.

CHAPTER 17

DOS Versions 2 and 3 Commands

Since we started the section of this book on DOS version 2, we have diligently traced our way through many of the complex features that the new version brought with it. This has been at the expense of the various upgrades that have happened to the everyday DOS commands that are not quite as revolutionary as many of the new features. So, this chapter will focus on the DOS commands themselves.

The changes that have been made between the two major versions of DOS lend themselves very well to categorization. There are, in fact, four categories of changes that have been made at the command level.

The first category of changes includes the commands that appear to have remained the same between the two versions. While many of the commands appear to exhibit exactly the same behavior as they did before, a quick comparison of the files will reveal that the sizes of the commands have almost universally become larger in version 2. The reason for this is obviously that they have been improved, either in speed or in efficiency. They have managed to accomplish this without placing any additional burden on the user. The changes are essentially transparent.

Included in this category are commands such as **sys, diskcopy, diskcomp, date,** and **time.** Since the differences are all transparent, there is very little need to discuss any of them further.

The second category of changes between the two versions of DOS includes all of the commands that made use of file names or filespecs in DOS version 1. Since DOS version 2 now includes the facilities to build hierarchical directory structures, the concept of the path, or path name, has been introduced. This obviously has a bearing on any command that previously used a file name as an argument. These commands have all been extended to manage the range and complexity of full path names, as well as simple file names.

This category includes commands such as **rename, copy, erase, type,** and the like. Since the only difference in the operation of these commands is the inclusion of one or two optional path names where they once used simple filespecs, they essentially perform the same as they did under DOS version 1.

Once you have a firm grasp on the concepts behind tree-structured file systems and their hierarchical directories, the operation of any of the commands that fall into this category should be easy. The only change to their operation is that wherever a filespec was used before, a full path name can now be applied.

For example, the **copy** command can work between two different directories in much the same way as it always worked between two different drives. The old version of **copy** was simply

```
copy filespec filespec
```

whereas the new version is slightly more complex, in that is can also contain path names:

```
copy [path]filespec [path]filespec
```

As an illustration, let's take a look at this command in its most complex form, where a group of files is to be copied from a directory on one drive to a different directory on a second drive.

If we were to copy all of the .com files from a directory in drive A: with the path name **\usr1\files\system** to a directory on drive B: with the path name **\backup\usr1\files\system,** the full command syntax would be:

```
copy a:\usr1\files\system\*.com b:\backup
\usr1\files\system
```

Although it looks somewhat complex, it follows all the rules of DOS that we have learned so far.

There are also several other rule changes and additions in this category of commands. However, they are all direct consequences of the new tree-structured filing system. One example that immediately comes to mind is that you are not allowed to erase files that are actually directories when the contents of the directory are not empty. This is an entirely new situation, a consequence of hierarchical directory structures, and had no analogy in DOS version 1.

Once the manipulation of hierarchical directories is mastered, the use of these commands should also be mastered. They all follow the same set of logical rules as they always have, but with one or two additions. Since many people will not use hierarchical directories, these additions are not all encompassing, and to many should not even matter. Users who will make extensive use of the facility are those who have purchased a PC-XT system that already contains a fixed disk, or regular PC owners who have attached an expansion chassis or a non-IBM-supplied fixed disk. Complex hierarchical directory structures are not really appropriate for floppy-disk-based systems, although they can be put to good use to hide large numbers of infrequently used files, such as the DOS files themselves. However, hierarchical directory structures more than two levels deep should only be found on fixed disk systems.

The third category of changes to DOS commands brought on by DOS version 2 includes all the commands that have been deliberately enhanced in their later incarnations. This type of upgrade has no single attribute that can be pointed to and used to describe the entire category, other than the fact that the command simply does more than it did before.

We've already seen that the **format** command has been upgraded to handle the various types of disk formats that can exist under DOS versions 2 and 3. **Format** can now work with either the older eight-sector-per-track format or the more compact nine-sector-per-track format. It can also work with single-sided and double-sided disks, high-density disks, and, of course, with the IBM fixed disk.

The changes that the **format** command have undergone for DOS version 2 are true upgrades to the command itself. They take the form of new switches that can be tacked on to the end of the command. These new switches were not available under DOS version 1. Likewise, the **chkdsk** command has undergone major surgery in its new form. As we saw earlier, the new form of **chkdsk** has been substantially improved to handle several new functions that it could not handle in its previous incarnation.

*The **Mode** Command*

Another command that falls into this category is the amazingly resilient **mode** command. **Mode** is one of the more interesting commands of DOS in that it seems to have been developed as a medium for change. The changes to the **mode** command between DOS version 1.0 and DOS version 1.1 allowed the PC to work with many new options. The upgrade to DOS version 2 seems to be another staggering leap.

A quick look at the purpose of the **mode** command will reveal the reasons for the accelerated growth of this command. **Mode** was designed to allow the user to configure certain aspects of the system to work with different sets of peripherals. In its original form, **mode** was a very simple command with two options that allowed the printer to be set up and the color graphics monitor to be set to either 40 or 80 columns and to be aligned correctly.

Under DOS version 1.1 **mode** went through a complete transformation, resulting in two new options being added to allow the asynchronous communications adapter to be configured so that it could be used with many different communications peripherals, and to allow a serial printer to be addressed by the system.

Although no new options for its use were added, under DOS version 2 **mode** has again undergone several significant changes. Obviously, as the PC market matured, IBM realized that many people were opting for what were considered nonstandard configurations of their PCs. Particularly so, since there were many options, such as a letter-quality serial printer, that IBM did not offer and which had to be supplied by third-party vendors.

Although IBM's official position is that it does not support any non-IBM-supplied hardware, it makes it possible to address many other devices through proper use of the **mode** command. As time goes on, and more and more people use different types of peripherals on their systems, you can expect the **mode** command to be upgraded accordingly.

Let's take a closer look at the upgrades so that we can see exactly what direction **mode** is taking. The command has been broken down into four different options for its use. The first is its use in configuring the standard line printer for character size and spacing. Under DOS version 1.1 the generic form of the command was

```
mode lpt#: n,m
```

where

is the printer port number (1, 2, or 3)
n is the number of characters per line (80 or 132)
m is the number of lines per inch to be printed (6 or 8)

Under DOS version 2 there has been added another parameter to this list. The new option takes the generic form:

```
mode lpt#: n,m,p
```

The new parameter, *p,* is not a variable like the other parameters. Instead, it works more like a switch: it is either there or it isn't. You may now have two forms of the command:

```
mode lpt1: 80,6
```

or

```
mode lpt1: 80,6,p
```

The *p* parameter is used to override the time-out condition which causes an error message in some cases. It arises when a peripheral device that is attached to the PC fails to respond when the PC talks to it. The PC allocates a specified period of time to the device, and if it does not respond within that time period, a DOS "time-out error" message will be generated, and control will be returned to the operating system.

Systems that do not have this time-out mechanism frequently hang or freeze when data are sent to a device that has not been attached correctly or has not been turned on. In these situations the computer will just sit there and merrily wait for the delinquent device to answer back. Often the only way to remedy the situation is to shut down the entire system and restart it, thereby sending all the data that were in memory at the time into the proverbial bit bucket, never more to be seen.

Luckily for us, DOS makes frequent use of the time-out mechanisms. However, there may be situations where you want to deliberately override the time-out system, such as when you have several devices attached to a single port. Many offices have two printers, one dot matrix and one letter quality, connected to a single parallel printer port. The dot-matrix printer is used for rough drafts while the letter-quality printer is used for final printout. This saves the expensive, nonreusable, single-strike ribbons frequently used in many letter-quality printers. It also allows more than one PC in the office to make use of the expensive features of the letter-quality printer.

If you use a setup like this, after you have sent a file to the printer you might find that the printer was not connected. Rather than have DOS generate a time-out error and have to deal with going through the entire sequence again, you can simply turn off the time-out system by making use of this new **mode** option. Then if the printer is not attached correctly or not turned on, the PC will simply sit and wait for the appropriate action to be taken. Once communications between the PC and the external device are established, the task can be completed as intended.

Of course, if a situation arises where you don't want the PC to continuously retry on a time-out error, but it is already stuck in its loop, DOS provides a convenient method for pulling out of the loop and returning control. In a case such as this, the Ctrl-Break combination will cause the appropriate exit to be made. If this keeps happening to you, the only way to stop it is to reset the time-out mechanism to its original status by entering another **mode** command without the *p* parameter specified.

The second option for using the **mode** command is in configuring the system for a particular type of display device. Under DOS version 1.1 **mode** let you configure your system for either a 40-column or an 80-column system, and also supplied a test pattern to allow corrective action to be taken for monitors that were not properly centered. The generic form of the command was

```
mode n,m,t
```

where:

n is the number of characters to be displayed on the monitor per line (40 or 80)
m is the direction to shift the display (either *r* or *l*)
t is to request DOS to throw a test pattern on the screen for alignment purposes

The new form of the command under DOS version 2 does not include any new parameters, but simply enlarges on the number of options available for the *n* parameter. Whereas before, *n* could only specify either 40-column or 80-column operation, new parameter options have been added to allow use of the PC with a wider range of display devices.

The new options for the *n* parameter now include the following:

40— same as before, for use in regular 40-column operation
80— same as before, for use in regular 80-column operation
BW40— for use in a monitor that can only display 40 columns in black and white; turns off the color for a sharper display (best for small black-and-white televisions attached through an RF modulator)
BW80— for use in a monitor that can display 80 columns in black and white; turns off the color for a sharper display (best for black-

and-white, green-screen, or other composite monochrome monitors attached directly to the color/graphics adapter)

CO40— for use in a color monitor or television that can only display 40 columns (best for low-resolution color composite monitors or color televisions attached to the color/graphics adapter through an RF modulator)

CO80— for use in a high-resolution monitor that can display 80 columns in color (in general this is limited to RGB monitors)

MONO—switches the output to a monochrome adapter if one is included in the system

These new options have been included to allow the PC to be attached to a large number of different display devices, all the way from a small black-and-white television set at one extreme to an expensive RGB color monitor at the other. It is particularly useful for PC*jr* owners who do not use a monitor, but instead attach *jr* to a television set.

These options also allow the not-as-unusual-as-it-might-seem situation where two display cards are connected to the PC at the same time. As it turns out, there are a few applications where the user can see graphics displayed on a color display attached to the system while entering data on a monochrome screen. The new MONO variation lets the user switch between displays.

By specifying the command

```
mode mono
```

DOS will send all the screen information out to the monochrome display. To de-select this display, simply select any of the other variations, such as:

```
mode CO80
```

The reasons for the large number of options for this parameter have to do with the applicable resolution of a display device, usually referred to as the bandwidth. The bandwidth of a television or monitor is usually expressed as a frequency (hertz). It ultimately determines the resolution of the picture that can be displayed on its screen.

The resolution refers to the amount of detail that can be electronically "seen" by the video device. It can be measured either horizontally or vertically. Normally, bandwidth, and hence resolution, are also directly proportional to cost. Higher-cost display devices generally tend to have higher bandwidth and better resolution.

As a rule, monitors have higher resolution than televisions. Televisions can be connected to the PC via an RF modulator. The RF modulator converts the signal coming from the PC, which is in a form known as "baseband video," into the appropriate format in which televisions receive video information. It piggybacks the video signal on top of a video carrier signal that a TV can pick up on a specified channel, usually channel 3 or 4.

The best way to see the difference between a signal being sent to a high-bandwidth device and a low-bandwidth device is to attach an RF modulator to the color/graphics adapter, and run the signal to a television. At the same time, connect the composite video output to a black-and-white monitor, and then connect the RGB output to an RGB monitor. The results are self-explanatory. The TV will look fuzzy compared to the black-and-white or the RGB monitors. When color is applied, the difference between the black and white and the RGB will be further emphasized.

If you expect to be doing a lot of work in long stretches on your PC, it is best to purchase as high a bandwidth display device as your budget will allow, since it has been proven that long periods spent staring at a low bandwidth monitor can cause eye strain—and the associated stress and headaches.

One other interesting difference between composite monitors and RGB monitors is the strange case of what happens to the lower-bandwidth device when you try to plot two dots next to each other. On a nice crisp RGB monitor, two white dots exactly next to each other will produce exactly that. The composite monitor will display a single dot of another color, often blue or green. This is an interesting anomaly that many programmers make use of, commonly known as *artifacting*. The result is that certain commercially available programs (e.g., Microsoft's *Flight Simulator*) will produce stunning colors on a low-cost, low-bandwidth monitor, while those who opted for a high-cost RGB monitor will have to make do with black and white or very unusual colors. The way around this is to attach a low-cost RF modulator to the color/graphics adapter and run the output to a color television. The TV can now be used with color programs that use artifacting effects, while the RGB can be used for other programs.

The MONO option allows the system to house both a color/graphics adapter as well as a monochrome adapter, and switch between the two at will. The other additions to the **mode** command are simply convenience features for those who want them, adding better control of the display device attached.

The other two versions of the **mode** command—for use in configuring the asynchronous serial port and for use in redirecting the printer output to a serial printer—have not changed between versions.

The only other point that should be made about the **mode** command is that it is specific to the operating system used on the IBM PC. Other systems that also make use of the MS-DOS operating system do not generally contain a **mode** command. As a rule, Microsoft does not supply a **mode** command with the operating system, and it is left to the manufacturer to include such a utility should there be a need for one. This may explain why certain aspects of the **mode** command, such as the *p* and the *t* parameters, work as switches although they are not defined as such, which does not follow the general rules for DOS commands.

The fourth, and by far the largest, category of changes to DOS version 2 includes all the new commands that were not available under earlier versions. Many of these new commands are here thanks to the new features of DOS. Obviously, hierarchical directories have brought with them a whole slew of new commands simply to create, modify, and remove hierarchical directories. So, too, the improved I/O redirection capabilities of DOS have brought many new commands with them. Many of these new commands were already seen when we reviewed the new features. However, several new commands have also appeared that have little or nothing to do with the new features.

The commands that are completely new with DOS version 2 include **ver, chdir, mkdir, rmdir, break, verify, path, vol, ctty, set, assign, backup, restore, tree, recover, print,** and **prompt,** as well as the new **sort, find,** and **more** filter commands. When we studied hierarchical directories, we were exposed to the **mkdir, chdir, rmdir, path,** and **tree** commands. Likewise, we saw the **find, more,** and **sort** commands when we looked at the improved I/O redirection features. There are also several new batch commands which we'll save for later.

Excluding the commands that we've already covered, the new internal commands include **ver, break, verify, col, ctty,** and **set,** while the new external commands include **assign, backup, restore, recover, print,** and **prompt.** First we'll take a close look at the internal commands.

The Ver Command

The inclusion of the **ver** command in DOS version 2 is a reaction to the confusion that was sure to arise due to the three different versions of the operating system that were available, and more to follow. It is a simple internal utility that, when invoked, tells you which version of the operating system is currently being used.

In actual fact, since the **ver** command is an internal command, it can only work with version 2 of DOS (and greater). If you attempt to use the **ver** command with DOS version 1, you'll be given an error message, since the command was not built in and was not available as an external command. So, the only information that **ver** will supply is whether you are in DOS version 2 or greater. If a "Bad command or file name error" occurs, you are probably running DOS version 1.

If you are working with DOS version 2 and you enter the **ver** command, you will be rewarded with the copyright notice for the operating system. It will, in fact, print:

```
IBM Personal Computer DOS Version  2.00
```

The version number of DOS is a good pointer to show how dynamic the situation really is. It is interesting to note that between the word "Version" and the number 2.00 there are two spaces, which means that there is room left for lots of new versions of DOS. It is quite disheartening to think that shortly after you master the latest DOS version, you may be confronted with yet another new version.

The way the numbering scheme for DOS versions works is quite simple. The first digit, in our case *2*, represents the *version* number. Significant changes in the capabilities of DOS must occur before a new version number can be assigned. The other two digits after the decimal point represent *release* numbers. This was seen in action in the very earliest days of the PC.

Everyone by now has heard about how quickly the PC project was put together by IBM and Microsoft. When DOS was first released, it was called DOS version 1.00. Shortly thereafter, however, a new release, DOS version 1.05, was seen in some computer stores. This only lasted a few weeks before DOS version 1.10 was released. DOS remained in this release until DOS version 2.0 came along.

Between DOS version 1.00 and the highly elusive DOS version 1.05, there were no apparent changes. The new release simply cleaned up some minor inefficiencies, with the net changes being transparent. The hallmark of a new release of DOS should be that the changes are quite insignificant. When DOS went from version 1.00 to 1.05, the changes were insignificant. When it went from version 1.05 to 1.10, DOS supported the new double-sided disk drives. When it went from DOS version 1.10 to 2.0, DOS supported the new hard disk. It is interesting to speculate what future versions of DOS will bring.

*The **Vol** Command*

We saw the **vol** command in use when we were discussing the new version of **format.** It is a simple internal command that is used to show the volume label identifier that was given to a disk when it was formatted. In the **format** command there is a switch, **/v,** that, when set, causes the **format** command to prompt the user to enter a label for the disk. This label is written onto the disk and is displayed whenever a **dir** command is issued. It can also be accessed by applications programs to check to make sure that you have inserted the correct disk in the drive.

When invoked, the **vol** command will simply print out the volume name identifier for the specified disk, so you can tell which disk is in which drive without removing either of them. If, in formatting a disk, you assign a volume name of BACKUP, invoking the command

```
vol
```

will result in:

```
Volume in drive A is BACKUP
```

Or, if you want to check the volume name on a drive that you are not currently logged on to, you can enter

```
vol b:
```

which may result in the message

```
Volume in drive B has no label
```

if the disk was formatted without the /v switch being set in the **format** command.

*The **Break** Command*

The next command that we'll review is **break,** an internal command that made its first appearance with DOS version 2. The **break** command sets, resets, and reports on the status of the extended Ctrl-Break function. That sounds like a mouthful, as do most of the relatively obscure DOS commands. In order to understand the **break** command, you must first understand a little bit about the Ctrl-Break key set and the effect that it has on the operating system.

The Ctrl-Break combination is used to halt many of the DOS processes and is universally used by the languages operating under DOS as a halt function, allowing the user to break out of any process in as short a time as possible.

DOS is a single-tasking operating system, meaning that it can only do one thing at a time. Therefore, there must always be some time elapsed, and some DOS functions completed, before DOS has a chance to check to see if the Ctrl-Break combination has been pressed. This is so because DOS has to poll the keyboard processor to find out if any keys have been pressed while it was off performing the last function. If a key (or key combination) has been pressed, it needs to determine what that key (or key set) was.

As a matter of fact, DOS deliberately checks to see if the Ctrl-Break combination has been pressed every time it services certain devices. However, this is really not as often as is appropriate for certain operations. To grasp this concept firmly, you need to understand the "other" way to talk to DOS.

Most people are familiar only with the standard keyboard and file method of passing information through DOS and commanding it to perform its tricks. Communications with the operating system take place entirely through the command line processor, or shell. This is the part of the operating system that puts the familiar A> prompt on the screen and interprets the commands entered at the keyboard. However, there is a whole world that sits beneath this level which a skilled programmer can access.

The lower levels of DOS are structured as a series of "system calls." A system call is simply a method of addressing the operating system that specifies one particular action. For example, there are DOS system calls for opening and closing files, for reading and writing blocks to and from the disk, for putting a character on the screen, for getting a character from the keyboard, and so forth.

During the operation of even the most simple program, there are a very large number of DOS system calls made by the program. During only some of these system calls does DOS check to see if the Ctrl-Break key combination has been pressed. If it were to check for the Ctrl-Break during every DOS system call, the operating system would be much slower than it is.

The type of DOS system call that flags a check for Ctrl-Break includes any time that DOS sends a character out to the video screen (which is obviously very often), whenever it is instructed to get a key from the keyboard (which is almost as often) whenever it sends a character to the printer, and whenever it sends or receives a character from any of the auxiliary peripheral devices attached. This type of DOS system call is known as character device I/O. Although this seems like a staggering number of times for DOS simply to check for a key combination, there are times when it may be best for DOS to check more often.

For example, any computer operation that does not require input or output for long periods of time may be a candidate for extended Ctrl-Break checking. Examples of such activities include the compiling or assembly processes associated with program development. During these processes the computer is simply given a file, called the *source file,* containing information and it is expected to transform that information and create a second file called the *object file.* The process could go on for hours with a particularly slow compiler or assembler without a single instance of DOS looking for a key being pressed on the keyboard or sending a character out to the screen or any other device. Obviously, there is a need for a method of stopping such a process.

The answer is supplied by the **break** command. When the extended break check is turned on, DOS will check to see if the Ctrl-Break combination has been pressed every time the program makes a system call to the operating system. This means it will check every time the disk system is called, or the operating system is called to handle a memory management function. In fact, it will check anytime the operating system is called to perform any function.

With the simple utilities supplied by DOS, there is no good way to demonstrate the use of the **break** command. Suffice it to say that the types of PC users who are most likely to take advantage of the **break** command are programmers who, no doubt, will have access to compilers and assemblers that eat up large chunks of processing time on their PCs.

To turn on the extended Ctrl-Break checking, simply enter:

```
break on
```

To turn it off, enter:

```
break off
```

If you cannot remember what the current status of the break checking is, simply enter the single word:

```
break
```

DOS will respond by telling you either

```
BREAK is on
```

or

```
BREAK is off
```

As with many of the commands that are oriented toward the more technical user, the **break** command is a very suitable candidate for inclusion in a batch file, although it is not, in itself, regarded as a batch command.

*The **Verify** Command*

The next new DOS internal command that we should take a look at is the **verify** command, which, like the other commands in this category, was not present in DOS version 1—or was it? You may remember from our discussion of commands such as **copy** that there is a **/v** switch that can be tacked on to some commands to force them to verify a writing process.

A computer verifies a writing process by reading it back into memory and comparing the written image with the original. If there are any discrepancies, it will retry the process. After a specified number of retries, it will generate an error message and proceed to the next step. Usually, that would involve printing the "Abort, Retry or Ignore" error message that we have all come to know. We shouldn't take this process for granted, though, since many of the older operating systems simply aborted the process and were incapable of recovering, leaving the astonished operator to figure out where all the data went.

With the new **verify** command, the operating system can be told to verify every writing process, thereby eliminating all errors created in that stage. To do this, simply turn the **verify** command on by entering

```
verify on
```

When it is turned on, all disk operations that involve writing will be noticeably slower than with it turned off. However, the integrity of the data being written will be guaranteed to a much greater extent than with it turned off. To turn it back off, enter:

```
verify off
```

As with other DOS commands of this type, if you need to know the current status—either on or off—enter the command with no arguments:

```
verify
```

This will return either

```
VERIFY is off
```

or

```
VERIFY is on
```

Once set on, the verify state will stay on until the computer is turned off or until the state is reset by means of another **verify** command. One fact that you should be aware of if you plan to use the **verify** command is that an applications program may turn off the verify state through a DOS system call, without first warning the user. Therefore, if you are preparing to **copy** some very important files, it is best to deliberately set **verify** to on immediately before you **copy** the files. In fact, it may be beneficial to create a batch file for the process that contains the **verify on** command.

*The **Set** Command*

The **set** command is yet another new internal command. Its full name is the "set environment" command, and in the IBM manual it has been promoted to the status of an advanced DOS command. The function of the **set** command is to allow the environment—the particular setup of the operating system—to be customized by using string variables in much the same way as a programming language.

The format of the **set** command is quite simple. It is very like the **let** command used by many programming languages, notably BASIC, although in DOS, numerical variables have no place whereas string variables can be used in many situations. The generic form of the command is

```
set $1=$2
```

where *$1* is the ASCII string that is to be set and *$2* is the ASCII string that $1 is to be set to.

This explains *how* it is used. *Why* it is used is probably a more complex question. **Set** has been placed among the advanced DOS commands because it tends to be very obscure in its use. It really falls into the domain of the applications programmer, or a maintenance group involved in debugging or setting up a system for an inexperienced user.

Once a string has been set in the environment, the "alias" that it has been set to can be used by any applications program that uses the environment. This may seem a little strange at first, particularly since an applications program must be set up to make use of the environment. Once an environment has been set, the information is passed through DOS to whatever program is to make use of it. In technical terms, the code segment (or program segment as IBM calls it) prefix contains a pointer to the environment table.

Besides any variables defined by the user through the **set** command, the environment table also contains other information that is important to applications programs running under DOS. For example, have you ever wondered how programs manage to keep track of where the appropriate command.com file is located? Or, similarly, if you set a path or two for DOS to make use of, how is that information passed to an applications program? The answer is, of course, through the environment table.

To see this information for yourself, the **set** command has a mode whereby the contents of the current environment can be checked. To do this, simply enter the command **set** by itself, with no other parameters. This should have the following results:

```
set
PATH=
COMSPEC=A:\COMMAND.COM
```

This is the raw, unmodified environment that DOS defaults to when it is first booted. As you can see, there is no path set. If you define a new path using the **path** command, the environment will be modified accordingly. Try it.

```
path=\usr1\files
set
COMSPEC=A:\COMMAND.COM
PATH=\USR1\FILES
```

The path variable was reset and moved to the end of the list. Now, when DOS, or an applications program running under DOS, is searching for a file, it will look along the specified path if it does not find the file in the currently logged directory. It is through this environment table that DOS passes this information to an applications program.

Similarly, the **comspec** variable that is automatically set in the environment points to the path along which the proper command processor (command.com) will be found. This will usually be the root directory on the drive from which the system was booted. This parameter is used by DOS to reload the command processor when it needs to.

To set and reset environment parameters using the **set** command, there are two forms of the command. The first form is used for aliasing variables. For example, to set the string usr1 to be debug1, the command

```
set usr1;debug1
```

is used. If we now look at the environment table, we will see that the string usr1 = debug1 has been added.

```
set
COMSPEC=A:\COMMAND.COM
PATH=\USR1\FILES
USR1=DEBUG1
```

The new addition to the environment can be used to alias the string usr1 to debug1 in an applications program. This would allow the programmer to, say, switch directories for debugging purposes at run time.

There are other uses for the **set** command, particularly with batch files, as we'll see later when we take an in-depth look at the new, improved batch facilities of DOS version 2.

The Ctty Command

The last of the new internal commands to appear along with DOS version 2 is the powerful **ctty** command, which is used to change the command console. This command is particularly useful in those configurations where a remote terminal is attached to the PC through a serial line, or where a printer that also has a keyboard is attached.

This differs from simple I/O redirection in that all input and output are redirected to the auxiliary console, including error messages. Under standard redirection, of course, the error messages would still be displayed on the console screen. The **ctty** command actually tells DOS to completely replace the standard keyboard and screen with whatever device it is assigned to. Obviously, then, the auxiliary device must be a character-oriented device like the main console and must have both character input capabilities—i.e., a keyboard—and character output capabilities—i.e., either a screen or a print-out device.

It doesn't make any sense to change the command console to a disk drive or any other device that is block oriented and not character oriented, and it also doesn't make any sense to change it to a device such as a printer that does not have a character input facility. A block-oriented device is a peripheral that works in blocks of data at a time rather than a character at a time. A disk drive is the best example of a block-oriented device, whereas a printer is the best example of a character-oriented device.

When a remote terminal is attached to the PC through a serial port, and the port is configured through the **mode** command to work with the terminal at the correct speed, it is perfectly feasible to have the PC operated from either the main console or the remote terminal. Of course, you have to manually tell DOS to switch control before you leave the main console; otherwise it will ignore whatever is entered on the remote console.

The **ctty** command along with the reserved device names tells DOS to switch command consoles to the remote device. The generic format is

```
ctty device
```

where *device* is one of the reserved device names **aux, com1,** or **com2.** Invoking the command will cause the main console to go dead and all activity to be directed to the remote device. To return command to the main console, you need to enter the command

```
ctty con
```

on the remote terminal. This will effectively restore the status quo and direct all communications through the main keyboard and screen.

As we'll see later, DOS also lets you create and install new devices on your own. The new devices are interfaced to DOS through an installable device driver. If a new character-oriented I/O device is installed, DOS can direct main I/O to it through the **ctty** command. This, however, is well beyond the capabilities of most users, since it involves the creation of complex device drivers in assembly language. If a manufacturer ships such a device driver with its hardware, then it is possible to direct I/O to the device through the installed device driver. For information on how to do that you should first consult the manufacturer and confirm that the device driver conforms to all the requirements of DOS.

*The **Prompt** Command*

The **prompt** command is unusual because the DOS version 2.0 manual says that it is an external DOS command and yet an examination of the two disks supplied with the DOS package reveals that there is no such command file. If there were, the file prompt.com would be seen on the disk. As it turns out, the **prompt** command is an internal command and works without DOS having to access anything from the disk system.

The purpose of the **prompt** command is to change the command prompt that DOS puts on the screen when it is free and waiting for the user to enter the next command. In its default condition, the standard DOS prompt is the one we all immediately recognize.

```
A>
```

The first character is always the default drive letter and it is followed by the > character. Very convenient and informative. Why, then, would anyone want to change it? The answer is that computer people tend to be very particular about their prompts, and everyone has a different prompting system that he or she likes and feels familiar with.

Unfortunately, just about every major operating system in use has a different prompting system, and many people use them so much that they begin to feel comfortable with a particular scheme. This is especially true of users on mainframe or minicomputer operating systems, such as UNIX, TOPS-10 and TOPS-20, OS, RSTS, etc., who become locked into a particular prompting scheme and complain that their PCs are inferior because they don't have the capability to emulate their favorite flavor of prompting. Now, through the **prompt** command, DOS supplies a do-it-yourself prompt-generating kit.

The simplest way to use the **prompt** command is to enter

```
prompt text
```

where *text* represents the string that you would like the new prompt to be. For example, if you are the dominant type who prefers to have a master/slave relationship with your PC, you could use the **prompt** command as follows:

```
prompt Yes, Sir?
```

This would have DOS prompt you in all future cases with the prompt:

```
Yes, Sir?
```

If you are changing your prompt to something such as this, you should be careful to leave a blank space at the end of the command before pressing the Return key so that there will be a space at the end of the prompt. Otherwise, when you enter commands it will be difficult to differentiate the command from the prompt. In other words, the command line can look like either of the following when the **dir** command is entered:

```
Yes, Sir?dir
```

or

```
Yes, Sir? dir
```

It depends on whether or not a space was left at the end of the **prompt** command.

The only limits to the type of prompt that you can design using this method are the 127 characters that can be entered on the command line, and your imagination. Of course, since the word *prompt* takes up 6 of the 127 characters available on the command line and the space takes up another, the longest prompt that you can have is limited to 120 characters. However, that is certainly enough to tickle even the most bizarre and/or devious sense of humor.

For those who prefer their prompts to be something other than simply humorous and actually like to have them do something, DOS provides a menu of options that can be applied to the prompt. These options include everything from the current time of day to the version number of DOS. These special features are entered by means of a cute little prompt-construction meta-string language.

For example, one of the capabilities of this system is to be able to display the currently logged disk drive, in much the same way as the default prompt. If you wanted to describe a new prompt that reads

```
You are currently logged on to drive x
```

where *x* is the current drive, you could enter the command:

```
prompt You are currently logged on to drive $n
```

The dollar sign, *$*, is used in this prompt kit to specify a particular system function that is available. The *n* that follows the $ means that you want the currently logged disk drive letter to be displayed in that position. There are a total of thirteen different functions available from which the prompt can be built. These functions are all single characters that follow the $ and include:

t	the current system time
d	the current system date
p	the currently logged directory path name
n	the currently logged drive letter
v	the version number message of the active DOS
g	the standard > symbol
l	the opposite < symbol
b	the bar | symbol
q	the = symbol
$	the $ character
h	when used causes a backspace character
e	the escape character
_	the carriage-return/line-feed sequence which goes to a new line

If you wanted to create a prompt that contained both the system time and the standard system prompt, you would use the command

```
prompt The time is $t $n$g
```

which would result in the prompt

```
The time is 9:59:38.28 A>
```

As you can see, the various functions that are available are positioned in the prompt wherever the $ is located.

The first five functions in the list are quite self-explanatory. The **$t** inserts the current system time at that position. The time is entered in the usual format of hh:mm:ss.xx, where the xx represents hundredths of a second. The **$d** inserts the current system date in its standard format Tue 8–09–83. The day of the week is calculated by DOS.

The third function is **$p,** which inserts the currently logged directory path name into the prompt, which is a convenient method of tracking which directory you are logged on to. Those who make frequent use of tree-structured filing systems might want to consider building a more functional prompt to show the current position in the file system.

The **$n** function inserts the currently logged drive letter into the prompt in exactly the same manner as the standard prompt. The **$v** function inserts the standard DOS version number message into the prompt. In DOS version 2 the message is:

```
IBM Personal Computer DOS Version 2.0
```

The next four options are simply methods whereby you can place certain characters into the prompt without confusing DOS. For example, the < and > characters are generally parsed by the DOS command line processor as being I/O redirection symbols to tell DOS to redirect the standard input and output to and from various files or devices. If they were to be entered on the command line in the **prompt** command, DOS would make a false assumption. Therefore, they can be included in the prompt by placing the appropriate symbol after the $.

Therefore, in a totally worthless, but highly illustrating, attempt to create the standard DOS prompt through the **prompt** command, the following should be entered:

```
prompt $n$g
```

This tells DOS to construct a prompt that contains the currently logged disk drive letter immediately followed by the > sign, which is the standard DOS prompt. Similarly, the pipe symbol | can still be included in the prompt by using a **$b,** which will tell DOS to insert a | character at that position.

For some strange reason, the equal sign = appears not to be an allowed character in the **prompt** command. However, if you attempt to enter the following

```
prompt 1+1=2
```

you will be rewarded with the appropriate prompt

```
1+1=2
```

Why, then, is there a problem with entering = in the prompt line? The answer is that if you attempt to enter the **prompt** command with the single character = in order to make the cursor an = by itself, you will reset the prompt to the standard DOS prompt. Try the following:

```
prompt This is a test
This is a test prompt =
A>
```

Therefore, if you wanted to create a prompt that was simply the equal sign by itself, as some operating systems do, you would have to enter the $9 combination after the **prompt** command.

Last, but not least, is the $ itself. What if you wanted to create a prompt that included the $ by itself, or with other text. Obviously, Microsoft would never leave all the devoted, if not fanatical promptwise, UNIX and XENIX hackers out in the cold. No, now DOS can even look like the UNIX shell. The way to do this is simply to enter two dollar signs in a row at the appropriate position. For example, to create the single, UNIX-like dollar sign prompt, the following command would be entered:

```
prompt $$
```

Indeed, with this capability DOS again proves that it has rapidly become the Cadillac of single-user operating systems.

The other three characters that perform specific functions in the prompt construction kit are all powerful features that further enhance the capabilities of the **prompt** command. The first of these, the **$h** combination, causes a backspace character to be generated. This is fairly easy to remember if you know that the standard ASCII backspace character is the **Ctrl-h**. Try typing Ctrl-h in the middle of a command line and see it at work for yourself.

The backspace character is a creative tool that you can use to construct prompts in several ways, some of them useful, others more in the comic vein. The more useful methods include the shortening of other standard functions. For example, the date function **$d** will always display something that looks like this:

```
Tue 8-09-1983
```

If we were to tack five backspace characters onto it, the prompt would end up being

```
Tue 8-09
```

and ten backspace characters would produce a prompt that specified only the first three characters of the day of the week—pretty handy. The latter would be entered as:

```
prompt $d$h$h$h$h$h$h$h$h$h$h
```

By combining these functions, complex prompts can be created. For example,

```
prompt $d$h$h$h$h$h$h$h$h$h$h$t$h$h$h $n$g
```

would produce a prompt that contained the day of the week, the current time less the hundredths of a second part, and the standard DOS prompt

```
Tue 2:01:42 A>
```

As you can see, there is a little flashing going on in the prompt as the backspace characters erase previously printed characters. This is also an effect that can be put to use in a somewhat whimsical manner. For example, try the prompt:

```
prompt this is a test$h$h$h$h$h$h$h$h$h$h$h
$hat's all, folks
```

Or, if you can handle it, try the somewhat more complex and artistic prompt:

```
prompt $n$g$h $g$h $g$h $g$h $g$h $g$h$h$g$h
$h$g$h$h$g$h$h$g$h$h$g
```

This goes through a lot of trouble to create the standard DOS prompt, but adds a little animation along the way. It should be more than enough to delight your friends and astonish your local IBM expert.

The function of the **$e** combination is to place an escape character into the prompt. The reason for doing this may not be apparent at this time. However, we'll return to this capability later and discover how it can be used to actually position the cursor on a specific location, such as at the top of the screen, and how it can be used to perform such tasks as clearing the screen and setting colors.

The last of the prompt creation tools that we need to look at is the **$_** (underline character, which is shift-minus on the PC keyboard). This causes the prompt system to place a carriage return in the middle of the prompt. The best way to illustrate this is simply to create the most extravagant superduper granddaddy prompt of them all, using all the bells and whistles available to us.

To create the prompt, enter the following:

```
prompt hello, this is the $v$_The time is
$t$_The date is $d$_You are logged onto drive
$n$_Your directory is $p$_$$
```

This will result in the most unlikely of prompts

```
Hello, this is the IBM Personal Computer DOS
Version 2.0
The time is 2:26:19:17
The date is Tue 8-09-1983
You are logged onto drive A
Your directory is a:/usrl/files
$
```

If all of this gets too much for you, you can return to the very simple but standard DOS prompt by entering the **prompt** command with no argument. This seems to have exactly the same effect as the **prompt** = command we saw earlier.

As a final word to tie two of these new concepts together, it is worth mentioning that the prompt information is made part of the environment table. If we do indeed change the prompt, and then take a look at the environment table by issuing the null **set** command, we will see that the prompt information is included.

```
Prompt $t$h$h$h$_$n$g

4:31:15
A>set
COMSPEC=A:\COMMAND.COM
PATH=\USR1\FILES
PROMPT=$t$h$h$h$_$n$g
```

As you can see, the **prompt** command is one of the more fun commands of DOS. There are few rules, except that your prompt should be recognizable as such.

*The **Graphics** Command*

The **graphics** command is one of the best of the new DOS commands. It allows a user with a PC equipped with a color/graphics adapter and an IBM-supplied dot-matrix printer, or an Epson-supplied equivalent, to produce several different types of graphics dumps. A graphics dump is simply a translation of the bits that make up the screen into a string of bytes that will produce a similar display on the printer. The result of which is that the screen is reproduced dot-for-dot on the paper.

As with most of the fun commands in DOS, the IBM manual is woefully lacking in details. It covers the entire command in one single page. The **graphics** command is a passive command that actually installs a driver into DOS which allows it to work with the dot-matrix printer. Of course, to take advantage of these features you need to have the graphics option installed on the IBM printer, or the equivalent Graftrax option on the Epson. Without the addition of these ROMs, you will only be able to use the text-printing features of the command.

Assuming that you do actually have the proper ROMs installed in your printer, enter the command

```
graphics
```

on the keyboard. That is all there is to it. As a passive command, all it has really done is add some more capabilities to your system. Without the **graphics** command being installed, you would be able to dump the *text* screen to the printer at any time. You can do this by pressing the Shift key and the PrtSc key at the same time. However, if you have a graphics image on the screen at the time, you won't get much of a printout.

You can attempt this for yourself by booting with the DOS master disk and, when the **A>** prompt appears, entering the following command:

```
basica
```

This will load the Advanced BASIC language. The BASIC copyright notice will appear and you will also see the BASIC prompt which is OK. You should notice at this point that you have something like 60,865 bytes free. This number will vary depending on how much memory is in your system, but you should make a note of it anyway.

At this point, remove the DOS master disk and replace it with the second disk supplied in the DOS package, "Supplemental Programs." This disk contains all the BASIC example programs, many of which produce graphics. Once you have switched disks, enter the following:

```
run "art"
```

This tells BASIC to load and run the BASIC program called art. It will then prompt you to press the spacebar and the program will run.

At any point while it is running, try pressing the Shift-PrtSc combination and watch the results on your printer. It will print only the characters that are displayed—"press Esc key to exit" and "The City." It won't print any of the graphics that are displayed. Press the Escape key and you'll return to the BASIC prompt. To return to DOS, you need to enter the command **system** into BASIC.

Once you are back in DOS, replace the DOS master disk in drive A: and invoke the new **graphics** command. It will appear that nothing happens. However, now that you have installed the new graphics driver, which is essentially all that the **graphics** command does, you are ready to retry the BASIC arts program.

Return to BASIC and step through the same procedure as before. If you have a system with less than 96K of memory, note that when you enter BASIC, the amount of free memory available will most probably be less than it was before. This is the memory space that the printer driver has taken up. Continue on and step through the sequence the same way you did before. This time, however, when you press the Shift-PrtSc combination, you should be rewarded with a printout of the graphics screen, frozen at the instant when you pressed the keys. While the graphics screen is printing, the BASIC program will remain frozen and will return to action as soon as the dump is completed.

With the graphics driver installed in DOS, you can print two different types of graphics dumps. These two types correspond to the two graphics modes that are available and supported by BASIC. The first graphics mode is the one that you have just seen. This is a representation done in the 320-by-200 graphics mode. In this mode there are four colors available on the video display. When you dump a screen in this resolution out to the printer, the driver will assign a different shade of gray for each color.

The second graphics mode that the **graphics** command will support is the high-resolution mode that has 640-by-200 resolution. In this mode there are only two colors available on the video display—usually black and white. When the graphics command driver is told to dump a high-resolution screen to the printer, it will turn it sideways. This is so that the full resolution of the printer can be put to best use, and also to preserve the *aspect ratio,* which is the ratio of height to width (when it is not exactly 1:1 it causes a circle to be printed as an ellipse).

As you can see when you examine a printout from the graphics driver, it makes no attempt to use the maximum resolution of the printer. It simply takes the dots that are on the screen and multiplies them to make bigger dots for the printer. Each of these bigger dots is actually a solid rectangle consisting of several smaller dots. This is not exactly the best method of printing out graphics with a printer that has as high resolution as the IBM or Epson, but it is free with DOS.

Like many of the other commands of DOS that are not part of the MS-DOS operating system, the **graphics** command seems to have come from a source other than the originators of DOS. Essentially a driver, it does not seem to follow the rules that DOS lays down for installing device drivers. It also does not work very well with BASIC. Since BASIC has such good graphics capabilities, it would benefit tremendously from this feature, but unfortunately it cannot.

In order for **graphics** to work with BASIC, you have to either catch the graphics display on the fly as was demonstrated, or actually insert a special command in the program that halts the graphics display. Then, while it is stopped, the screen can be dumped, and finally the program restarted. There is no way that the driver can be called by a BASIC program.

If you have need of a graphics dump program, then this one will probably do the job. However, if you are looking for something more sophisticated, there are several others available on the open market that may better meet your needs—but at a cost.

The **Assign** *Command*

The **assign** command seems to have been designed to overcome a frustrating limitation that many inexperienced applications programmers have created—they write a piece of software and hard code into the program all of the disk-drive information. These programs force the user into, for example, always using drive A: as the drive that holds all the program information, and drive B: as the drive for all data disks. This may have worked just fine on the programmer's system, but may not be appropriate for your system. You may have a hard disk drive that you have set up as drive C:. You may also want the hard disk to be the receptor of all data, instead of a floppy disk in drive B:. However, the programmer has set up, and hard coded, the drive designations into the program.

The way out is through the simple little **assign** command. **Assign** lets you instruct any drive in your system to behave as though it were physically connected to any other slot. The answer to the problem just described would be to assign all information that is being sent out to drive B: by the applications program to the hard disk in drive C:. This is done simply as:

```
assign b=c
```

Note that in the **assign** command there is no need to include the colons usually associated with the drive-designation letters. In fact, if you attempt to include the colons, you will be rewarded with an "invalid parameter" error message.

One clue to this strange behavior is that the **assign** command is also not generally distributed with versions of MS-DOS for other computers, indicating that the source of this command (and a few others that seemingly break the DOS rules) was probably not the same as the rest of the operating system. It may have been added as an afterthought by popular demand.

However, if you use the correct form and then do a directory of drive B:, you will be shown a listing of the files on drive C:. In the directory listing you will be informed that the information came from drive B: by the usual

```
Volume in drive B has no label
Directory of B:\
```

directory listing header, proving that even DOS believes that the information is actually coming from drive B: instead of drive C:. In fact, if you do a directory of drive C:, you will be given exactly the same listing but with the B: in the header replaced by a C:.

Aha! you might say. This is a way to fool DOS. If I copy a file from drive B: to drive C:, I could get two files on the same directory with the same name. Not so. If you do tell DOS to copy a file, it will simply overwrite the original. The result is that you will still be left with the same file.

Not a very exciting command, **assign** should be used sparingly. It apparently has some very strange side effects when used with the **print** command—a combination that is to be avoided, as we'll see later.

One of the pitfalls of the **assign** command that most people will innocently waltz into is the effect that happens when you boot your system with the DOS master disk and then decide to try out **assign** for yourself. Of course, since most people have systems with two disk drives, the most logical choice is to assign A: to B: by the command:

```
assign a=b
```

Doing this places you in an unrecoverable situation, since the **assign** command is an external command. The only way out of this is to physically switch disks, so that the master or any other disk with a copy of the file assign.com on it is placed in drive B: where it can be accessed.

Alternatively, you can reboot your PC and start all over again.

In general, the **assign** command should be avoided. It is shipped with DOS as a convenience to those inconvenienced by sloppy programming, but is itself an example of sloppy programming. Programmers developing software to run under DOS should be aware of the following quote from the IBM DOS manual:

> If you will be developing an application program, we recommend that you avoid using specific drive assignments within your program, but instead, allow the user to specify the drive(s) to be used.

Wise words indeed. If all programmers would follow this simple rule, there would be no need for commands like **assign.**

The **Recover** *Command*

The **recover** command is one of those DOS commands that you'll be glad you have but hope you never have to use. Its purpose is to reconstruct a damaged file from the information contained in the directory and the file allocation table. It is a brutal command that has saved many a day, and proved ineffective on many others.

You may remember from an earlier chapter that DOS keeps track of where files are located by entries in a directory that are linked to a file allocation table. From this information, DOS knows exactly where on the disk each file is located. During the file-loading process, DOS looks up these tables and retrieves each of the disk sectors that contain a part of the file. It then strings them all together in memory and recreates an exact duplicate of the file as it was originally created. The problems start when one of the sectors becomes damaged.

When DOS encounters a bad sector that it cannot read, it will always give the user the option of retrying, ignoring, or aborting the attempt. If you make several attempts at reading the sector by retrying over and over again, and fail to read it, you have experienced a bad sector.

There are two types of bad sectors that you can experience. The first and most devastating is when a sector that is actually part of the file is destroyed. If DOS cannot read the sector, the information is lost. There is little that any program can do at this point. If the sector that is damaged is in the directory or file allocation table (FAT), all is usually salvageable. DOS can, on most occasions, reconstruct the directory or FAT, thereby retrieving all the information that appeared to be lost.

In the first case, where a sector containing part of the file is damaged, the **recover** command can only do so much. After all, if the sector cannot be read, then it cannot be read. Those data are lost. **Recover** can only attempt to salvage the rest of the data in the file. Therefore, if the file contained program data, the entire program is rendered unusable in the majority of cases. If the file contained any kind of structured information, such as formatted records from a database program, or any kind of encoded or compacted data, then, again, the recovered file will probably be useless.

Recover is only really good at saving files containing text. The data that were in the bad sector will not be recovered, but the rest of the file should be usable. Therefore, it can do little more used in this way than you can do by yourself if you just ignore any file-reading errors when they are discovered.

If you suspect that a file has become damaged, you can try to use the **recover** command as follows

```
recover badfile
```

where *badfile* is the name of the file that has become corrupted. **Recover** will make its best attempt to reconstruct the file from the pieces that it can read. The bad sectors will be marked as used so that they will not be reallocated to another file later. The net result is that another file with the same name as badfile will be created. If it is a text file it will be fully readable, but will not contain any of the information that was lost.

The other use of **recover**, which is infinitely more effective, is in the reconstruction of directories—particularly now since DOS version 2 makes extensive use of hierarchical directories. Imagine, if you will, the following scenario. You have set up a hierarchical directory structure as follows:

```
                     Root
                      |
      ---------------------------------------
      |               |                     |
    usr1            usr2                  usr3
      |               |                     |
    files           files                 files
```

In the directory called \usr3\files, you have the following files:

```
letter.mom
income.82
inventry.1st
insrance.1st
```

These files all contain very valuable information. However, one day you discover that you cannot log on to the directory \usr3. You should remember that any directories that you create are actually stored as normal disk files and are subject to the same wear and tear as any other disk file—more so, in fact, because they need to be accessed more often than other disk files.

Obviously, if you cannot log on to the \usr3 directory, all the information stored in that directory and all directories beneath it is inaccessible. It is in a situation like this that the **recover** command earns its living. If you discover a problem with a directory, using **recover** without a file name argument will reconstruct the files on the disk.

One of the basic assumptions that **recover** has to make is that none of the information in the directory is correct. So, it throws it all away, including any subdirectory structures that you've built, and starts from scratch. That means that it throws away all the names that were initially assigned to files and subdirectories alike. In fact, since it has discarded all the original directory information, it has no way of making a distinction between actual files and subdirectories, and will treat them both as regular files. It then proceeds to construct a new root directory, containing all the files that were on the disk, from the scratches of information (such as the FAT) that it has available to work with.

As it reconstructs the directory, it arbitrarily assigns new names to the files that are recovered. These files are given names following the scheme

```
filennnn.rec
```

starting at file0001.rec and increasing.

Once the directory has been reconstructed, it will be necessary for you to go through the files and rename them to what you remember the original names to be. Although this is somewhat of an inconvenience, it does result in the recovery of valuable data.

You may want to see the **recover** command in action in a simulated situation so that you are prepared for its use should you ever have to rely on it. The best way to do that is to construct a simple three-level tree and place a single file at the bottom. To do this, you should format a blank disk and place it in drive B:. Then, log on to it and enter the following sequence of commands:

```
mkdir dir1
chdir dir1
mkdir dir2
chdir dir2
mkdir dir3
chdir dir3
copy con: testfile
This is a file.
^z
```

This creates a three-level directory tree and places a solitary file named testfile at the lowest level. If you remain in the dir3 directory and list its contents, you will find that the file named testfile is only about 17 bytes long.

Having done this, you then issue the **recover** command. Since it is an external command, the DOS master disk, or a duplicate, will have to be placed in drive A:. Enter the following command

```
a:recover b:
```

to which DOS will respond:

```
Press any key to begin recovery of the file(s)
on drive B:
```

As soon as you press a key, the **recover** program will go to work. It takes an alarmingly short time to work, and when it is done, it will report on how many files were recovered—in our case:

```
4 file(s) recovered
```

This may surprise you, since we only created one file. The other three are, of course, the files that were once used as the directories dir1, dir2, and dir3. If we take a look at the new root directory that **recover** creates, we will see something like the following:

```
dir

        Volume in drive B has no label
        Directory of B:\

file0001 rec   512    1-01-80    4:53p
file0002 rec   512    1-01-80    4:53p
file0003 rec   512    1-01-80    4:53p
file0004 rec   512    1-01-80    4:53p
        4 file(s)    177664 bytes free
```

Confused? Probably so. **Recover** has taken each of the files that were on the disk and created a new root directory with all the files in it, including what were previously directory files. It cannot assume that the information in the supposedly damaged directory is correct, so it redoes everything from scratch.

The problem now is to determine which file is which. The **type** command presents the best method of determining this. Simply **type** the contents of each file onto the screen. It will be immediately obvious that the recovered files 1 through 3 are what remains of the old subdirectories. The file named file0004.rec is the file that we had created earlier.

This raises the issue of file size. When we initially created the file testfile, it was only about 17 bytes long. The recovered version is now 512 bytes long. Where did all the extra space come from?

The **recover** command will, in most cases, return a fixed-up file that is longer than the original file. This is because it works with blocks of disk space at a time. These blocks are the equivalent of the DOS allocation unit. You may remember that when we looked at the directory structure and the file allocation table, we saw that as storage space is required, DOS parcels it out in allocation units, or blocks at a time. The allocation unit is the smallest unit that the **recover** program can work with.

This extra space at the end of the file will often contain garbage. In the case of text files, it will probably be necessary to edit the file and remove everything that has been added. This should not present a major problem, though, considering the alternatives. If you had .com or .exe files on the disk, they can be used to check themselves out. Simply rename each file one by one to a name such as test.com (or test.exe if it is a large file) and issue the command **test.** If the file contains a program, it will probably run with no trouble. You can then identify the program and rename the file accordingly.

After seeing how the **recover** program works, it is easy to establish a set of rules for its use. As you can see, the changes that it makes to the files on the disk and the directory structure are drastic. It would be best if you could salvage whatever information is still intact before using **recover**. The basic steps that you should take when you discover a disk error are as follows:

1. Try to load the damaged file several times before determining that you have a problem. Try several different methods of loading the file (**copy, diskcopy, type,** etc.).
2. If step (1) fails, try loading it from another disk drive.
3. If steps (1) and (2) fail, you probably have a damaged sector. Try to load other files on the same disk.
4. If step (3) fails, you have a bad directory sector. This spells trouble. Proceed to step (6).
5. If step (3) succeeds, immediately **copy** all the files that you can onto a backup disk and then delete the originals. This will make for fewer files on the recovered disk and help you to identify which files are which. Use the **recover** command in the individual file mode (**recover badfile**).
6. Your disk is seriously damaged, and you must use the full power of the **recover** command (**recover B:**, for example). When it is done, you will have to search through the rubble and see what pieces you can pick up.

Hopefully, you will never need to use the **recover** command. However, digital accidents are frequent and often cannot be avoided. But don't let the existence of the **recover** command serve as an endorsement of sloppy media management. The best way to recover from an accident is to pull out your backup disk and use it instead. All important data should be backed up and verified frequently. There is simply no substitute for it.

That about wraps up the new external DOS commands. There are still a few others that we have not covered, but they will be addressed in later chapters. Those commands include ones that are specific to fixed disk operation, the new, improved batch language features and the **print** command, which will be the subject of the next chapter.

CHAPTER 18

Background Printing

For the past few chapters we've been looking at many of the new commands that are part of DOS version 2.0. This chapter will continue on that track, but the command we'll look at in depth is more than just another DOS command. The **print** command introduces us to a whole new ball game—multitasking.

Without a doubt, one of the most heralded of the new DOS features is its ability to perform background printing. This new feature is brought to us courtesy of the external DOS **print** command. **Print** allows the user to specify and queue a number of files that are to be printed. Then, as if by magic, the printer prints the specified files while returning control to the user, so that he or she can run other DOS commands or programs simultaneously. Multitasking? The answer is actually yes, but in a limited manner.

Background printing is not exactly a new feature for the PC. Many word-processing programs have been using the facility since they were announced. Print spooling as it is generally known has always been a particularly easy task for a personal computer to run in the background. What does it mean, though, for a task to be run in the background, and why are print spoolers so popular? To answer these questions, you first have to understand how computers generally approach the problem.

One of the more interesting facets of computer operation is the concept of an "interrupt-driven" system. Interrupts are signals generated inside the computer that are often used to inform the central processing unit of the completion of certain tasks, usually those managed by a peripheral processor. It is really considerably more complex than any simple description, but this approach makes the printer interface very easy to understand. The best way to see how the system works is to walk through the steps involved in one everyday task that the PC can do.

The process of sending a file to the printer is a very illustrative process and suits the requirements of our example very well, especially so because the computer can operate at much higher speeds than the printer. The internal speeds of the computer are measured in millions of cycles per second, whereas the speed of the printer is measured in characters per second. The standard dot-matrix printer supplied by IBM, and its Epson counterpart, are capable of delivering only about 80 characters per second (cps). Obviously, then, there is a great capability gap between the printer and the PC.

Inside most printers there is a small amount of memory called a buffer that is used to hold the information waiting to be printed. There is usually a direct connection between the PC and the printer's memory—either serial or parallel. Suppose that the printer has a buffer capable of holding only one line of 80 characters, and we have just instructed the PC to print a file containing four such lines. The first thing the PC does is to send a signal, called a "request to send," to the printer. If the printer is prepared to receive information, it will acknowledge the request and send back the computer equivalent of an okay. This is part of the protocol generally known as "handshaking."

Whenever the PC receives the okay-to-send signal, it sends the first line. At that point, the printer buffer is filled, and the printer sends a message to the PC telling it to stop sending any more characters. When it receives this message, the PC will then sit around and wait for space to be cleared in the printer's buffer so that it can send the next line. Whenever the coast is clear, the printer sends the okay back to the PC, which repeats the process until the entire file has been transmitted and then printed.

Very efficient you might think, and it is, if there is a high-speed device such as another computer, or a smart printer with a very large buffer, on the other side of the communications link. In the case of a slow-speed printer, however, the PC is spending over 90 percent of its time just sitting around waiting for the printer to send back an okay signal. There has to be a better way.

The answer to this dilemma is to have a small piece of software in the PC that allows it to go about its other business while waiting for the printer to send out an okay-to-send signal. This is done entirely in software using the process of interrupts. The PC's normal business is only momentarily interrupted when the printer is ready for some more data to be sent. This frees up large amounts of time during which the user can have the PC run other tasks.

When a second task is running in the PC, there exists the possibility of a conflict. What happens if both of the programs need to access some resource at the same time? To guard against this, the tasks are given priorities. Usually one is called the foreground task and the other the background task. Since the process of print spooling involves the use of a very slow physical device—the printer—it is usually safe to assume that the printing task is relegated to the status of a background task, with a relatively low priority.

In the DOS **print** command, however, this is not the case. The printing is actually done in foreground, having a very high level of priority. This is somewhat backward from the traditional approach of running the print spooler in the background. There is essentially no difference from the user's perspective, with the exception that any task being run by the user while a **print** is in progress may be subject to some inefficiencies and/or noticeable slowdowns. However, for the sake of efficiency, we will always refer to concurrent printing as in the background.

The **print** command itself is really quite powerful, but it does have some limitations. It is simply a utility, although it demonstrates quite nicely the fact that the PC is fully capable of running multitasking operations.

Using the **print** command is quite easy. To print a file, use the command:

```
print filespec
```

Again, the best way to learn how to use the **print** command is actually to create some dummy files and sit down and play with them. To create a dummy file, a word processor or text editor is needed. If you do not have access to either of these, you can always use the **edlin** mini editor supplied with DOS. The object is to create four files with the names file1.txt, file2.txt, file3.txt, and file4.txt.

To create these dummy files, simply enter one line into the text editor and use the editor's facilities to duplicate it over and over so that the final document is longer than a single page. Every editor and word processor has a different way of doing this, but the results are always the same. The line that you enter into the files should identify the file name so that when you look at the printout, you will know which file is currently being printed. To make things simple, you should use a line like

```
This is the file named file1.txt
```

which will allow you to use the editor to globally substitute a 2 for a 1, and so forth, when you are creating the other files.

If you use a word processor to prepare the files, make sure you use the mode that writes an ASCII file to the disk. If your word processor does not have this facility, you should use its "print to disk" command, which has the same result. To check your results, you should use the **type** command to send the contents of the file across the video screen. This will let you see if you have actually created ASCII files or not. If the file appears as gibberish on the screen, you have not created an ASCII file. If it appears as plain text, you have succeeded.

With these four files created, you are now ready to take on the **print** command. The first exercise is to enter the command

```
print file1.txt
```

and see what happens. If all goes well, you should be rewarded with a prompt from DOS requesting

```
Name of list device [PRN]:
```

which means that DOS needs to know how your printer is set up, or indeed which printer to send the file to if you have more than one connected.

If your printer is connected to the standard parallel printer port and is usually addressed as the standard device **prn,** you can simply press the Return key to continue. If your printer is connected to any of the other ports, enter the reserved name for the port—**com1, com2, aux, lpt1, lpt2, lpt3**, etc., and press Return.

When this is done, DOS will print the message:

```
Resident part of PRINT installed
```

You need to go through this process only when you start your system. Any time from now on that you use the **print** command, you will not need to go through it again.

DOS then displays the message

```
A:FILE1 .TXT is currently being printed
```

to show exactly what is happening. Whenever the printer starts up, the DOS prompt will return and you can operate your PC as though the printing weren't happening. Try some of the usual DOS commands like **dir** and **type** and see the effect that it has on the printer. You will see that when some commands are going on, the printer will come to a halt, since the processor is busy tackling another job.

This is all very nice. We have just experienced real multitasking on a PC. But what happens if, while the background printing is in progress, we issue a second **print** command? Let's try it and see. (If the printing stops before you get a chance to enter the second command, simply reenter the command, immediately followed by a second **print** command.)

```
print file1.txt
A:FILE1    .TXT is currently being printed
print file2.txt
A:FILE1    .TXT is currently being printed
A:FILE2    .TXT is in queue
```

What happens is that there is obviously a problem with trying to run two separate **print** commands at the same time. So, DOS queues the files. That simply means that DOS creates a list of files that are to be printed. If we were to immediately add a third **print** command, DOS would add that file to the queue.

```
print file3.txt
A:FILE1    .TXT is currently being printed
A:FILE2    .TXT is in queue
A:FILE3    .TXT is in queue
```

Whenever a file has finished printing, the **print** command will cause a page eject to be sent to the printer, which ensures that each file will be started on a new page; it then removes the completed file from the queue and bumps each of the lower-priority files up one level.

If we want multiple copies of a file, it is easy to simply enter the command twice, or as often as we want.

```
print file1.txt
A:FILE1    .TXT is currently being printed
print file1.txt
A:FILE1    .TXT is currently being printed
A:FILE1    .TXT is in queue
```

Of course, while this queue is being printed, you are free to run other programs on your PC. You should, however, be extremely careful and make sure that the program you are running while a background print is in progress is a program that works through the operating system. Many programs do not work through DOS to conduct their input and output, but rather bypass the operating system and work directly with the hardware. It is unfortunate that you cannot queue up a whole slew of files to be printed and then sit down to a session on Microsoft's *Flight Simulator* while you are waiting.

Which raises the issue—just how many files can be placed in the print queue? The answer is ten files. Once the print queue is full, it will not accept any other files. Multiple file names can be entered on the **print** command line at the same time. For example, if you wanted to print all four of the files that you created, you could enter the following:

```
print file1.txt file2.txt file3.txt file4.txt
```

Instead of typing this long line into the command line interpreter, however, you could make use of the wildcard characters, replacing the 1, 2, 3, and 4 in the file names with a single ?. To demonstrate this, as well as what happens when the print queue becomes full, try entering the following command three times in quick succession:

```
print file?.txt
```

One convenient method of entering a command more than once is to use the F3 special function key, which repeats the last command entered on the keyboard, and then press Return.

The first time you issue the command, **print** will search the directory and determine that there are four files that meet the wildcard specification, since it will accept any file with any character where the question mark character is located. It will then place all four files into the print queue.

When you issue the command for the second time, **print** will again place the four files in the print queue, for a total of eight. On the third instance, however, there should be room for only two more files. **Print** will add the first two files that it finds that match the wildcard search, and then close the queue. To show that the queue is full, it will print the message

```
Print queue is full
```

on the screen, and then list the contents of the queue as is normal. It will not accept any more files to be printed until a space becomes available in the queue. The queue itself follows a first-in, first-out (fifo) sequence.

A quick look at what you have just done will reveal that you probably just cost yourself half a box of paper and tied the printer up for about half an hour or so. It would be nice if you could stop it before you wasted any more paper, wouldn't it? However, while the queue is full you have a good opportunity to see some of the other **print** features at work.

If you are ever confused at any time about just which files are in the print queue, or if you are smart and have placed your printer off in another room and would like to check the status of the print queue, you can enter the **print** command with no arguments. This will print a status report on the screen which might look something like this:

```
print
A:FILE2    .TXT is currently being printed
A:FILE3    .TXT is in queue
A:FILE4    .TXT is in queue
A:FILE1    .TXT is in queue
A:FILE2    .TXT is in queue
A:FILE3    .TXT is in queue
A:FILE4    .TXT is in queue
A:FILE1    .TXT is in queue
A:FILE2    .TXT is in queue
```

We see from this report that **print** has finished printing the first document and is currently working on the second.

Before you waste all that paper and cause severe strain on your printer ribbon, now is the time to discover how to abort the **print** command and empty the queue. The normal method of entering a Ctrl-Break combination has no effect on the **print** command; it will only affect any other command that is running concurrently. The key, then, is to enter the following version of the **print** command itself:

```
print /t
```

The **/t** switch is added to the **print** command to tell it to immediately *terminate* the process. **Print** will respond by immediately stopping the print in progress and ejecting the page currently in the printer. It will then ring the printer's bell (or beep the printer's beeper, whichever is the case), empty the print queue, and terminate the entire print. It will also cause the message

```
All files canceled by operator
```

to be printed on the printer.

Another switch that can be used with the **print** command is the **/c** switch, which causes it to *cancel* specified files. For example, if, after you had queued all four files for printing using the

```
print file?.txt
```

you decided that you didn't really want to print the file named file3.txt, you could always enter the command:

```
print file3.txt /c
```

This would cause **print** to remove file3.txt from the print queue. If there was more than one file in the queue with that name, it would remove all the occurrences of that file.

The third switch that can be used with the **print** command is the **/p** switch, known as the *print* switch. This causes all the file names that precede it to be printed. Use of this switch allows you to set up complex print situations with a single command. For example, suppose that you wanted to print the three files named file2.txt, file3.txt, and file4.txt. Rather than having to enter three different **print** commands—one for each file—or entering a global print command and then a second command to cancel the printing of file1.txt (which would be difficult since it would have started to print already), you can accomplish the whole thing with one command:

```
print file?.txt /p file1.txt /c
```

This will load the three files into the print queue and cause the message:

```
A:FILE1    .TXT canceled by operator
```

to be printed on the printer.

Unfortunately, the **print** command is one of those innocent little commands that is extremely vulnerable to deliberate and accidental sabotage. There are many cases where the poor thing can become incredibly confused, because of the fact that while it is off doing its thing the operator is free to wreak as much havoc as possible. For example, what happens if you queue a file for printing and then change its name? The best way to see the result is simply to try it.

Enter the command:

```
print file?.txt
```

When control returns, sneakily change the name of file2.txt as follows

```
rename file2.txt somethn.els
```

and observe the reaction. **Print** will plod along on its path printing the first file. However, when it comes to the second file, it should not be able to find it. But for some strange reason it sometimes does find the file, and it does print it out correctly! Strange goings on indeed.

To further provoke the situation, make a backup copy of the file named file2.txt under the name file2.bak. Then issue the **print** command as before

```
print file?.txt
```

and very quickly erase the file file2.txt. A quick look at the print queue will reveal that the file was not removed from the queue. This situation should give the **print** command some headaches, since the second file in its queue does not now exist. As though to make a mockery of the situation, **print** will, on some occasions, print out the file, or at least a part of it.

What this all means is that it is best to avoid any situation where a file is tampered with once it has been queued for printing. The results are totally unpredictable. It is simply not good practice to have two processes act on the same file at the same time—under any circumstances. Since concurrency seems to be a coming attraction on the PC with new versions of DOS, it behooves us to adopt these good practices early on and establish good habits now. Otherwise, when we are faced with the opportunity of running several tasks concurrently, we will discover many new and wonderful methods of destroying our work.

There are several other situations besides tampering with queued files that are to be avoided when using the **print** command. For example, first invoking **print,** and then sending information out to the printer via another command, such as **type** with the output redirected to the printer, can have devastating effects. So too can use of the PrtSc key, which dumps an image of the screen out to the printer, or use of the BASIC command **llist** which sends a program listing out to the printer. The best rule is to avoid using any command or program that uses the printer while the **print** command is doing its stuff.

For some strange reason, **print** cannot work in different directories at the same time. Again, the rules for how **print** works on various directories are vague, and putting the command into a situation where it is forced to work with multiple directories can be dangerous. From a little experimentation you can find out that if you log on to another directory and issue a **print** command, and then return to the root directory, everything appears to work just fine. However, if you try to issue a **print** command that includes a path name for a file, you will be given an error message.

Print also ignores the search path set by the **path** command. For example, if you are in the root directory and you set the search path to be \backup, and then tell **print** to print a file that is in that directory, you will be given a "file not found" error message, and the file will not be printed.

Print seems to work perfectly when you are using files on two disk drives and you enter full filespecs for the files to be printed, including a disk identifier. **Print** stores the disk identifier along with the file name in the queue, as can be seen on examination.

Another interesting discovery can be made when you attempt to redirect the output of the **print** command to a disk file. Enter the command:

```
print file?.txt >myfile
```

What happens in this case is that the file named myfile is actually created. However, the **print** command merrily sends the contents of the specified files out to the printer as it normally would, instead of to the file as we had seemingly requested.

When we examine the new file named myfile, we will see that it contains the following:

```
type myfile
A:FILE1    .TXT is currently being printed
A:FILE2    .TXT is in queue
A:FILE3    .TXT is in queue
A:FILE4    .TXT is in queue
```

From this we can see the **print** does not send the output to the printer through the standard output. However, the screen messages are all standard output. On the same track, it is very illustrative to send the output of a file through the **print** command and then pipe it to a filter.

The **find** filter lends itself very well to this. First, copy the file find.exe onto your disk, and then issue the command:

```
print file?.txt | find "2"
```

In theory, this should only pass the lines that contain the character "2." The **print** command will print all four files intact, however. Not surprisingly, what it does is send the output that is going to the screen through the filter, resulting in only one line being displayed

```
A:file2   .txt is in the queue
```

instead of the entire list of queued files. If we were then to look at the listing of items that have been queued, we would see that all four files are indeed in the queue. The filter has only filtered the output that was sent to the screen.

That is really all there is to know about the **print** command. It can be made to work very effectively, but as yet, has some limitations. Hopefully, these barriers will be removed in the future—if they haven't been already.

CHAPTER 19

New, Improved Batching

With DOS version 1, the batch capability, as we saw, was very powerful. Batching allows a series of DOS commands to be stored in a file and executed by entering one single command. It provides a method of customizing DOS for particular operators, and at the same time can be used to simplify very complex systems so that an inexperienced operator can control the entire system by simply turning it on.

Another popular use of batch commands is to automate frequently used tasks so that they can be invoked quickly and easily. Programmers often use batch files when they are working with compilers or assemblers, since they drastically reduce the number of keystrokes required to invoke a complex and often repetitious process.

As if the batch capabilities in DOS version 1 were not enough, even for the most discriminating hacker, DOS version 2 brings with it a whole slew of new commands and capabilities, adding intelligence and iterative capabilities where there were none before.

With DOS version 1, we had only two commands that were designed specifically for use in batch files. The first of these is the **rem** command, which lets you pepper your batch files with remarks so that when you come back to them in six months you will be given clues about what the files do. The second is the **pause** command which, when placed in a batch file, causes all action to halt and the message

```
Strike a key when ready
```

to be printed on the screen. By placing some text after the **pause** command, you can also issue a prompt to the user to change disks, or whatever.

The other two features of the batch facility that were seen in DOS version 1 are the replaceable parameters and the autoexec capability. Replaceable parameters let you define and use variables so that you can use the same batch files for various processes. The autoexec feature can be used to automatically run a batch file by the name of autoexec.bat whenever you first start your system, thereby allowing "turnkey" capabilities to be added.

Even with these scant features, the batch capabilities of DOS version 1 proved to be both very powerful and very popular. Hopefully, the additions that DOS version 2 has brought will prove to be even more so.

Under DOS version 2 there are six new commands available for use in batch files. These commands are **echo, for, goto, if, shift,** and **cls.** The last of these is technically not a batch command, since it can be used outside of batch files, but it will most often be used within batch files. Most of the others are used to control the logical flow through a batch file, adding conditional branching capabilities and iteration.

*The **Cls** Batch Command*

The **cls,** or clear screen, command is the most simple of the new commands. When it is used, it will cause the screen to be blanked. Since the DOS version 2 batch language is much more complex than its earlier incarnation, it is only appropriate that some cosmetic commands be added to help create a tidier environment. Which is exactly the purpose of the **cls** command. Its operation is so simple that nothing more need be said about it.

*The **Echo** Batch Command*

The **echo** command is another cosmetic command. It has several modes of operation, but its purpose is simply to enable or inhibit the display of batch commands while a batch file is running. Under the normal state of affairs, all commands that are stored in a batch file are displayed on the screen as they are executed. While having the screen scroll in the manner of a printer may have been just fine for older operating systems, some of DOS's new capabilities allow very accurate cursor manipulation through some of the advanced features. This places a greater burden on the new DOS to manage the screen much better. Therefore, better screen-management commands such as **echo** have been added.

The first form of the **echo** command has two main modes. These are simply

```
echo on
```

and

```
echo off
```

The former returns DOS to its default state where all executing batch commands are "echoed" to the screen. The latter version inhibits this. Turning off the screen echo lets you set up batch files that have a much more professional look to them.

When you set **echo off,** only those commands that are contained in a batch file will not be displayed. All other commands typed at the keyboard will be displayed as usual. If you plan to use this feature, you should consider placing the **echo off** command as the first command in your batch file. Since it is the first command, it *will* be displayed as usual. You should, therefore, follow it immediately with a **cls** command if you don't want the **echo off** statement to be seen.

Echo only has an effect on the statements in the batch command itself; it has no effect whatsoever on the screen output from the command. For example, if you include an **echo off** command followed by a **dir** command in a batch file, you'll still see the directory listing on the screen. However, you will not see the **dir** command itself.

If you use the **echo** command without an argument, the current status of the echo, either on or off, will be displayed. One minor frustration that you might encounter is that **echo** is always set back on when the batch command terminates, meaning that you need to put the **echo off** statement at the beginning of each batch file if you want to use it. You cannot simply turn it off once and leave it off.

You can see this for yourself by creating a simple batch file containing the statement **echo off** by itself. Execute the file and then enter the argumentless **echo**. You'll see that the **echo** is back on again.

The second mode of the **echo** command allows the sending of messages to the screen when **echo** is turned off. By placing a text message after the word **echo,** you can have that text displayed, regardless of whether the echo is on or off. Keep in mind that when **echo** is turned off, messages contained in **rem** statements will not be printed.

So, too, any messages that are contained in **pause** statements will not be printed on the screen while **echo** is off. The entire operation of the **echo** command can be demonstrated by entering and running the following batch file:

```
copy con: mytest.bat
rem the echo is on
pause this message should be displayed
echo off
rem the echo command has been turned off
pause this message will not be displayed
echo
^z
```

When you invoke the batch file, you should see the following:

```
A>mytest

A>REM the echo is on

A>PAUSE this message should print out
Strike a key when ready . . .

A>echo off
Strike a key when ready . . .
ECHO is off
```

Notice the effect on the **pause** command. If the echo is off, any message associated with the **pause** will not be displayed, although the "Strike a key when ready . . ." message will always be displayed.

*The **Shift** Batch Command*

The **Shift** command is an extension of the replaceable-parameter feature. It allows more than ten replaceable parameters to be used in batch processing. You should remember from the discussion of replaceable parameters under DOS version 1 that we can assign meanings to the symbols %0, %1, %2 . . . %9 from the command line. These dummy parameters are placed in a batch file, and when we invoke the file, we can determine the real parameters that are to replace them.

Any string can be assigned to a replaceable parameter, starting with the dummy %1. The %0 parameter is reserved for the name of the batch file itself. One of the examples that we used to demonstrate this feature was the file that many people who use the macro assembler package could make use of:

```
rem this is asmfile.bat
rem first make a backup copy
copy %1.asm %2.asm
rem next assemble the source file
masm %2,%2,%2
rem finally read the assembler listing
type %2.1st
```

Instead of entering a long-winded string of commands to make a backup copy of the source file, assemble it, and list it, the entire process can be invoked with one simple command, for example:

```
asmfile a:source b:backup
```

In this case, the name of the batch file itself would be assigned to the *%0* dummy parameter, which is not used in this example, the parameter *a:source* would be assigned to *%1,* and *b:backup* would be assigned to *%2*. When these parameters are placed in the batch file, it will result in the equivalent of:

```
rem this is asmfile.bat
rem first make a backup copy
copy a:source.asm b:backup.asm
rem next assemble the source file
masm b:backup,b:backup,b:backup
rem finally read the assembler listing
type b:backup.1st
```

With up to ten replaceable parameters available, arbitrarily complex batch processes could be constructed. However, for many people, ten was just not enough. DOS's solution is the **shift** command. When **shift** is placed in a batch file, the order in which the dummy parameters %0 through %9 are replaced is changed.

With each **shift,** every parameter is shifted down one. This happens to be one of those features that is very difficult to explain, but can be easily demonstrated with a simple example. The example is best prepared with a word processor—in ASCII mode—or text editor, since it is very repetitious. The final product should look like this:

```
echo off
rem this is fun.bat
echo %0 %1 %2 %3 %4 %5 %6 %7 %8 %9
shift
echo %0 %1 %2 %3 %4 %5 %6 %7 %8 %9
shift
echo %0 %1 %2 %3 %4 %5 %6 %7 %8 %9
shift
echo %0 %1 %2 %3 %4 %5 %6 %7 %8 %9
shift
echo %0 %1 %2 %3 %4 %5 %6 %7 %8 %9
```

With a file such as this we can actually enter more than the allowed nine parameters on the command line. In this case we've used **shift** four times, so we can actually enter thirteen parameters. To demonstrate the workings of **shift,** try entering the following command:

```
fun 001 002 003 004 005 006 007 008 009 010
011 012 013 014
```

This should result in the following:

```
A>echo off
fun 001 002 003 004 005 006 007 008 009
001 002 003 004 005 006 007 008 009 010
002 003 004 005 006 007 008 009 010 011
003 004 005 006 007 008 009 010 011 012
004 005 006 007 008 009 010 011 012 013
```

This demonstrates how each of the replaceable parameters is shifted by one in the priority scheme each time a **shift** command is encountered.

The **shift** command is one of the few completely decadent commands of DOS. Very few people will ever build batch files that require more than ten parameters to be replaced. However, for those for whom plenty is never enough, there is always the **shift** command.

The If Batch Command

Ths **if** batch command is probably the most useful of the new batch features. It allows a programmer to insert conditional testing into a batch file. Now, using the **if** command, a programmer can build a batch file that can make internal decisions for itself, depending on whether or not a certain predefined condition is met. The condition to be met is built into the **if** statement itself.

The **if** command works in much the same manner as the **if-then** statement in BASIC. However, the general Boolean arithmetic conditions that the BASIC **if-then** statement is usually used with do not apply to DOS. Instead, DOS has its own set of conditions. The best way to think of the **if** command is as follows:

```
if (the condition is true) then do the
command x
```

There are three types of the conditions that the **if** command can check to see are true or not. The first of these is the **exist** condition. The **exist** condition checks to see if a specified file exists or not. If it does exist, the command at the end of the **if** statement will be executed. If it does not exist, the command will not be executed.

An example of such a command is:

```
if exist myfile.txt copy myfile.txt myfile.bak
```

The condition that is to be met in this command is the existence of myfile.txt. If it does exist, then the statement is true and the condition has been met. Therefore, the command will be executed. The command in this case is **copy myfile.txt myfile.bak.** In short, the command tells DOS that "if the file named myfile.txt exists then make a backup of it and call it myfile.bak." This has the benefit of not producing an error message if the file does not exist.

There is also another form of the **if** command that does precisely the opposite. That is the **if not** form. If the **not** is placed in the **if** statement, the DOS command at the end will be executed only if the condition is *not* met. This can be demonstrated by the command

```
if not exist myfile.bak copy myfile.txt
myfile.bak
```

which is a handy way for a batch program to check to see if a particular file name is already allocated before it copies another file and uses the name. When DOS is given a batch command like this, it will check to see if the file myfile.bak already exists. If it does, it will not copy the file myfile.txt over it. If the file does not exist, DOS will forge ahead and create it.

The second condition that DOS can check for is to see if two strings match each other. This way, the batch program can perform certain functions, based on what the operator enters on the command line. The general form of this conditional test is:

```
if string1 == string2 command
```

Note that in this command two consecutive equal signs are necessary to distinguish it from other commands. This version of the command can be used to make the PC simpler for an inexperienced user to operate. For example, if there are some programs that you do not want people to run, you can build a minimum security password scheme into a batch file. By constructing the following batch file, you can have a "secret" code that can be used to invoke a program:

```
echo off
cls
if %1 == swordfish basic payroll
^z
```

By calling the file password.bat, the user would have to enter the code

```
password swordfish
```

in order to run the payroll program. Of course, this is only for the sake of illustration; no one with a need for security would ever put together as minimal a security system as this.

This version of the **if** command also comes in very handy if children or people who are easily intimidated by computers will be using your PC. The **if** command permits you to construct a dispatching system that lets users enter very simple commands and have them translated into the long, complex commands often required to start DOS programs.

For example, if you have a number of programs that are easy to use, but difficult for an inexperienced user to start, you might want to place all the programs on a special disk or a special directory on a hard disk, and then construct a batch file dispatching system to control their operation. Suppose, for our example, that there are four programs that a child likes to play with. Assume that they are a word processor called miniword, an electronic spreadsheet program called minicalc, a drawing program called minidraw, and a great game called minigame. It would make things a lot easier if you placed the following file on the disk.

```
copy con: i.bat
echo off
cls
if %3 == type miniword
if %3 == count minicalc
if %3 == draw minidraw
if %3 == play minigame
^z
```

It is then very easy to teach the inexperienced user how to load the correct programs. For example, to invoke the batch file, all you have to do is enter the letter *i*. This is a good lead in for sentences. Since the batch file is looking for a match on the third replaceable parameter, sentences such as

```
I want to play
```

can be entered into the command line interpreter. This would cause the batch file i.bat to be invoked, and the words "want," "to," and "play" to be assigned to the replaceable parameters %1, %2, and %3, respectively. DOS would then replace all the occurrences of %3 with the word "play" in the batch file. It would therefore find that the statement

```
if play == play
```

is true and would then issue the command:

```
minigame
```

This would run the appropriate program. Similarly, if the user were to enter any of the other keywords in the right position, DOS would load and run the correct program. This new form of a mini command interpreter would also be able to work with commands such as:

```
I want to type
I want to count
I want to draw
```

Again, this example serves merely as an illustration. It does point out, however, that it is very easy to customize batch files using the **if string = = string** construct to perform just about any function you can imagine. As an exercise you might want to develop a batch file using this form of **if** in conjunction with the **shift** command to create something that will appear a little more clever.

The third condition that the **if** command can check for is called **errorlevel.** Some DOS commands, and, in time, many applications programs will support the DOS **errorlevel** scheme. This scheme allows a program that fails to operate correctly to return a code that can be used to determine why it failed.

There is a table of error codes available for applications programmers to use. When a program that is written correctly finishes, it should return to DOS with an error flag set. If the error flag is not set, DOS will assume that all went well and the program ran correctly. If the error flag is set, DOS looks at a specified location to find out what the error code is.

The only commands that support **errorlevel** are the **backup** and **restore** commands for use in fixed disk operations, since only they are set up so that the return error codes can be checked. However, it is quite easy for any programmer to have his or her program support the error code system, and therefore work with **if errorlevel.**

The syntax for the **if errorlevel** command is

```
if errorlevel x command
```

where *x* is the designated error code number. The way it works is that if the returned error code is *x* or higher, the command will be executed. If there is no error code, or if it is lower than *x,* the command will not be executed.

Since **backup** and **restore** are the only commands that support the error code system, we will use them in our example. The following example illustrates its use:

```
backup
if errorlevel 1 echo - backup aborted -
```

The **backup** command returns one of four error codes when it exists. If a 0 is returned, no error occurred; if a 1 is returned, no files were backed up, since no qualifying files could be found; if a 3 is returned, it indicates that the user terminated the command with a Ctrl-Break; and if a 4 is returned, another type of error was encountered.

The preceding command checks for an error code of 1 or greater. If an error is detected, the message "-backup aborted-" is printed.

The **if errorlevel** condition is a new concept to DOS. It has been included so that programs developed in the future can take advantage of it. Hopefully, applications programmers will begin to use it, since it does add some capabilities that will simplify the use of the operating system.

*The **For** Batch Command*

The **for** command allows specified DOS commands to be iterated, or performed in a repetitive manner. The full syntax of the command is:

```
for %%x in (set) do command
```

The **for** command is one of the more complex of the DOS batch commands, but it is also one of the most powerful. It allows you to perform the same command on a list of files, directories, or whatever.

The *%%x* is simply a dummy variable that is associated with each local **for** command. It must consist of the pair of percent signs, followed by any valid character other than the digits 0–9. If one of these numbers is used, DOS will not be able to determine whether the command is a replaceable parameter or not. Also, the %% is needed so that after the batch parameter replacement is done there is still one % sign left. If only one % is included, DOS will look at it when it is in the process of replacing parameters and decide that it is a "bad parameter reference" error. It will then throw out the %x and invalidate the **for** command.

The *set* is simply a list of parameters that is passed to the command. It usually consists of a series of file specifications. The command at the end of the **for** statement is the DOS command that is to be repeated. As it is repeated, it is applied to each of the parameters in the set.

For example, if you wanted to type three files on the printer, and there was no way to include all three files in a wildcard parameter, the usual method would be to enter three separate commands, something like the following:

```
type thisfile.txt >prn
type thatfile.bak >prn
type another.fil >prn
```

If you look closely at these commands, you will see that we have entered *type* and *>prn* three times, which seems sort of redundant. However, there is no way to apply wildcards to shorten the process. To make matters worse, we have to sit and wait for each file to be typed before we can enter the next command. Of course, you could always use the "type ahead" feature of the PC, but since you can't see what is being entered, the chances of making a mistake are increased.

The answer is to use the iterative capabilities of the **for** command. The following batch command will do the trick.

```
for %%a in (thisfile.txt thatfile.bak another
.fil) do type %%a >prn
```

As you can see, the variable we use is *%%a,* and the command we use is *type >prn*. The *set* is simply a list of the file names that we want to **type.**

When you are entering the command part of the **for** command, be careful to include the second *%%x* in the appropriate position. Anywhere in which you want to substitute the name of the file from the set, you must use *%%x*.

One feature that makes this command particularly interesting is that, like all the batch commands, it is really an internal DOS command, and as such can be used on the command line rather than from a batch file. To use it as an interactive command, you simply use a single % instead of a pair.

The **Goto** *Batch Command*

The **goto** command is pretty much the icing on the cake as far as batch programming goes. Use of the **goto** command more than doubles the capability of the batch language, since it can be used with any combination of commands or conditionals to add logic flow to a batch command.

Goto requires the use of labels in your batch files so that a destination point can be defined. A *label* is a string of characters preceded by a colon and placed in a batch file. In the **goto** command, DOS, as in other commands, does not differentiate between lowercase and uppercase letters. In labels they are treated equally, so that the label :here is the same as the label :HERE. The following short batch file shows how a label can be used in its most simplistic form.

```
:start
dir
goto start
```

When executed, this batch program will ignore the first command, since it starts with a colon and is therefore a label. It will then proceed to the next statement and issue the **dir** command. When that has finished, it will step to the **goto start** statement. This causes control to jump back in the file to the line that contains the label :start and to then repeat the procedure. It will continue in this loop format until you deliberately break out of it by pressing the Ctrl-Break combination.

When used in conjunction with the **if** command, **goto** provides a whole new level of functionality for DOS batch processing. However, the one situation that you should avoid is placing two labels in a file that have the same first eight characters, since that is all that is significant in a label. If DOS encounters two labels having the same first eight characters, it will always **goto** the first occurrence. Therefore, it is best to keep the labels as short as possible.

Goto can be made to send control in the batch file either forward from the current line or backward as we saw earlier. The following file is an interesting little example of the type of functionality that **goto** can add to a batch processor.

```
Echo off
rem this is the file catalog.bat
:start
if %1 == #1 goto drivea
if %1 == #2 goto driveb
if %1 == . goto end
:bump
shift
goto start
:drivea
dir a:
goto bump
:driveb
dir b:
goto bump
:end
```

The file is stored under the name *catalog.bat*. Then, the user is given a simple rule. To get a directory listing of any disk drive, you only need to start the command with the word *catalog* and finish the command with the period preceded by a space. You can refer to disk drives as #1 and #2.

When the file is stored on the disk, try entering the following commands:

```
catalog the disk in drive #1 .
catalog the disk in drive #2 .
catalog the disks in drives #1 and #2 .
```

When these commands are entered, the batch file catalog.bat is executed. Then, the feature of replaceable parameters is used. Of course, %0 is the string "catalog." The only dummy parameter that we have used in the file, however, is %1, which is assigned the string "the." The batch file then compares the string "the" with the strings defined "#1," "#2," and "." to see if there is a match. Since there is no match, it will continue on until it reaches the command **shift.**

When everything is shifted, %1 will now be equal to "disk" in the first two examples and "disks" in the third. It then steps on to the command **goto start.** Control is then passed back to the :start label, and the comparison tests are run again. Still there is no match, so the **shift** command is activated for a second time, causing the %1 parameter to be replaced by the word "in" in all three cases.

Again, control is returned to the :start label and the comparisons are run for a third and fourth time, with no match being found. When the **shift** is encountered for the fourth time, however, the parameter %1 is replaced by either "#1" in the first and third examples, or "#2" in the second example. Since, in these cases, the **if** commands are true, the **goto** associated with the **if** will be executed, and control is passed to either the :drivea label or the :driveb label, depending on what the match is.

In either case, the appropriate **dir** command is issued, and when that is complete, a **goto bump** command is encountered. These commands send control back to the :bump label, which sends control back to the **shift** command in the initial loop. The process continues in this way, and in the third example, another match is found, and another **dir** command is issued.

Finally, in each of the three examples the parameters are shifted so that %1 is equal to "." and control is sent via the **if** %1 == **. goto end** command to the last statement in the file, thereby terminating the batch command.

Highly complex batch commands can be constructed with the **goto** command and labels. When used with conditionals, DOS becomes as powerful as many programming languages, particularly in the aspects of program flow control. Everyone will have a different use for these intelligent batch files. Programmers need them very often to assist in the construction of program files. Office managers or MIS groups use them to simplify the operation of a complex process for an inexperienced user, or even to check a user's actions and correct them if a mistake is made. Parents and teachers will find them useful in simplifying the operation of the PC for children. There are no rules to determine their many applications, only their proper construction.

As you can see, the new batch capabilities of DOS version 2 go well beyond the older version 1 capabilities. These new commands take a little getting used to, but most people will find that they are not as difficult as they seem once they begin to use them.

CHAPTER 20

Fixed Disk Operation

In this chapter we'll take an in-depth look at how DOS versions 2.0 and 3.0 fare with the fixed disk versions of the IBM PC—the PC-XT and PC-AT—as well as PCs equipped with other vendors' hard disks. By looking at some of the concepts behind the use of devices such as Winchester drives, we will see that DOS can be made to work with just about any device—in a very easy way.

For the time being we'll assume that you've been through the configuration procedure, as directed by the IBM DOS manual, and have opted not to partition your disk but to allocate all the space on the disk as a single DOS partition. The information supplied in the IBM manual is sufficient to do this and is very clearly written. Another discourse on this procedure would only serve to confuse the issue.

The first thing you should notice when you start the fixed disk version of the PC is that it appears to be identical to the floppy disk version, at least as far as DOS is concerned. The boot procedure is the same and the log-on sequence is identical. However, a little further probing will disclose that the fixed disk is usually configured as drive C:, with the PC thinking that the floppy disk is both drive A: and drive B:.

Of course, the sheer mass of the fixed disk lends itself very much to some of the more advanced features of DOS version 2, such as hierarchical directories. The operation, however, is identical to a floppy-based system. Besides the physical differences of a fixed drive—speed and capacity—DOS does not differentiate between them.

DOS, however, has a few commands that are specific to fixed disk systems. These commands are designed to address the problem of maintaining adequate backups of the information stored on the fixed disk. Ten megabytes or more is a lot of storage. It is the equivalent to over sixty single-sided diskettes. The problems of keeping adequate backups are nontrivial.

Some fixed disks supplied by manufacturers other than IBM offer their own proprietary methods of maintaining backups. Some of these involve removable media such as cartridges, some offer tape spooling, and some even make use of the Pulse Code Modulation storage features of videotape. The majority of hard disk users, however, are faced with their floppy disks as the only relevant method of backing up their data.

To address this problem, DOS version 2 has introduced two new commands, **backup** and **restore.** These commands are for fixed disk users only, and offer a relatively painless method of maintaining backups—if they are used properly.

*The **Backup** Command*

Many users do not quite understand the use of the **backup** command. Why should it be necessary when the **copy** command is available to copy files from one disk to another? The answer is evident when you consider the situation that arises when one single file becomes larger than the capacity of a single floppy disk. How can you create a backup copy of such a file using the **copy** command?

The best way to demonstrate this dilemma is to actually encounter it for yourself under simulated conditions before the real thing happens. First, of course, you need to have a file that is larger than the capacity of a single floppy disk. If you do not have such a file, you can always use the DOS file concatenation feature to create one. To do this, first you must create a small text file. Let's call it test. A single line of text, entered via the

```
copy con: test
```

command will suffice. Then, create the following batch file:

```
copy con: grow.bat
copy test + test test2
```

```
dir
copy test2 + test2 test
dir
pause press Ctrl-Break if the file test is
 large enough
grow
```

When you issue the command **grow**, the file test will grow very rapidly. After several iterations it will be larger than the size of a single floppy. When this point is reached, stop the growth process by using Ctrl-Break. The temporary file named test2 will also be created in this process. Once you have halted **grow**, you can delete test2, since it is not necessary for our purposes.

Next, format several blank disks. During this process make sure that you direct the **format** command to drive A:, and not the fixed disk. Unfortunately, many people have discovered just how easy it is to erase all the data on a fixed disk by a misapplication of the **format** command. When this is done, you have all of the tools that you will need to try out both the **copy** and the **backup** commands.

First, try to **copy** the file test onto one of the floppies. As soon as the disk is filled, you should get an insufficient disk space error, and the command will terminate, demonstrating that the **copy** command is functionally useless for this type of job. This is exactly the type of situation for which the **backup** command was created, and is indispensable.

Make sure that you have a copy of the file backup.com on your fixed disk before you start this next exercise. Then enter the following command:

```
backup test a:
```

The **backup** command will load and run, and it will prompt you to:

```
Insert backup diskette 01 in drive a:
Warning! Diskette files will be erased
Strike any key when ready
```

When you press a key, the message

```
**Backing up files to diskette 01 ***
```

will be printed, and DOS will go about its business of copying the information in the file test onto the floppy disk. Once the disk is full, it will stop and prompt you again:

```
Insert backup diskette 02 in drive a:
Warning! Diskette files will be erased
Strike any key when ready
```

Note that the number of the diskette has been incremented by one. Insert another formatted diskette, press a key, and again DOS will continue the backup process. It will keep requesting diskettes until the file test has been completely copied.

This use of the **backup** command is the only valid method of backing up files that are larger than a floppy. The process of reading them back in to the fixed disk is similar, and need only be used if the original copy on the fixed disk becomes corrupted. Hopefully, you will never need to use it.

There are several other options available on the **backup** command that are useful for certain procedures. As usual, they take the form of switches on the command line. Let's look at these in more detail. The full command syntax of the **backup** command is as follows:

```
backup filespec d:/s/m/a/d
```

Each of the switches is optional. The *filespec* defines the file, or files, that you want backed up, and can include a full path name and drive designator. The *d*: specifies the disk drive that contains the floppy disk to hold the backed up image. The purpose of the switches takes some explanation.

The /s switch, when included, tells DOS that you want to include all the files in any subdirectories in the backup procedure. For example, if you issue the command

```
backup c:\ a:/s
```

you are telling DOS to back up the entire contents of the fixed disk. The *c:* tells **backup** that the source of data is the root directory of the fixed disk. The *a:* tells it that the destination of the data is a diskette, or series of diskettes, in drive A:. The /s switch says to include any files found in any subdirectories in the **backup** process, thereby including all files on the disk.

If the /s switch was not included in the command, **backup** would only copy the files that are in the root directory, and would bypass any subdirectories.

The second switch, **/m,** tells **backup** that you only want to back up those files that have been modified since the last **backup.** Obviously, for this option to be functional, you need to have made a backup previously. You can try that out on the file test. Enter the command

```
backup test a:/m
```

and see what happens. When you insert the first backup diskette, DOS will check to see if the file has been modified since you last made the backup. Since, in this case, no changes have been made, DOS will issue the message

```
Warning! No files were found to back up
```

and terminate the command. If you want to, you can make a slight modification to the test file by concatenating something to it and trying it again. This time **backup** with the **/m** switch should work.

When it finds the **/m** switch, **backup** will check the directory on the fixed disk and compare it to a copy of the directory on the backup diskette. If it finds that the file has been written to since the last **backup,** it will copy it. If not, it will bypass it. If you are backing up multiple files, **backup** will simply bypass the files that have not been modified. This speeds up the backup process for those who use it on a regular basis, since it offers purely incremental backup capabilities.

The third switch, **/a,** when included on the command line tells **backup** to include any files that are to be backed up on a disk that already contains other backed up files. This switch ensures that **backup** will not erase any files on the backup disk, but simply use any leftover space. This minimizes the number of diskettes that are required to hold backups.

The final switch is the **/d** switch and tells **backup** that it should only back up those files that have been written to on or after a specified date. For example, the command

```
backup c:\ a:/d:08-13-83
```

tells **backup** only to copy the files that have been created or modified since the date 8–13–83.

By combining the switches on the **backup** command, you can effectively back up only the files that you deem important. Liberal use of this command is encouraged, for although the cost of the floppy disks may be substantial, the loss that can ensue from a damaged fixed disk can quite easily cause severe damage to a small business.

Files stored on a disk by the **backup** command are not stored in the regular file format, and are therefore not usable from DOS as commands, text files, or programs. They are simply backed up images of the original files, and before they can be used, they need to be replaced on the fixed disk using the

restore command. If you look at a directory listing of a diskette used to hold backed up files, you will see that they contain a file called backupid.@@@. This is the file that contains the information about the backed up files and is necessary to restore them on the fixed disk.

The **Restore** *Command*

The **restore** command is the functional and logical antithesis of the **backup** command. It is used to reconstruct the original files from the image stored on backup disks. It should only be used in a situation where the original data on the fixed disk are rendered unusable. It is not recommended that you use the **backup/restore** combination as a cheap way of increasing the capacity of your PC. There is no substitute for a fixed disk when large amounts of data are involved. The **backup/restore** system is simply an insurance policy against the accidental loss of valuable data.

To use the **restore** command, you should enter commands that are logically the opposite of **backup** commands. The full syntax of the command is:

```
restore d: filespec/s/p
```

The *d:* represents the floppy disk drive from which the previously backed up data will be read. The *filespec* tells **restore** which file or files to restore. It should include the drive designation for the fixed disk onto which you want to restore the files, and the appropriate path name if one is required.

The two switches that can be included in the **restore** command are also highly functional. The first of these, the **/s** switch, tells **restore** to include any files that are in subdirectories. If this switch is not included, **restore** will only operate on those files that are in the specified directory.

The command

```
restore a: c:\ /s
```

tells **restore** to bring back all the files that are on the floppy disks. This is somewhat similar to the **/s** switch that can be included in the **backup** command.

The second switch, the **/p** switch, tells **restore** to prompt before it restores any files that have been modified since they were backed up. It will also prompt before it restores any files that are marked as read-only files in the directory. This prevents the accidental replacement of good data by the earlier versions of the files.

This points to one of the limitations of fixed disks as compared to floppies. Since they are not removable, they have no physical equivalent of a write-protect notch. Consequently, they are much more vulnerable to physical abuse than are floppies. Although it is possible to determine that a file is to be read-only through software interaction, there is no direct physical protection. When this is combined with the storage capacity of a fixed disk, the problem is compounded and adds more ammunition to the argument for a regular backup procedure.

You may want to try the **restore** command on the file test that was created earlier. To do this, simply erase the file test, to simulate its accidental removal, and then enter the command:

```
restore a: c:test
```

You will then be invited to:

```
Insert backup diskette 01 in drive A:
Strike any key when ready
```

And when you do, the **restore** command will go to work. The first thing that it does is to print on the screen the date on which the version of the file was backed up. This lets you see how old the backup is. It will then copy all the data from the diskette and write it onto the fixed disk. When it has completed restoring the information on the first floppy, it will prompt for the subsequent disk to be inserted, and will continue doing so until all the information has been restored.

If, for some reason, you insert the wrong disk, or if the disks are out of sequence, you will be warned by the following error message:

```
Warning! Diskette is out of sequence
Replace the diskette or continue
Strike any key when ready
```

If you do not replace the disk with the correct one, and simply press a key, you will be given the message:

```
**restoring files from diskette xx ***
```

The *xx* is the diskette number in the sequence. Then, **restore** will stop and print the error message

```
backup file sequence error
```

and return you to the command line. This prevents you from compounding errors by getting the backup disk sequence out of order.

As was mentioned earlier, the **backup** and **restore** commands support the **errorlevel** condition that can be tested through the **if** statement in batch files. This means that batch files can be prepared that force the user to back up all data that have been entered before the system can be exited. It is recommended that this feature be put to use on a regular basis.

Now that all the commands applicable to fixed disk systems, be they supplied by IBM or not, have been covered, it's time to take a look at another feature of DOS that makes it possible to attach any manufacturer's fixed disk and have it work with the operating system as though it were a standard piece of hardware. This is done through the installation of programs known as device drivers.

CHAPTER 21

Installable Device Drivers

DOS version 2 corrects a problem, which existed in earlier versions, associated with the manner in which the operating system works with "foreign" devices. A foreign device is a peripheral that is not supplied by IBM, or is added as an afterthought by IBM. Third-party fixed disks are a good example of such devices.

In earlier versions, for a foreign device to work with DOS, a modified version of the operating system had to be used. Quite often, these modified versions were created by means of a "patch." A patch modifies the BIOS interface to DOS. This in itself does not necessarily create any problems for the user. The problems arise when more than one foreign device is used.

If more than one patch is made to DOS, there is always the possibility that a conflict can arise. This may happen when two devices try to patch the same part of DOS. The results may be catastrophic. If one of the devices is a fixed disk, it may result in the loss of all the data that it holds.

With DOS version 2 this problem was addressed by defining a standard method of interfacing any foreign device with the PC, through a program known as a device driver. The device driver manages all the communications between the PC and the device in a standard fashion. Another facility of DOS allows device drivers to be added to the system in an *ad hoc* manner through a very simple installation process.

When a manufacturer ships a foreign piece of hardware, a device driver stored in a disk file should be included with it. It is up to the user to add the device driver to the system. Since users are not necessarily systems programmers, the process of installing a device driver has been made reasonably painless. It involves typing characters on the keyboard, and perhaps the copying of a disk file or two.

When DOS is booted, it checks on the master disk to determine if there are any device drivers to be loaded, or installed as it is known. If it finds one or more, it will load them into memory and activate them, thereby attaching the peripheral that the device driver services to the PC. It is obvious, then, that there needs to be a method of informing DOS that there is one or more device drivers to be installed.

The installation process requires that a special file be created under the reserved name of config.sys. This file is used to pass the names of any installable device drivers to DOS so that it can load them at boot time. Config.sys is a simple ASCII text file that can be prepared with any ASCII text editor or word processor, or with our popular **copy con:** command. The format of the file is simply a series of lines that tells DOS which device drivers are to be loaded. There are also several other functions that it can be made to perform.

Suppose, for example, that you want to install a mouse on your PC. The manufacturer of the mouse should provide with the hardware a disk containing a device driver for it. If there is no device driver, it is doubtful whether commercially available software will work with the mouse, although it should be possible to write special software for it. Let's assume that the device driver is supplied, and it is stored on the disk under the file name mouse.sys.

To ensure that the device driver is installed each time the PC is started, the statement

```
device=mouse.sys
```

needs to be added to the file config.sys. If the file does not exist, it will be necessary to create it.

If you also use a clock, a mouse, and a RAM-based disk emulator, each of which has a device driver with it, the config.sys file might look like the following:

```
device=mouse.sys
device=clock.sys
device=ramdrive.sys
```

The three files

```
mouse.sys
clock.sys
ramdrive.sys
```

must also be present on the disk from which the PC will boot. If you have a peripheral from a knowledgeable manufacturer, the installation should be the same as the previous example. If it is not, you should question it.

If you are installing a hard disk supplied by a third party and it is functionally identical to the fixed disk supplied by IBM, it will not be necessary to use a device driver. If it is not functionally equivalent to the IBM drive, it should be installed through a device driver in the same manner as the preceding example. Fixed disks that do not use device drivers but instead modify DOS should be avoided like the plague if you plan to use other devices. Modifying DOS is extremely dangerous.

The file config.sys is something of a super-batch file that is always loaded and interpreted when the system is booted. Besides information about device drivers, there are also several other configuration parameters that can be set through its use. These parameters can be set by including some other special commands in the configuration file.

There are a total of five different commands that can be included in a configuration file. These five commands can be used to change some of the default settings that the PC uses when it is started. The first of these commands is the device= command that we just saw. The other four are somewhat more obscure.

*The **Break** Configuration Command*

The **break** command is used to set the default status of the Ctrl-Break checking. As we saw when we looked at the regular DOS **break** command, the level at which DOS checks for the Ctrl-Break key combination can be changed from its normal state to an extended state. This was done through the regular **break on/off** command. The **break** configuration command can also be used.

If you always want the extended Ctrl-Break check to be on as the default, you can enter the command

```
break on
```

in the configuration file. If you want, you can always turn it back off from the command line or from a batch file via the regular DOS **break** command.

*The **Buffers** Configuration Command*

Under normal circumstances, when started in the default mode, DOS creates two areas in memory that are used as buffers for passing data to and from disk files. The number of buffers used can be changed through use of the **buffers** command placed in the configuration file. Any number of buffers from 1 to 99 can be specified.

The more buffers that are available for DOS, the faster DOS is likely to operate when an applications program uses it. This is because it will probably make fewer attempts to read from the disk as the number of available buffers increases. On the other hand, there is a premium of 528 bytes from memory that must be paid for each buffer that is allocated. However, if you are using a PC with a large amount of available memory, you may be able to speed it up by allocating more buffers.

The way to allocate more buffers is to include the command

```
buffers=xx
```

in the configuration file, where *xx* can be a number from 1 to 99. If you are going to change the number of buffers available for DOS, you should note that it operates quite well with only two buffers in the default condition. Making available large numbers of buffers may or may not increase the read/write speed of the PC very significantly, depending on the applications program being used.

*The **Files** Configuration Command*

DOS version 2 provides a very convenient and efficient method for applications programmers to create and maintain files. It is technically a vast improvement of version 1. However, under the default settings of the operating system, only eight files can be open at any one time. This number is based on a practical, but somewhat arbitrary, conclusion about the nature of applications programs. Many applications programs work with multiple files simultaneously. Usually, if the maximum number of allowable open files is exceeded, an error condition will result, causing a program error. For the vast majority of applications, a maximum of eight files open simultaneously is more than enough. However, DOS makes it easy for more files to be open at the same time if it is deemed necessary.

This is done by placing a **files** command in the configuration file. This command is of the form

```
file=xx
```

where *xx* is a number from 1 to 99. The overhead associated with each file is only 39 bytes. However, it is not particularly useful to have a large number of files available for concurrent use unless problems have occurred. If you are using an applications program that will not run on a standard DOS system, or if you wish to create an operating environment that will allow more than eight files to be open at one time, you should make use of the **files** command.

*The **Shell** Configuration Command*

The last of the configuration commands is the **shell** command. **Shell** lets you change the name of the default command processor that is used by DOS. Normally the command processor is stored in the file named command.com. However, it is possible to replace this command processor with another.

The command.com command processor is a very integral part of DOS and cannot be replaced by just any old program. There are some very special functions that a command processor must perform. Still, it is possible for another command processor to be used. The way to do this is through the **shell** configuration command.

If you want to replace command.com with a different command processor, you can install it at boot time by using the statement

```
shell=filename
```

where *filename* is the file containing the new command processor.

If you do replace the command processor, any of the facilities of DOS such as internal commands, batch processing, etc., will not be available, unless they are duplicated in the new command processor.

The only time a new command processor should be used is if one is made available for a particular turnkey application. The creation of a new command processor is immensely complex, and so should only be prepared by an authority on DOS. The facility of replacing command processors is very similar to the shell facility of UNIX/XENIX, hence its name.

There are little or no rules about what can and cannot be done with DOS for a particular hardware configuration. If your PC is used to run standard canned, or off-the-shelf, programs, there is usually no need to change the default configuration. If you need your PC for some specialized application with more than standard requirements, it is possible to configure it for that purpose.

The capabilities of the configuration file are yet another pointer to the capabilities and power of DOS when compared to older microcomputer operating systems. No popular operating system has ever been this flexible and powerful, or so easy to customize. Many people will never need to know about configuration files. Many more will only experience them when installing device drivers for foreign components. However, for those who do need to make use of them, it is remarkably easy to change the default configuration by simply entering configuration commands into the config.sys file.

CHAPTER 22

DOS Version 2 Directory Structures

Here, finally, in this chapter, we've come full circle. We started by looking at all the features and commands of DOS version 1, and then we took an in-depth look at DOS version 2. Before we finished with DOS version 1, we peered inside and managed to make sense of the bits and bytes that DOS used to keep track of files on the disk. Now it's time to learn the mysteries of the interior of DOS version 2.

During a formatting procedure DOS version 2 creates a directory and FAT. The directory that it creates is initially empty and is referred to as the root directory. Other directories can be created at a later date and placed into the root directory. These are known as subdirectories. The FAT is the instrument that DOS uses to maintain information about which sectors on which tracks are used to store the data that are associated with each file. It works on a chaining scheme that we shall see later.

DOS version 1 created a directory and a FAT on the lowest-number tracks of each disk. The combination of those two allowed DOS to decide where to allocate space on the disk for new files, and where to find the various components of a file when it was time to retrieve them. The entire directory and FAT took up only a small portion of the disk and were encoded in such a way that there was literally not one single byte to spare.

Under DOS version 2, there is a new, more compact disk format. Where there used to be only eight sectors of 512 bytes each on a single track, there are now nine sectors, still of 512 bytes each. A quick review of the old methods of keeping track of files will immediately indicate that the new system is internally incompatible with the old.

For it to be compatible with DOS version 1's format, it would need to keep track of the additional storage in the same amount of space as it did before. Due to the increased storage capacity and the associated management requirements necessary for the use of mass-storage devices such as the fixed disk, this is physically impossible. Given the compact method by which DOS version 1 managed the storage requirements for 320K floppy disks, it would be ludicrous to assume that a scheme could be derived through which a 10-megabyte fixed disk could be managed in the same space. So, some changes had to be made, as we'll see.

The second major difference between the two revisions to DOS is the ability of DOS version 2 to host several directories on a single disk simultaneously. It is this facility that allows us to create a hierarchical directory structure so that very large fixed disk drives can be managed in a much simplified manner. This new feature obviously requires that more space be devoted to the storage of file name information. There is theoretically no limit to the number of directories that can exist under DOS version 2, although there are certainly many practical considerations. Each of these directories places a space requirement on DOS version 2 equivalent to the single directory that could exist under DOS version 1.

The third difference is DOS version 2's ability to work with the fixed disk itself, thereby having to work with much more data than it did in its previous incarnation. The theoretical upper limits of DOS version 2 are very high.

Practically speaking, DOS can now work with one or more large fixed disks. This capability has been added to the system without any visible burden or overhead to the operator. Fixed disks are treated in exactly the same way as floppy disks—at least it looks that way on the outside. Therefore the changes that have been made to DOS are quite transparent as far as you are concerned.

Each of these has had some effect on the requirements of DOS by demanding more performance and storage capabilities. DOS version 2 has risen to the situation in what appears to be a very elegant manner. As we did before when we examined the inner workings of DOS version 1, let's take a look at the implications of these changes on the directory and the FAT.

The Directory

When a disk is formatted under DOS version 2, there is only one single directory created. This is the directory that we know as the root directory. However, when the **format** command is run on a floppy disk, we can choose from two different disk formats, eight sectors per track and nine sectors per track. Couple this with the fact that disks can be either single sided or double sided, normal density or high density, and there are now many different types of diskettes that DOS will recognize.

Nevertheless, DOS version 2 requires the same amount of space as DOS version 1 did to maintain its root directory. Of course, under DOS version 1 there could only be one single directory, whereas DOS version 2 allows multiple directories. Directories other than the root directory are stored in a somewhat different way, as we'll see, while the root directory itself takes up the same amount of disk real estate as the one single directory possible under DOS version 1. That is, it requires either four sectors or seven sectors, depending on whether the disk is single sided or double sided.

These requirements are the same for disks that are either eight sectors per track or nine sectors per track. The number of entries that can be placed in the root directory has not changed between versions. Again, there can be 64 entries for a single-sided disk and 112 entries for a double-sided disk.

When we looked at DOS version 1, we also saw that disk space is allocated one cluster at a time. For single-sided disks, a cluster is the equivalent of a single sector. For double-sided disks, clusters of two segments are allocated. There has been no change in the cluster allocation scheme for floppy disks between DOS versions.

The only major difference in disk-space requirements between the two versions lies in the FAT. Under DOS version 1 only one single sector was required for the FAT, whereas DOS version 2 requires double this amount for any disk that is formatted for nine sectors per track. This seems a small price to pay for the additional 12 percent storage that DOS version 2 brought with it.

In the directory itself, there have been several significant enhancements made to DOS version 2. Each directory entry is 32 bytes long, as it was under DOS version 1, and the positional information has not changed. However, there have been several additional codes allocated to new features that are available under DOS version 2. Each directory entry is still mapped as follows:

Bytes	Meaning
0–7	file name, stored as an 8-byte ASCII string
8–10	file name extension, stored as 3 ASCII bytes
11	file attribute byte
12–21	reserved for future use
22–23	file creation or last change time
24–25	file creation or last change data
26–27	file starting cluster number
28–31	file size in bytes

As you can see, the actual layout of the directory entry has not changed between versions.

The first byte of the file name field had a special significance under DOS version 1. If it contained a hexadecimal E5, it indicated that the file had been erased. This made the process of erasing files very simple and consequently very fast. DOS simply had to locate the file name in the directory and change one single byte. The actual contents of the file were never physically removed from the disk.

Under DOS version 2 the first byte of the file name still plays a significant role. An E5 in that byte is still used to indicate that the file has been erased. Two additional codes have been added to this, however. If the first byte contains a hex 00, it indicates that the entry has never been used. This permits DOS to speed up certain functions.

The manner in which DOS allocates space for files is always the same. If the file already exists, DOS will simply determine where the next available cluster is located and will allocate that. If the file needs to be created, it will search through the directory until it finds the first available directory entry.

DOS only needs to read the first byte of each directory entry to determine this. If it discovers an E5 in the first byte, it knows that the file that used to reside in this directory entry has been deleted. It has therefore found the first available directory entry, and will allocate space from the FAT—in its usual first available basis—to the file that will occupy this directory entry. If it discovers a 00, it knows that no file has ever been allocated to that directory entry. In either case it will allocate the directory entry.

Since a 00 will always indicate that DOS has just entered virgin territory—i.e., no files have ever existed this far into the directory—it knows there is no need to search any further through the directory for any more file information. It can therefore terminate any action (such as that required to produce a directory listing for the **dir** command) as soon as it finds a zero byte in the first position. This simple addition greatly speeds up any directory searching process that DOS undertakes during a command, or under the control of a program, since it never needs to search through meaningless information. This is particularly appropriate given the fact that the number of files that can be managed by DOS version 2 is far greater than earlier versions.

The other code that has been added is a hex 2E. If DOS discovers a 2E in the first position, it knows that the directory entry represents a subdirectory. Subdirectories are stored in what resemble regular disk files, and are treated as such in the directory. The current directory, i.e., the directory onto which you are currently logged, will be given the highest priority to remain in memory. Therefore, there is little performance degradation, if any, in running programs out of a subdirectory rather than the root directory.

If the second position in the file name is also a 2E, this indicates that the starting cluster number field in the directory entry actually points to the cluster number of the parent directory. This provides a road-sign mechanism that allows DOS to find its way back to the root directory or to any other point in the directory tree from wherever it is currently located in the hierarchy.

There have been no changes to the file name extension field. However, the twelfth position (byte 11) has gone through several changes and additions. Under DOS version 1 only the values of 00, 02, and 04 were valid for the attribute byte. These are still valid; however, four additional attribute-byte codes have been added.

The attribute byte works on the bit level. In the byte there are 8 bits that can be turned off and on (0 and 1). A 00 attribute byte (00000000) still represents a normal file. A 02 bit (00000010) set in the attribute byte still represents a hidden file. Hidden files will not be displayed during a directory listing. A 04 (00000100) bit set in the attribute byte still means a system file as it did under DOS version 1.

The new representative bits in the attribute byte represent new file types and indicators that can be set and checked by DOS. The 01 bit (00000001), when set in the attribute byte, indicates that the file is a read-only file. Any attempt to write to the file will produce an error message. There is no way for an operator to directly influence the setting of this byte from the keyboard through any of the DOS commands. Its purpose it to allow applications programs to "lock" files so that they cannot be accidentally written to.

When the attribute byte has its 08 bit (00001000) turned on, it indicates that the directory entry does not contain the name of a file per se, but is actually the depository for the volume name that was allocated to the disk at format time. Since any volume name associated with a disk is 11 characters long, the ASCII characters can be stored in the fields that are usually reserved for the file name and extension, since these also total 11 bytes.

In the root directory, since one entry is allocated to hold the volume name, it is obvious that the numeric file capacity of the directory is reduced by one. With the capability of DOS version 2 to create hierarchical directories, this does not appear to be much of a trade-off. Volume name entries can only be stored in the root directory, and there can only be one per disk. All the other fields in this type of entry do not, by definition, contain useful information.

If the attribute byte has its 10 (00010000) bit set on, it indicates that the directory entry is for a subdirectory. This type of file is excluded from any normal directory searches, although it is included in directory listings through the **dir** command.

Finally, if the attribute byte has its 20 (00100000) bit set on, it indicates that the file has been written to. This bit is known as the "archive bit." It is used by commands such as **backup** and **restore.** Whenever a file is backed up, the archive bit is set back off. The next time the file is written to and closed, the archive bit is set back on. By examining the archive bit, a DOS command or any other program can determine whether or not the file has been modified since it was last backed up. Programs can therefore be written to manage only the information that has been incrementally added. Those files that have not changed since the last backup will not be operated on, while files that have their archive bit set on can be backed up or written to a tape streamer, or whatever the user needs.

In many cases, several different bits in the attribute byte are set at the same time. For example, the system files (ibmbio.com and ibmdos.com) are marked as system files, hidden files, and read-only files. Therefore, their attribute bytes would read 00000111, indicating all three states existing simultaneously. There are, however, many combinations that do not make sense, such as volume names and subdirectories in the same entry.

This leads to a truly remarkable, and completely undocumented, feature of DOS that lets it meet many of the requirements that security-minded individuals have. Since subdirectories are actually stored in regular DOS files, DOS version 2 is capable of living and working with *hidden directories*. However, these strange animals cannot be created directly by DOS, although if you have access to one of the various utility programs that allows you to modify the contents of a sector, you can create a hidden directory.

First, create the directory in the normal manner using the **mkdir** command:

```
mkdir private
```

Then, using a sector examining and modifying utility, examine the directory sector on track 0, and notice that the attribute byte for the file containing the new directory has indeed been set to 10. By changing this to a 12, the directory can be hidden from view. A directory listing will confirm that.

Like any other directory, a hidden directory can be logged on to using the standard

```
chdir private
```

command. Once you are logged on to the directory, it behaves as any normal directory would. However, when you return to the parent, the subdirectory will appear to have vanished.

This feature is practical for the type of applications program that requires sensitive data to be placed into a public situation, such as accounting or payroll applications. The applications program can use the contents of the directory, whereas casual users do not even need to know that the data are on the system. Such a modification does require that DOS be made to run in a nonstandard fashion. However, there are no caveats in the DOS documentation that indicate that it cannot be used in this way.

The other fields in the directory entry have not been the subject of change between versions. The reserved fields must not be used by applications programs, or modified by the user. They are marked reserved and must be respected as such. The starting cluster number is still normally set at 002, and the file-size bytes are still 4 bytes, or 32 bits, long, indicating that file sizes up to 2 to the power of 32 can be stored under DOS.

The File Allocation Table

The file allocation table (FAT) has been the subject of some change between DOS versions 1 and 2. First, the space-management requirements for very large fixed disks demand that the size of the new FAT be variable on demand. Second, new codes have been added to define the additional device types that DOS can now work with. Otherwise, the fundamental methodology under which the FAT works has been maintained.

The FAT is still the road map through the various clusters on a storage device that DOS uses to store and retrieve file data. However, the concept of a cluster has been enhanced somewhat. As we saw when double-sided disks were first introduced, clusters are created on the lowest track number of disk side 1 first, then the next disk plane (side 2) is addressed. This minimizes the amount of thrashing around that the disk head has to do to load or save a disk file, since it is most likely that the data will all be stored on adjacent tracks, although not necessarily on the same disk surface.

With the move to large fixed disks, the need to minimize the disk head's movement becomes even more important. The plane priority that was first seen with double-sided disks has therefore been extended to the multiple platters that make up a hard disk. Essentially the concept of a *cylinder* has been introduced. A cylinder is a series of like-numbered tracks on each of the platters of the disk drive. Under this scheme, a cluster now becomes a single sector on each of the disk surfaces of the drive. The actual size of a fixed disk cluster is determined at format time, and is determined by the amount of disk space that is allocated for DOS use.

Entries in the FAT still consist of a 12-bit block (1.5 bytes). This block can be thought of as three hexadecimal digits. Each of these 12-bit blocks represents a cluster on the disk, so that the actual size of the FAT can be determined by finding the number of clusters available for DOS. With floppy-based systems this is quite easy, although with fixed disk systems it is again entirely dependent on the amount of fixed disk space allocated for use under DOS.

The first two FAT entries are still dummy entries, used to determine the type of disk media used. These two FAT entries consist of a total of 3 bytes. The first byte contains the device code, while the second and third bytes always hold a hex FFFF. The device codes that are currently (officially) recognized by DOS are:

Code	Device Type
FF	double-sided disk, eight sectors per track
FE	single-sided disk, eight sectors per track
FD	double-sided disk, nine sectors per track
FC	single-sided disk, nine sectors per track
F8	fixed disk

As with DOS version 1, this media ID FAT entry maps over part of the disk that is not available for disk storage—the boot record, directory, and FAT. This assures that a file-creating or modifying program can never accidentally damage a disk by writing over these disk sections, or by writing into the wrong FAT entry. The next FAT entry begins the mapping of the available data segment of the disk.

As before, a FAT entry can exist in one of three states. The first is where it contains a 000. This means that the cluster associated with this entry is not currently in use, and is therefore available for DOS. DOS allocates clusters on a first available basis, so that the first entry in the FAT that contains a 000 will be the first cluster allocated on demand.

The second state that a FAT entry can exist in is where the represented cluster has been allocated. In this state, the FAT entry would contain a number that points to the next cluster in the file. This allows the FAT to mark that the cluster is in use and to point to the next cluster in the chain.

If there is no next cluster in the chain, which would mean that the current cluster is the last cluster associated with the file, the FAT entry would contain a hex number between FF8 and FFF. This is really the third state that a FAT entry can exist in.

When a FAT overflows the single sector that is initially allocated for its use, it will grab a second sector, which will be contiguous with the first, and so on as it grows. As with DOS version 1, two copies of the FAT are always maintained on the disk for safety's sake. The FAT is usually maintained in memory on a high-priority basis within the buffers allocated by DOS for disk input and output. This means that DOS can achieve a relatively high performance, since it does not have to read the FAT every time it needs to allocate disk space or retrieve a file.

Whenever there is a change in the FAT, as with a new file being created or a file being updated, the new version of the FAT is written out to the disk. This does not represent much of a performance degradation, since much of the time associated with disk input or output is simply used to bring the disk-drive motor up to speed, and for DOS to find its initial starting point.

Since the disk is always brought up to speed during a write, there is little overhead associated with updating the disk version of the FAT. This means that the latest version is always stored—in duplicate—on the current disk. It also means that the disk can be physically removed from the disk drive without damage. In some older, less-sophisticated operating systems, disks could not be removed from the disk drives in this way.

As you can see, the new file-management scheme used by DOS version 2 is predictably more complex. Many of the features added to the later version have direct consequences on the directory and FAT structures. DOS has grown a generation older, and better, and the internal structure of the file system has been upgraded in a logical enough way. Hopefully, other radical new features will be added to future versions of DOS in such a straightforward and upward-compatible manner.

Glossary

Applications program a program designed for a specific task, such as payroll or accounting.

ASCII stands for American Standard Code for Information Interchange. It is a numerical coding scheme of letters of the alphabet, numbers, and all other printable characters. This scheme makes for easy conversion to binary numbers.

Assembler a program that takes symbolic instructions written by a programmer and translates them into a form that the computer can understand.

Assembly language the symbolic instructions that a programmer writes to feed into an assembler.

Asynchronous one of the two ways by which computers communicate with intelligent peripherals and other computers. This method involves a single bit at a time being transmitted and received. See also *serial port* and *RS-232C*.

Backup the process of making a second copy of computer data for security purposes.

BASIC acronym for Beginner's All-purpose Symbolic Instruction Code, the most popular computer language. A version of BASIC is contained in the ROMs within the IBM PC. An extended version is included on the DOS master disk.

Batch a process whereby one or more commands are stored in a file for later use. Since many commands can be placed in a file and operated by a single command, batch command processing is a very efficient method of programming.

Baud a transmission rate of 1 bit per second; 1,200 baud is the equivalent of 1,200 bits per second, or roughly equivalent to 120 characters per second.

Binary a form of arithmetic where there are only two digits, 0 and 1. Binary arithmetic is particularly well suited for computers since it can be represented easily by electrical circuits. An open switch can represent a 0, while a closed switch can represent a 1. Similarly a voltage in a wire can represent a 1, while no voltage can represent 0.

BIOS the basic input/output system. This is a part of DOS that is specific to the hardware and is the mechanism through which the operating system controls the hardware. While other computers may make use of the same operating system as the PC, they will most likely have a different BIOS.

Bit stands for binary digit; it is the lowest component of the binary arithmetic system. A bit can exist in only two states, 0 or 1. Series of bits are strung together to form larger units that can represent larger numbers.

Boot the process of starting a computer.

Buffer a portion of a computer's memory that is allocated for input or output operations. This memory holds the data that are to be transmitted until the receiving device is ready. Some intelligent peripheral devices also have buffer memory. In general, the larger the buffer, the faster the device will operate.

Bug a term generally used to denote a flaw or an error in a computer program.

Byte a series of 8 bits. Since each bit can be in one of 2 states, a byte can exist in one of 2 to the power 8, or 256 states. Any character in the English language can be stored in a single byte. In microcomputers a single memory location is analogous to a byte. See also *character*.

`Character` a single alphanumeric digit. A single character can represent any of the alphabetic, numeric, or punctuation symbols on the keyboard. The ASCII character set defines numeric equivalents for 128 characters.

`Cluster` a unit of disk storage that is allocated when the operating system requests it. For a single-sided disk a cluster is a single sector. For a double-sided disk a cluster is two sectors. The cluster size for a fixed disk is dependent on how much of the disk is allocated for use with DOS.

`.com file` the type of disk file in which the simplest DOS commands and programs are stored. Programs stored in .com files can usually be made to operate in less than 64K of memory.

`Command` a word or series of words that is used to tell a computer what to do.

`Command interpreter` the part of the operating system that recognizes commands typed at the keyboard and passes the appropriate information to the other parts of the system.

`Compiler` a program that analyzes a computer program written in a computer language and generates the appropriate machine instructions.

`Composite video` a video signal that contains a sum of the red, green, and blue components of video. Composite video is also used for many component television systems and videotape recorders.

`Concatenate` to merge two or more files together into a single, larger file.

`Control character` a special nonprinting character used to specify information to the system, such as carriage returns, line feeds, tab characters, and bells (beeps).

`Cursor` a special symbol on the video display that indicates the current screen position. Different programs can use different cursor characters. Many systems use a flashing cursor character.

Debug the exercise of removing bugs or errors from a program, usually requiring much repetition and limit testing.

Device driver a program that controls the transfer of data between a computer and a peripheral. In DOS version 2, drivers are dynamically installable, which means that they can be added to a system by the user when the peripheral hardware is physically attached.

Diagnostic a program that tests the various components of a computer. The PC has many diagnostic routines built into the ROM which are run every time the system is switched on. This accounts for the long delay between the power being turned on and actual operation of the computer.

Directory the part of a disk that holds the name and location information for each of the files on the disk. Each directory entry contains information about the name of the file, the date and time on which it was either created or last modified, the type of file that it is, the size of the file, and information about where the file is stored on the disk.

Disk drive a mechanical device built into the PC that can read and write information to and from floppy disks. It does this by magnetically encoding the information in much the same way as an audio recorder stores music on cassette tape, although the disks bear more physical resemblance to record disks.

Disk operating system the software that makes a computer behave like a single unit rather than a collection of modules. The DOS supplies all the fundamental operations that are needed to make applications programs work in a coherent fashion. The DOS that is used on the PC was developed by Microsoft Corporation and is available on other personal computers under the name MS-DOS.

DOS master disk the disk included with the DOS package as sold by IBM, or a perfect copy of it. This disk contains all the files and programs necessary to operate the PC.

Dot-matrix printer a low-cost printer that creates characters on paper by means of a matrix of dots. Dot-matrix printers such as the IBM 80 cps printer provide low-quality output at very low cost.

EBCDIC a code system, similar to ASCII, used primarily in large IBM mainframe computers. In general, EBCDIC is not used on the PC.

Edit computer term for the action of creating or modifying a text file.

Editor a program used to create or modify a text file. Editors, also known as text editors or line editors, come in many flavors, ranging from the simple **edlin** program included with DOS all the way up to the most advanced word processors.

End-of-file marker a special character used to mark the end of a DOS file. Usually DOS uses the Ctrl-z character. The F6 special function key can be used to enter such a character into a file.

Escape a special key on the computer's keyboard marked "Esc" dating back to the old Teletype days. A special ASCII code associated with Escape is also used for cursor-positioning sequences and other advanced uses.

.exe file a file used to store many of the more complex DOS commands and programs. Programs stored in .exe files generally require more than one single 64K memory segment to work in.

External command a DOS command that is not resident in the core of DOS, but rather stored in a disk file. When the command name is entered into DOS, the program will be loaded into memory before it is run. External commands are generally used for many of the more obscure DOS commands, and also for many commands that require a lot of memory to operate.

File a part of a disk that contains a coherent unit of information. Files can contain either program information or data. Under DOS, files are referred to by the name that they are given and are manipulated by many of the DOS commands.

File allocation table (FAT) the table that keeps track of where on the disk each file is located. In conjunction with the directory, the file allocation table determines where each newly created file is placed on a disk.

File name — the name that is given a file when it is created. Under DOS a file can be given a name up to eight characters long. An additional three characters can be used in the optional file name extension. The extension is normally used to indicate what type of file it is.

Filter — a special program that takes its input from the standard input and sends its output to the standard output, modifying the data in the process. Filters can be used to search for information or for other more complex functions such as sorting.

Fixed disk — a high-capacity disk drive whose media cannot be removed. The IBM fixed disk consists of multiple platters onto which data can be written.

Flag — a bit that is set to either 0 or 1 to signal a specific state. Flags are generally used in DOS to indicate file attributes such as read-only files or system files.

Floppy disk — a removable and inexpensive device for storing computer information through magnetic encoding. The PC uses a 5¼″ disk format.

Formatting — the preparation of a new disk for use with DOS. The formatting procedure writes magnetic information onto the blank surface of a disk so that DOS can find its way around. These magnetic markers are arranged into tracks and sectors. The formatting process also creates the directory and the file allocation table.

Hardware — the physical components of a computer system. The hardware on the PC includes the main system unit, the disk drives, the video display, the keyboard, the memory chips, etc. See also *software.*

Hexadecimal — a number system based on the number 16, which is 2 to the power of 4. A single hexadecimal digit is represented by the numbers 0–9, and then A–F to represent the numbers 10–15. Hex, as it is known for short, is a very convenient method of displaying the contents of memory locations, etc.

Hierarchical file system — a structure for a filing system that is similar to a tree. Each directory can have one or more subdirectories associated with it so that data can be logically structured according to importance or function.

High-density disks the disks supplied with the IMB PC-AT that are capable of storing almost twice as much information as a regular PC disk. These disks are capable of having ninety-six tracks per inch in the disk surface.

High-level language a general-purpose computer language such as BASIC, COBOL, FORTRAN, Pascal, C, Logo, Ada, Forth, APL, and Modula 2. See also *BASIC, compiler*, and *interpreter*.

Input the process of entering data into a computer. People usually input data through a keyboard, although reading disk files and sensing a mouse position are also considered input.

Internal command a command that is built into the memory resident portion of DOS. Whenever an internal command is invoked, it can be run immediately without any disk accesses. Many of the most popular and useful DOS commands are internal commands.

Interpreter the design for a computer language where the instructions are interpreted each time the program is run. This differs from a compiler where the instructions are translated into machine language only once. See also *BASIC, compiler, high-level language.*

Interrupt a signal to the central processing unit to stop what it is doing and service some other request. Many simple processes such as pressing a key on the PC's keyboard generate interrupts. The use of interrupts in a computer program assures that the processor is never redundant.

I/O short name for input/output. Used to signify the transmission of data to and from a computer.

K a shorthand method of denoting a unit of 1000, generally used with memory descriptions—64K refers to 64,000 units. In actuality, a K is really 1,024 (which is 2 to the power of 10), so that 64K actually refers to 65,536.

Letter-quality printer a high-quality printer that uses a hammer mechanism similar to a typewriter. More expensive than dot-matrix printers, letter-quality printers generally produce higher-quality output.

Mass storage generic name given to peripherals such as fixed disks that can store large amounts of computer data.

Memory the silicon chips in the main system unit in which the PC stores transient information such as computer programs and data. Computer memory is organized in bytes of 8 bits each. Large units of memory are referred to in units called K. See also *bit, byte, random-access memory, read-only memory,* and *K.*

Microprocessor the chip at the heart of the PC that performs all of the arithmetic and comparison functions that give the PC its computing powers. The PC uses an Intel 8088 microprocessor and the PC-AT uses an Intel 80286; both essentially computers-on-a-chip. The 8088 can externally manipulate 8 bits of data at a time, although it can manipulate 16 bits of data internally. The 80286 can manipulate external data 16 bits at a time. This leads to some contention as to whether the 8088 is an 8-bit or 16-bit processor. The 8088 is software compatible with several other microprocessors manufactured by Intel, including the more powerful 80286 chip.

Parallel printer adapter a peripheral card that allows the PC to be connected to a parallel printer. Parallel communications between devices allow multiple bits of information to be transmitted simultaneously (in parallel). See also *asynchronous.*

Parity a scheme used to eliminate memory and transmission errors, involving an additional bit that is used to set the total number of bits in a byte so that they are always even or always odd. If any bit changes, the computer can detect the error using the parity scheme.

PC short for personal computer. Generally used to refer to the IBM Personal Computer.

Peripheral a piece of hardware that is physically attached to the PC. Peripherals include add-on memory cards, printers, video displays, etc.

Pipe two or more commands connected together so that the output of one command is the input of another. Pipes, or pipelines, are a feature of DOS that is derived from the UNIX operating system.

Port used to refer to a communications channel of a computer used for input or output. Ports are usually either serial (asynchronous) or parallel. See also *serial, asynchronous, parallel printer adapter*, and *RS-232C*.

Program a series of codes that instructs a computer how to operate to perform a particular function. DOS is itself a program, as is the BASIC language and any of the applications that run on a computer.

Prompt a special character or series of characters that a computer displays to let the operator know that it is waiting for input.

Random-access memory (RAM) also known as main memory, user memory, and read/write memory, RAM is the type of memory that can both be written to and read from by a computer. RAM is used to store transient programs and data, and must usually be loaded from disk before it can be used. When the power is removed from the computer, the contents of RAM are lost. It is RAM that gives computers their inherent general-purpose nature. See also *read-only memory*.

Read-only memory (ROM) the type of memory that is permanently programmed and cannot be erased or modified. ROM is not dependent on the application of electrical power, so that its contents are not lost when the computer is turned off. The ROM in the PC is used to store the diagnostic routines, the BIOS code, and the BASIC language. See also *random-access memory*.

Redirection the facility whereby input or output comes from or goes to a source or destination other than the standard input and output.

Resolution the level of detail available on the video display measured both horizontally and vertically. The PC is capable of 640-by-200 resolution with the color/graphics adapter.

RF modulator a device that processes a composite video signal into a signal suitable for use with a standard television. It does this by piggybacking the video signal on top of a carrier signal.

RGB monitor a high-resolution color monitor in which the red, green, and blue signals are kept separate.

RS-232C the electrical specifications for a simple serial (asynchronous) interface that have been adopted as an industrywide standard.

Sector a block of storage space on a diskette. DOS formats disks with either eight or nine sectors on each track. Each sector is capable of holding 512 bytes of data.

Segment a region of memory controllable as a block by the microprocessor. The Intel 8088 and 80286 cannot address all of memory at one time. Instead, they require that memory be broken up into segments of 64K each. The processor can work with up to four of these segments at one time.

Serial port a peripheral card containing an RS-232C asynchronous channel for serial communications. See also *asynchronous* and *RS-232C*.

Single sided a term used for a disk where information is written on and read from only one plane.

Software the generic term for program information. Software is the coded instructions that are used to operate a computer. Software can reside in memory or can be transferred onto permanent media such as floppy disks, audio tape, or ROM chips. See also *hardware*.

Source code the human-readable program instructions written by a programmer for use with a compiler, interpreter, or assembler.

Storage a term for a medium that can be used to store computer data or program information. It is generally used to refer to disk or tape. See also *mass storage*.

String a sequence of characters strung together.

Subdirectory a directory within or below another directory in a hierarchical file system. See also *hierarchical file system*.

System disk any disk that contains the system file necessary to start or boot the computer from scratch. See also *DOS master disk* and *boot*.

`Terminal` — a device consisting of a keyboard and a video display. The PC can be used to behave like (emulate) a terminal, and under certain circumstances a remote terminal can be attached to the PC.

`Text file` — a file containing ASCII information that can be read and understood as text.

`Track` — a concentric circle or ring around a diskette surface used to locate and store data. Each track consists of either eight or nine sectors of 512 bytes each. A normal DOS diskette is capable of holding forty tracks on a side. See also *sector*.

`Utility` — a program often supplied with an operating system for simple functions.

`Winchester` — the name for the technology used in the IBM fixed disk. See also *fixed disk*.

Index